THE BC
Tweak
Unleas

DATE DUE

DEMCO 38-297

THE BOOK OF OVERCLOCKING

TWEAK YOUR PC TO UNLEASH ITS POWER

**Scott Wainner and
Robert Richmond**

NO STARCH
PRESS

San Francisco

Publisher: William Pollock
Editorial Director: Karol Jurado
Cover and Interior Design: Octopod Studios
Composition: 1106 Design, LLC
Developmental Editor: Heather Bennett
Proofreader: Robyn Brode
Indexer: Broccoli Information Management

Distributed to the book trade in the United States by Publishers Group West, 1700 Fourth Street, Berkeley, CA 94710; phone: 800-788-3123; fax: 510-658-1834.

Distributed to the book trade in Canada by Jacqueline Gross & Associates, Inc., One Atlantic Avenue, Suite 105, Toronto, Ontario M6K 3E7 Canada; phone: 416-531-6737; fax 416-531-4259.

For information on translations or book distributors outside the United States and Canada, please see our distributors list in the back of this book or contact No Starch Press, Inc. directly:

No Starch Press, Inc.
555 De Haro Street, Suite 250, San Francisco, CA 94107
phone: 415-863-9900; fax: 415-863-9950; info@nostarch.com; http://www.nostarch.com

Library of Congress Cataloguing-in-Publication Data

Wainner, Scott.
  The book of overclocking : tweak your PC to unleash its power /
Scott Wainner and Robert Richmond.
        p. cm.
Includes index.
  ISBN 1-886411-76-X
1. Microcomputers--Upgrading. 2. Computer organization. 3. High performance computing. I. Richmond,
Robert, 1980- II. Title.
  TK7887 .W85 2003
  621.39'16--dc21
                                                                                          2002152911

DEDICATIONS

For Bill Turney, Phyllis, and Robyn.

—S.W.

To Doreen, for believing in me.

—R.R.

BRIEF CONTENTS

CONTENTS IN DETAIL

1
WHAT THE COMPUTER INDUSTRY
DOES NOT WANT YOU TO KNOW

2
OVERCLOCKING VERSUS INDUSTRY HYPE:
TECHNICAL BACKGROUND

3
TECHNICAL THEORY:
EVOLUTION OF THE INTEGRATED CIRCUIT

4
HOW TO OVERCLOCK

5
COOLING

6
INTEL OVERCLOCKING

7

AMD OVERCLOCKING

8

VIA/CYRIX OVERCLOCKING

9

BENCHMARK TESTING

10

TROUBLESHOOTING

11
FINAL THOUGHTS

Appendix

Index

1

WHAT THE COMPUTER INDUSTRY DOES *NOT* WANT YOU TO KNOW

Everyone understands the potential for increased productivity or enhanced entertainment afforded through computers, but most users often view the technologies and hardware driving the phenomenal demand for desktop computers as "behind the scenes" components. Indeed, computers are often regarded as mysterious or even troublesome devices. A significant number of computer users do not understand the workings of a computer system's internal hardware beyond the minimal basics.

This lack of knowledge is often a byproduct of the computer industry itself. Technology follows a consistent evolutionary path, with the arrival of new architectures and platforms every 6 to 12 months. The backlash of this process is the users' inherent belief that systems are outdated as soon as they are purchased. This never-ending cycle fuels the computer technology industry, thus leading to ever increasing costs associated with upgrades, or even complete system replacement.

The upgrade cycle forces computer users into a price-concentric upgrade path based on what the industry wants the user to believe, thus leading to the increased demand for upgrades or system purchases. This model does not benefit the end user, as hardware costs are increasing at an exponential rate for those hoping to keep pace with the public relations hype generated by the industry. (The impact of the current industry model is not meant to be negative or malicious toward the end user; it is simply the marketing approach being adopted in nearly all industries these days.)

In order to sustain their business models, many corporations within the computer industry often prey upon the fact that the vast majority of end users have limited hardware knowledge. *The Book of Overclocking* dispels the myths surrounding the politics of the technology business and fully equips you with a cost-effective alternative to upgrading by extending the life of your current hardware while increasing your satisfaction with your existing PC's level of performance. Why purchase expensive upgrades when increasing your current PC processor's clock speed could be the key to realizing your desired level of performance?

Current Industry Players

Many computing enthusiasts choose not to conform to the tech industry's upgrade path propaganda by implementing overclocking techniques. Overclocking is the process of increasing the speed or clock frequencies of devices, such as processors, beyond their factory defaults.

Our primary concern in this book is with extending the processor (CPU) clock speed and examining the intricate relation it has with the computer system's other components. The procedures involved with the overclocking process can vary according to different system architectures, but the basic concepts remain essentially the same. We'll focus on desktop personal computing, with the IBM compatible being the dominant market player.

The term IBM compatible has undergone a radical departure from the early days of desktop computing, but the fundamental concepts behind the technology remain essentially the same. The entire range of desktop systems once designated under the blanket umbrella of IBM compatibility can now be referenced to the base architecture being utilized, in this case, "x86," a derivative of the naming process applied to system architectures from the original 8086 in the early 1980s through the release of the 80486 nearly a decade later. While different manufacturers and developers have adopted various naming strategies to increase market differentiation, all current so-called IBM-compatible desktop platforms remain nothing more than extensions to the x86 core processor architecture.

The market has witnessed the rise and fall of a variety of processor manufacturers over the years. The three remaining x86 market players are Intel Corporation, Advanced Micro Designs (AMD), and VIA Technologies, and their major product offerings are listed in Table 1-1.

Table 1-1: Major Processor Manufacturers and Product Offerings

Manufacturer	Architecture	MHz Rating
Intel Corporation	Pentium	60 – 200 MHz
	Pentium MMX	133 – 233 MHz
	Pentium Pro	150 – 200 MHz
	Pentium II	233 – 450 MHz
	Celeron	233 – 333 MHz
	Celeron A	300 – 533 MHz
	Pentium III Katmai	450 – 600 MHz
	Pentium III Coppermine	500 – 1133 MHz
	Celeron II	533 – 1100 MHz
	Pentium III Tualatin	1100+ MHz
	Celeron Hybrid	1200+ MHz
	Pentium 4 Willamette	1300 – 2000 MHz
	Pentium 4 Northwood	1600 – 3000+ MHz
	Pentium Xeon	All Pentium Ranges
Advanced Micro Designs	K5	75 – 117 MHz
	K6	166 – 300 MHz
	K6-2	266 – 550 MHz
	K6-3	350 – 450 MHz
	K6-2/3+	450 – 550 MHz
	Athlon K7	500 – 700 MHz
	Athlon K75	550 – 1000 MHz
	Athlon Thunderbird	600 – 1400 MHz
	Athlon Duron	600 – 950 MHz
	Athlon 4/MP	1200 – 1400+ MHz
	Athlon Duron Morgan	1000+ MHz
	Athlon XP	1333+ MHz
VIA Technologies/Cyrix/ National Semiconductor	686 M1	80 – 150 MHz
	686MX M2	133 – 300 MHz
	Cyrix III	350 – 450 MHz
	VIA C3	533 – 933+ MHz

Intel remains the dominant player across all ranges of the desktop computing marketplace, and has retained its significant market share ever since the first implementation of its 8086 processor within IBM's earliest x86 desktop computing systems. The architectures driving competition from other manufacturers are extensions to technologies pioneered by Intel over the past 30 years.

The Pentium 4 represents Intel's current flagship platform. The Pentium 4 platform is based on a radical departure from its earlier P6 architectures, though binary compatibility is maintained with nearly all 32-bit x86 programming code. The older P6 core technology is still represented through Intel's active support and manufacturing of the Pentium III and Celeron microprocessors.

AMD has rapidly gained market share over the past decade due to its superb architectural designs and dedication to cost efficiency. This increased competition is a welcome addition to the computer markets, as AMD can effectively influence the pricing strategies across the entire microprocessor market, thus leading to decreases in end-user pricing due to increased competition for Intel's product offerings.

AMD's core business model is based around the Athlon series microprocessor, which has undergone a multitude of revisions since its first inception just a few years ago. The Athlon remains the most efficient x86 architecture currently available in terms of raw per-MHz performance, regardless of the marketing hype and paranoia generated by competing manufacturers. The current AthlonXP, AMD's flagship product series, represents a pinnacle of x86 computing not even conceptualized just a decade ago.

Once popular processor favorites like National Semiconductor's Cyrix and IDT Centaur's WinChip are now only memories, though both of these corporations still live on through acquisitions by the Taiwanese technology giant VIA Technologies. VIA has resurrected the technologies from these manufacturers with its C3 series of processors. The C3 is a relatively underpowered chip compared to competing entry-level designs, though its architecture does offer a good performance to price ratio for users interested only in basic desktop applications.

Additional Architectures

Other manufactures have come and gone, but their processors have been only of mild interest to most end users, so we won't discuss them here specifically. Still, the techniques we'll address are often applicable to additional architectures not directly covered because most X86 platforms are similar. Older processors often overclock like their later siblings, the only difference being the operating speeds and other architectural values.

Topicalities to Be Presented

Your path to understanding overclocking begins with a view of today's market in Chapter 2. This background information explains how you can use overclocking to offset the increasing costs of computing. We'll do a cost analysis of common overclocking scenarios versus the actual monetary cost of both purchasing a prebuilt PC and upgrading individual hardware components, so that you can better appreciate the fundamental benefits of overclocking.

Chapters 3 and 4 provide the concepts that create the foundation of overclocking. We'll cover the basic techniques and ideas required to attain a successful overclock without concentrating on platform-specific data.

Chapter 5 covers perhaps the most important factor in attaining a successful overclock: cooling. Proper thermal regulation of both the microprocessor and the entire system is required to maintain stability at extended operating speeds, especially as the latest 1+ GHz architectures push the envelope in terms of extreme heat generation. The overclocking of a processor without proper cooling is tempting fate, as this is the leading cause of component failure when pushing systems beyond their factory defaults.

Chapters 6 through 8 offer extended information about each of the latest platforms from the three primary manufacturers: AMD, Intel, and VIA. Topics include platform specifics and detailed information about the latest generations of processors. We'll cover background information, architectural data, operating speeds, and detailed overclocking procedures for all current, popular platforms.

Chapter 9 tackles troubleshooting, which is often required to diagnose potential instabilities or device failures within an overclocked computing system. Overclocking increases the possibility of instability because it places additional stress on the various system components. The majority of problems arise from mismatches in the communication rates between each of the PC's components.

Chapter 10 discusses benchmarking applications and procedures, the ability to assess the performance return offered by overclocking. We'll look at the intricate testing and analysis of system performance at all component levels with a balance of both synthetic and real-world benchmarking routines. A complete system benchmark testing process can also offer you the ability to determine the proper mixture of various overclocking procedures for maximum performance.

Chapter 11 offers advice on whether or not you should overclock once you know how, as well as smart shopping tips, and what to do with your PC's increased performance. Just because you know how to overclock, doesn't mean that it's right for you, since overclocking can increase system instabilities and the potential for data loss. And of course, it may make more sense for you to buy cheap and fast components rather than overclock your existing hardware, so the smart shopping tips section will help you find the lowest prices on quality hardware from the best retailers.

The Appendix answers your most frequently asked overclocking-related questions, defines terms, and provides a list of resources where you can further advance your knowledge and overclocking skills. You will also find a list of software applications to help you diagnose, benchmark, and overclock your PC. Several retailers are listed that provide overclocking equipment such as water coolers, fans, Athlon unlocking kits, and PC cases.

2

OVERCLOCKING VERSUS INDUSTRY HYPE: TECHNICAL BACKGROUND

The popularity of overclocking has undergone extensive growth within the tech enthusiast community as a response to the increasing costs of maintaining a cutting-edge yet affordable PC. Overclocking serves as a solution to the high prices associated with today's latest processors. Trying to keep pace with the latest releases in processor technologies can become costly, as new releases of increased speed ranges become available at an exponential rate compared to just a few years ago.

No longer do just a few megahertz (MHz) separate the fastest processors from the slowest within a single processor family. For just one processor design, today's market offers processor speed ranges of several hundred MHz, though the manufacturer's associated pricing strategies of this business model do not benefit you. Processor manufacturers spend millions of dollars to hype the "latest designs," when in reality the newest processors are little more than the same processor core operating at a higher MHz rating. The pricing of each speed-rated processor varies as widely as the hype surrounding the MHz rating game. As illustrated by Figure 2-1, where we look at the Intel Pentium 4 processor as an example, the cost of the higher-speed processors often exceeds the cost of the lower-speed processors of the same processor family by hundreds of dollars. Overclocking successfully circumvents the industry's hype by working to obtain maximum performance from the more cost-efficient lower spectrum of a particular processor family.

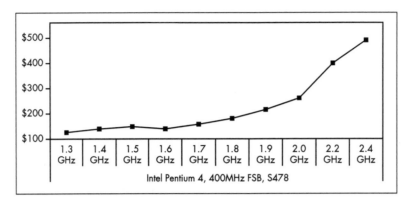

Figure 2-1: Intel Pentium 4 retail pricing and speed range

Overclocking allows users to select lower speed, and thus lower cost, grades of a processor family, then increase the clock speed of the processor core to a level that is comparable to the upper-range processors of that processor family. A properly designed overclocking implementation can often exceed the speed ratings of the latest processors available while utilizing much lower-cost processors to minimize expense. Overclocking existing systems may prove more problematic compared to building a system with overclocking in mind, but the potential for increasing operating speeds by several percent still remains a reality for the widest range of designs.

Processor manufacturers are well aware of the overclocking community, but most do little to circumvent such efforts, since the majority of mainstream computer users know little about the processes and procedures involved in overclocking. Still, the industry has implemented various features to deter overclocking attempts over the years. Such attempts have been implemented across all stages of processor design, from the earliest engineering to the latest fabrication stages of production. Some manufacturers have even attempted complete locking of processor core operating speeds, known as clock locking. Fortunately, the cost of implementing clock locking has limited its introduction within the retail market segment of the industry.

Prebuilt Versus Custom Systems

Preconfigured systems from original equipment manufacturers (OEMs) offer clear pricing advantages for initial retail cost, though the long-term maintenance and upgrade costs may be significantly higher compared to a custom configured system from a smaller system integrator, local vendor, or self-build. OEM-assembled systems are clearly not the choice for maximum overclocking potential, but the possibility of successfully overclocking these systems remains high due to increased efforts of the enthusiast community to provide overclocking-related information, custom software, and hardware hacks for OEM-assembled computers.

OEM systems are commonly built atop hardware with minimal overclocking capabilities to minimize costs associated with supporting end-user overclocking attempts. Owners of such systems must often look to online enthusiast communities for specialized procedures and tricks for successful overclocking. Thus, it's trickier to overclock OEM-configured systems, but the rewards in terms of increased operating speeds and improved performance can rival that of a custom-built overclocking system.

NOTE   *OEMs have no desire to support overclocking options within their system designs. Overclocking not only voids component warranties, but also it can lead to system instability and component failures for those users unwilling to undertake the precautions required for successful overclocking. Integrating support for overclocking would lead to a customer support nightmare for these large corporations.*

Table 2-1: The Pros and Cons of OEM- and Custom-Configured Systems

System Type	Pros	Cons
OEM Configured	• Low upfront cost • Easy to acquire	• Higher upgrade cost • Difficult overclocking
Custom Configured	• Superior overclocking potential • Every component tailored exactly to your computing needs • Less expensive upgrades	• Self-build requires some specialized knowledge to select and assemble system components • Increased upfront cost

The cost of implementing overclocking-friendly components within a system would serve to increase retail prices for the consumer market segment. Overclocking-capable systems are generally built atop quality hardware developed for direct retail sales to consumers, while OEM systems are usually built utilizing mass-produced, off-the-shelf components in the hopes of lowering production costs. While overclocking is still a possibility for many OEM system owners, aftermarket custom-configured systems offer superior overclocking potential for enthusiasts.

A custom-configured (or self-built) system can provide optimum tweaking options to offer the most potential for successful overclocking. The effort required to either build or attain overclocking-friendly systems is more intensive than an off-the-shelf retail system from a major OEM manufacturer, but the enhanced overclocking potential is clearly evident. When building your own custom-configured system, you can also precertify each of the system's components for its "overclockability" by researching product reviews and articles from a variety of publications, such as popular hardware review websites like those in Table 2-2.

Table 2-2: Recommended Websites for Precertifying the Overclockability of Hardware Components

Website Name	Website Address
Ace's Hardware	http://www.aceshardware.com
AnandTech	http://www.anandtech.com
HardOCP	http://www.hardocp.com
TechIMO	http://www.techimo.com
Overclockers.com	http://www.overclockers.com

Overclocking Examples

Examples of typical overclocking scenarios offer better illustrations of the cost savings and performance improvements than any amount of technical data. Table 2-3 reflects a substantial savings in cost for an overclocked slower-speed-rated processor versus a nonoverclocked faster-speed-rated processor, for both AMD and Intel processors. Both the AMD Athlon and the Intel Pentium 4 represent the latest architectures from each of the largest industry players. Each platform offers rated processors that scale several hundred MHz within the same model family, with prices varying widely from the lowest to highest MHz offerings.

Table 2-3: Cost Analysis of an Overclocked, Slower-Rated Processor Versus a Nonoverclocked, Faster-Rated Processor

Processor to Overclock	Market Price*	Potential Overclock**	Equivalent to Overclocked Speed	Equivalent Cost*	Comparative Savings
Intel Pentium 4 2000 MHz	$143	2600 MHz	Intel Pentium 4 2600 MHz	$378	62%
AMD Athlon XP 1600+ @ 1400 MHz	$53	1800 MHz	AMD Athlon XP 2100+ @ 1800 MHz	$141	62%

* Average market prices as of 11/2002.

** May not be typical of all processor samples.

The Athlon Thunderbird series of processors offers a great example of over-clocking potential. A typical entry-level AMD system now comes configured with a 1000 MHz Thunderbird processor, as this chip offers a great price to performance ratio. However, overclocking can serve to further extend that ratio by allowing the processor to operate at a speed beyond the factory-defined 1000 MHz rating. For example, many of the best 1000 MHz Thunderbird processors can be overclocked to 1200+ MHz with little more than a minor change in the system's user-configurable BIOS configuration setup or motherboard jumper settings. The potential exists for even higher overclocking ranges with additional user effort, such as improving case or processor cooling to maintain better thermal regulation in order to reach higher core processor operating speeds.

Intel's latest Pentium 4 platform offers superb overclocking potential assuming the user thinks ahead when designing and assembling a custom-configured system. Even the earliest Pentium 4 1.5-GHz processors can usually attain 1.7+ GHz with little effort beyond a single change in the system's BIOS setup or motherboard jumper settings. As with the first example, those willing to undertake additional effort to increase cooling capabilities and other system design aspects can often witness much improved overclocking potential. Many of the best Pentium 4 1.5-GHz processors can attain operating speeds upwards of 2 GHz with a careful and patient system design plan.

3

TECHNICAL THEORY: EVOLUTION OF THE INTEGRATED CIRCUIT

Learning about the terms and technologies associated with overclocking will help you understand the techniques involved. PC performance depends not only on the technology of the processor itself, but on a number of subsystems as well.

Measuring Processor Performance

Early processor performance was measured in terms of how many instructions per second the architecture could execute on a standard set of data. As processors evolved and increased in complexity, a new approach was required. Frequency (the ability to switch a circuit quickly) became the popular measurement of computational speed.

Frequency is best described as the rate at which an IC can change between its two states in a given period of time. Computer processor frequency is generally measured in megahertz. The term *megahertz* refers to millions of cycles per second, and the abbreviation is expressed as MHz. *Gigahertz* (expressed as GHz), or billions of cycles per second, is becoming the de facto standard due to significant speed gains in the latest generation of processors.

Physical Properties of Integrated Circuits

Several physical properties directly influence a processor's speed potential, but the die fabrication size of the processor's core circuitry is the most important. The core die size represents the actual physical distance between each trace signal route used to construct transistor pathways within the processor. A smaller die size means that the processor can generally operate at higher clock frequencies while using less voltage and producing less heat.

The current industry standard die size is .18 micron (μ), which represents a balance between electrical and thermal constraints, yet retains scalability beyond 1 GHz. Popular designs using the .18-micron die size include Intel's Pentium III Coppermine and Pentium 4 Willamette, and AMD's Athlon Thunderbird.

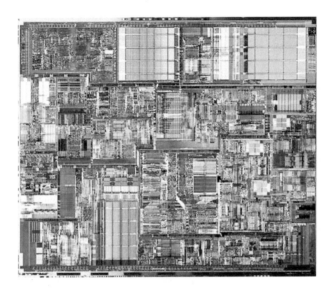

Figure 3-1: .18-micron Pentium 4

A significant number of PCs still in use contain processors fabricated with the much older .25-micron core die size. These include processors like the Pentium II and K6-2. Massive cooling systems are needed when overclocking .25-micron processors, because these chips demand much higher voltage levels compared to those required by their .18-micron counterparts. It is difficult to scale these older designs beyond 600 MHz.

The core die size for the latest generation of processors, like Intel's Pentium III Tualatin and Pentium 4 Northwood, is the radically small .13 micron. These chips offer relatively low thermal dissipation rates (up to 50% lower than .18-micron models), as well as significantly lower core voltage requirements. Improved MHz scalability is the direct result of these advancements, and many .13-micron designs are expected to scale to 3 GHz and beyond before the next-generation fabrication process, which should be in the range of .7 to .9 micron, is introduced.

These overclocked chips need more power to keep them stable at extended MHz operating speeds. Current designs are built atop a split-voltage architecture. Core voltage represents the internal electrical properties of the processor and corresponds with the die size employed during fabrication. Input/output voltage represents the operational voltage of the processor-to-chipset bus. It usually includes the power levels of other front-side bus components within a traditional system configuration.

Thermal Dissipation Rate

The *thermal dissipation rate* is a measurement of heat generated within an electrical circuit. The actual thermal unit employed in this measurement is watts. Assuming that the core die size remains consistent, the thermal rate increases proportionally to rises in operational speeds and core voltage levels. The processor's heatsink cooling mechanism is worth examining in any PC.

Figure 3-2: Processor heatsink cooler

Most designs use a large metal heatsink coupled with a fan to provide a forced-air cooling system for maximum heat dissipation at a relatively low cost. Other cooling systems are available, including vapor-phase and thermoelectric technologies, but their associated costs are usually prohibitive for the average desktop PC user. Whatever the cooling system, efficient thermal regulation is an important factor in successful overclocking. If core temperatures exceed normal operating specifications, the system can become unstable. Circuits can also be damaged during prolonged periods of intense heat.

Fabrication

While overclocking is often regarded as a rogue process, the premise behind it is well documented within the computer industry. Once a particular processor design has been finalized and taped out for silicon production, the manufacturer moves into the production and marketing phase of development. The manufacturing of processors or of any circuit device, is known as *fabrication*.

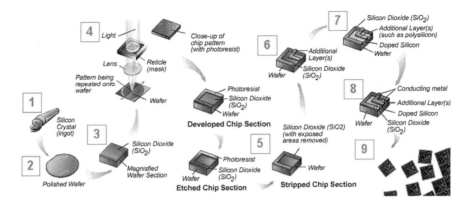

Figure 3-3: Processor fabrication process

The fabrication of an integrated circuit device begins with the selection of a substrate material. The substrate provides a base for the layers of electrical circuits that create transistor pathways. Both the type and quality of the substrate are important in determining maximum operating speed for a given processor design.

Silicon Substrate

All commercial processors currently on the market are built atop a silicon substrate. Silicon is a readily available element with good electrical isolation properties. It can be harvested from a variety of sources, and can even be obtained from common sand. The use of silicon minimizes production costs for processor manufacturers.

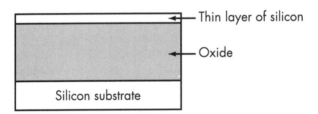

Figure 3-4: Silicon substrate circuit

Silicon substrates in today's processors contain impurities left during the extraction process. These limit the substrate's electrical insulation efficiency, and lead to lower yield rates and slower core operating speeds.

CMOS fabrication techniques will likely change to accommodate upcoming generations of processors. Processors are currently manufactured using aluminum or copper metal layers within the transistor gate array. Copper offers less resistance and better conductivity than its aluminum counterpart. Nearly all newer processor designs therefore incorporate copper trace-route technologies, though an evolution in substrate technologies will be required to consolidate the gains in speed and efficiency.

The SOI Standard

Silicon-on-insulator (SOI) is primed to be the next substrate manufacturing standard. It differs from CMOS in that it places the transistor silicon junction atop an electrically insulated layer, commonly of glass or silicon oxide. *Capacitance*, a measure of ability to store an electrical charge, can be minimized in the gate area using the SOI switching technique.

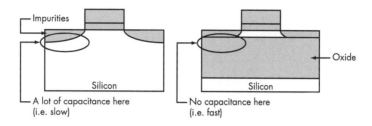

Figure 3-5: Silicon-on-insulator circuit

Any transfer medium that can conduct electricity will exhibit capacitance to some degree. A MOS transistor is regarded as a capacitance circuit, implying that the MOS circuit must actually charge to full capacitance before it can activate its switching capability. The process of discharging and recharging a transistor requires a relatively long time compared to the time needed to switch the voltage state of a metal layer within a traditional transistor architecture. SOI is an attempt to eliminate this capacitance boundary: a low capacitance circuit will allow faster transistor operation. Accordingly, the ability to process more instructions in a given timeframe increases as latency in the transistor array decreases.

New Technologies

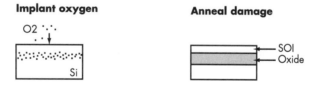

Figure 3-6: IBM SIMOX process

IBM has pioneered research into SIMOX, a silicon purification method that uses a high-temperature injection to introduce oxygen into a silicon wafer and thus purify the substrate material. Oxygen bonds with silicon at high temperatures; thus a thin layer of silicon oxide film is formed. This nearly perfect layer allows for direct bonding of a pure crystalline silicon substrate. The greatest advantage of SIMOX is its significantly lower production costs compared to crystalline-based SOI methods that use expensive ruby or sapphire design materials.

Silicon-on-insulator is not the only upcoming technology to revolutionize the substrate production process. Perhaps the most promising future technology involves the compression and purification of nitrogen. In this process, purified nitrogen gas is compressed and tempered into a solid form. Once depressurized, the nitrogen remains in a solid state. Substrates produced from this technique are expected to be almost perfectly pure, while the abundant supply of nitrogen within our atmosphere could lower production costs.

Light Lithography

Light lithography is used to etch specific circuit pathways within a processor core. A shadow mask is created from a scaled blueprint of the processor's core circuitry. This shadow mask is then used in conjunction with a light etching process that literally burns the circuit pathways into the processor substrate. Additional shadow masks are then applied to create the complex multilayer circuitry found within a processor. Figure 3-7 shows a silicon wafer being tested after etching.

Figure 3-7: Silicon wafer being tested after etching

Etching can lower production costs by producing multiple processors at once. A large wafer of silicon is placed within the light masking system, which produces a "batch" of processors during a single pass. Each processor shares a common circuit design, with certain fail-safe and redundancy features embedded into the core architecture. Variation in quality among processors is due to the physical limitations involved in production.

Figure 3-8: Intel processor fabrication lab

Silicon-on-Insulator Processors

AMD is scheduled to release a silicon-on-insulator processor based on its popular Athlon architecture before the end of the year 2002. This new Athlon design should arrive under a development project codenamed Thoroughbred, the first introduction of SOI technologies into the mainstream computing market for x86 architectures. Assuming the Thoroughbred design proves successful, other manufacturers, including Intel, will move quickly to adopt similar production techniques to extend the operating speed of current processor designs.

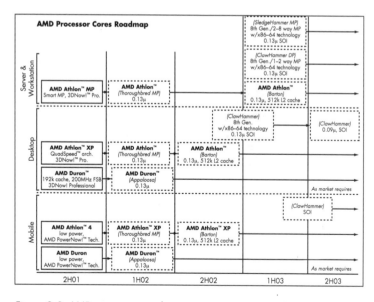

Figure 3-9: AMD processor roadmap

Laboratory testing shows that SOI-based processors can achieve up to a 25% improvement in transistor cycle time compared to the same architecture manufactured with more traditional CMOS fabrication techniques. Performance gains can average 25 to 35% when SOI is employed. Considering the efficient scalability of such an advanced design, the upcoming Athlon Thoroughbred could rapidly emerge as the dominant choice for overclocking enthusiasts.

Quality Control and Overclocking

As with any fabrication process, the actual quality of each unit in production can vary under the influence of numerous variables, both internal and external. For example, consider automobile manufacturing. Thousands of vehicles are manufactured during every production year. One individual vehicle may outperform another of the same make and model simply because no two cars rolling off the assembly line are exactly the same.

Assembly lines operate within tolerances. Designers set base specifications that represent a minimum standard of quality before the product can be sold in the retail market. Let's take the automotive industry example to the next level. Assume that each vehicle within a given model line must perform at a specific minimum miles-per-hour rating before being released for retail consumption. Imagine that a speed limit of 100 miles per hour is such a minimum. In order to test the production quality, designers could sample two individual vehicles of the same model manufactured on different days. Vehicle A reaches maximum performance at 100 mph, so the designers are satisfied. Vehicle B offers even better performance, reaching 105 mph during testing. While both vehicles were produced at the same plant with the same materials, small differences between them can result from even smaller variances in the manufacturing process.

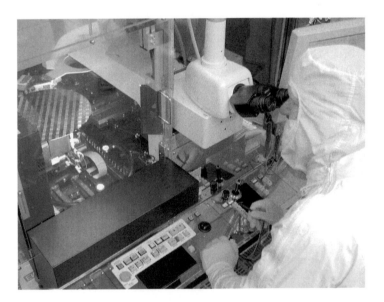

Figure 3-10: Intel quality control testing

Most computer processor manufacturers use more exacting tolerances than those illustrated in the automobile example, though the general analogy holds. Because the average processor is comprised of millions of microscopic transistor circuits, the possibility for variances is considerable. For example, each speed grade of the Athlon XP processor from AMD is fabricated to essentially the same expected tolerances. Minor fabrication differences among units may lead one processor to reach a maximum stable operational speed of 1.4 GHz, while another chip of the same design may operate at 1.6 GHz.

The Economics of Speed Binning

Automobile companies sell all comparably equipped vehicles of a particular model at the same base price, while a processor company can choose to sell the better performing chip at a higher price to maximize profit yields with lower capital costs. If the automobile manufacturer in the above example operated like a processor manufacturer, it would sell the car that reached 100 mph at one price and the car that reached 105 mph at a higher price, even though both vehicles were essentially identical in every other respect. Conversely, a processor manufacturer like AMD could behave like an automobile maker, offering each CPU without any performance rating beyond the flat minimum speed requirement. This marketing strategy would yield the same base revenue for all processors. Profits would decline due to the standard economies of supply and demand.

Offering varying speed grades of the same product means maximizing profit. Most computer users exhibit a consistent *desire* for better performance, whether they *need* it or not. Computer performance is dictated by megahertz ratings, assuming all other subsystem characteristics are identical. Most buyers equate MHz ratings to performance, though many other aspects of processor design contribute to performance. The cost of acquiring higher MHz models can prove limiting, which leads some consumers to investigate the benefits of overclocking.

Popular fabricators and chip suppliers like Intel and UMC produce millions of circuit-based devices each year. The trend toward bulk fabrication techniques leads to a practice known as *speed binning,* which allows the computer industry to differentiate cost and performance characteristics while protecting profits. Still, the sheer number of chips being produced each year prevents manufacturers from testing every individual processor for its maximum operating speed potential.

Figure 3-11: Intel quality control testing

In Speed Binning, the manufacturer selects processors from a given production batch and puts those processors through reliability testing to determine the maximum reliable speed that is common to all processors in that batch. The processors in the batch are then usually marked for sale at the speed rating determined in the testing process.

Even though speed binning is a well-developed and highly efficient process, quality variances still exist among processors in any given batch. These variances often allow processors to be overclocked beyond their rated speed, since the speed rating for any given batch must be such that all processors in the batch can operate at the speed rating, even though each and every individual processor is not speed tested.

Speed binning produces unique benefits for both manufacturers and consumers. Manufacturers can charge higher selling prices for better performing processors. Consumers can opt for lower speed grades to minimize costs, while enthusiasts among them may obtain an even greater performance-to-price ratio if they are willing to push the stability envelope and overclock their processors.

Processor-to-Chipset Relation

The frequency of a processor represents only the core operating speed; each subsystem within a computer may operate at various other rates. It is important to understand how these frequencies interact with each other before embarking on the overclocking process. Additional factors related to the processor's physical properties play a key role in understanding the process. These include core die sizes, electrical aspects, and thermal regulation.

Figure 3-12: Traditional motherboard layout

PLL Circuit

A *phased locked loop* or PLL circuit resides at the simplest level of the frequency generation equation. Some older designs were based around a set frequency crystal, though PLL circuits have been the mainstay logic timing control technology for many years now. The PLL acts as a base frequency synthesizer by cycling its generated signal according to a preprogrammed routine. The locking of the circuit in a specific pattern creates a phase shift in the signal, thus producing a cycling effect that drives the frequency generation scheme. The PLL signal travels across a motherboard bus, dedicated to timing, to dictate the frequency needed for the operation of other buses. The primary recipient of the PLL signal is the motherboard's main controller, known as the *chipset*.

Chipset designs differ greatly across the wide range of platforms available, though the basic concept is shared. The frequency rate at which the chipset operates is the motherboard's primary operating speed. The chipset provides a communications hub for all of the system's various components. It also controls routing and logic for most primary control operations, ranging from memory addressing to data transfers across different bus standards.

The term *front-side bus rate* is widely used to describe the motherboard's frequency rate, as this same rate is often also used for the memory and processor buses within a traditional system design. To confuse matters, many of the latest architectures like the AMD Athlon or Intel Pentium 4 blur the relationships among each of these three primary buses by separating each bus at the chipset connection point. The *back-side bus,* on the other hand, is generally composed of additional input/output mechanisms, such as PCI and AGP connection buses.

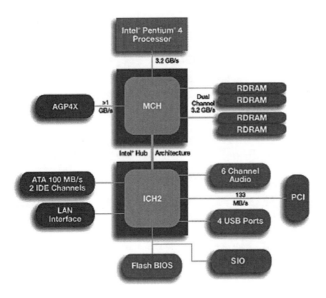

Figure 3-13: Intel i850 chipset diagram

Upon receiving the base PLL signal, the chipset generates a signal to the other buses. The most important signal to overclockers is the processor bus rate of the front-side bus, as this directly determines the central processing unit's core operating speed when combined with the processor multiplier value. The PLL circuit provides the base timing signal for the motherboard chipset, which in turn passes the value to the processor. The processor then internally multiplies this clock rate to derive its core clock operating frequency.

Frequency Timing Scheme

The best way to describe this process is to refer to a common system design, such as the Pentium III platform. A quick examination of a common chipset, such as the VIA's Pro133A model, shows how the process actually works. The Pro133A chipset is built primarily for a 100-MHz operation, though the Pentium III processor itself features a much higher operating speed. The core processor rate is determined by inserting a multiplier into the timing signal. Thus, a Pentium III 650e processor uses a 6.5x clock multiplier, given that the chipset is operating at 100 MHz. Multiplier values are generally spaced in .5x increments; this scheme allows for a wide range of operating frequencies when speed-binning processors.

Most platforms use the timing scheme presented in the Pentium III example, though some of the newer architectures, notably AMD's Athlon and Intel's Pentium 4, can alter the interpretation. The x86 Athlon uses a modified bus architecture developed from a non-x86 DEC Alpha EV6. The Athlon inserts a double data rate (DDR) signaling pattern into the processor-to-chipset interconnect bus. DDR signaling uses the rising and falling edges of the base clock signal to effectively transfer twice as much data as traditional buses can transfer in a similar period of time.

Quad Data Rate

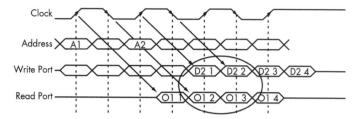

Figure 3-14: QDR signal pattern

The Pentium 4 goes one step further with a pseudo quad data rate (QDR) processor bus design. Without going deeply into deeply technical issues, the P4 processor bus can be viewed as implementing DDR signaling across two 180-degree co-phased timing signals that travel essentially the same bus pathway. More about each of these platforms can be found in the architecture-specific overclocking sections of this book.

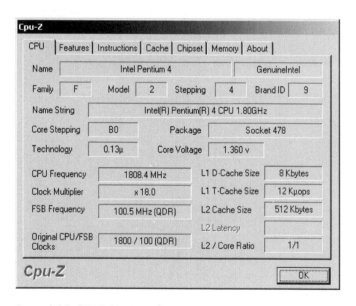

Figure 3-15: CPU-Z CPUID application

A software application called CPUID can help you determine the particular model and speed grade of your PC processor if you are unsure of its configuration. CPU-Z by Frank Delatree is a popular freeware example. This valuable utility can be obtained at http://www.cpuid.com/cpuz.htm. CPU-Z can provide information about multiplier values, bus rates, and various other technological aspects of most currently available processors.

4

HOW TO OVERCLOCK

Motherboard Configuration

Overclocking involves manipulating the processor's multiplier and the motherboard's front-side bus speed, in small increments, until a maximum stable operating frequency is reached. The idea is simple, but variation in both the electrical and physical characteristics of x86 computing systems complicates this process. Processor multipliers, bus dividers, voltages, thermal loads, cooling techniques, and many other issues can affect your ability to push any given system to its maximum potential.

On most systems, processor multiplier values, motherboard bus speeds, and voltage levels can be adjusted, either through hardware-level jumpers and dip-switches or firmware BIOS settings. The brand and model of the motherboard determine how easy and effective the process will be. Most boards allow you to configure at least a portion of these settings, though many low-end and original equipment manufacturer (OEM) designs opt for autodetection routines that prevent manual manipulation.

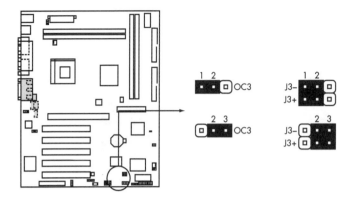

Figure 4-1: Jumper configuration

Jumpers and dipswitches are the predominant methods for adjusting motherboard values in many computing platforms. *Jumpers* are small electrically conductive devices that push into place over a series of pins to establish an electrical connection (essentially, a removable on/off switch). Jumper points are usually arranged in block patterns, each jumper connecting two pins within the series. Connecting a series of pins in a specific sequence within the block creates the signaling data required to set parameters for proper motherboard operation.

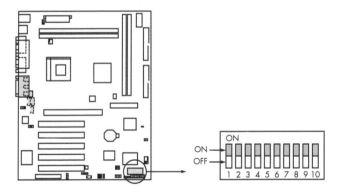

Figure 4-2: Dipswitch configuration

Dipswitches are tiny switching devices, usually found in groups among a single interface block. Electrically, dipswitches work the same way their jumper cousins do. The dipswitch design was introduced to simplify the motherboard configuration process. Dipswitches are available in a variety of sizes. The smallest types require particular care because they can be damaged easily, especially after multiple changes in position or through the overexertion of force.

Many of the latest motherboard architectures allow for advanced hardware configuration through the system's CMOS BIOS Setup. Methods of entering the BIOS interface vary according to brand, but basic procedures are generic. Most systems prompt for a specific keystroke to enter the BIOS Setup menu. The most common of these are DEL and F2, but others include DEL-ESC, CTRL-ESC, and F10, F12, CTRL-ALT, ESC, CTRL-ALT-ENTER, CTRL-ALT-F1, CTRL-ALT-S, and simply ESC. If your system boots with a custom graphics screen, you can often press the ESC key to bypass it and view the standard interface. Custom boot screens are common in OEM-built systems.

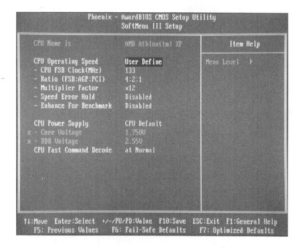

Figure 4-3: Award BIOS configuration

No two motherboards are alike, so it is nearly impossible to determine how to alter hardware settings without researching the documentation provided by the motherboard manufacturer or system integrator. Some companies even choose to implement a combination of hardware and BIOS-level configuration options. They may use *both* jumpers or dipswitches *and* a BIOS Setup menu in order to appeal to both the OEM and retail markets.

Preferred Motherboards

Retail-level manufacturers usually want to maximize system configuration options, so their motherboards are likely to be easier to tweak. In contrast, pre-built systems from larger OEMs and system integrators often lack advanced user-definable options. Prebuilt systems are engineered for maximum stability across the widest range of users, so the incentive to allow user configuration of hardware is limited.

Taiwan-based Abit Computer Corporation is perhaps the most popular of these retail-level companies. Its motherboard designs support many customizable options. Companies like Asus, Epox, Gigabyte, and Transcend also offer great designs for the enthusiast market. Nearly all motherboards allow some overclocking, either through hardware or software. Feature sets vary widely, however, even among similar motherboard models from the same manufacturer.

Motherboards may contain only some of the features that would facilitate overclocking. Optimal support would include the ability to manipulate the processor's multiplier, configure processor-to-chipset bus speeds, and set processor core and motherboard input/output voltages. A feature called active thermal monitoring, which uses onboard sensors to maintain optimum temperature at extended operating speeds, also promotes stability and improves overclocking capability.

Overclocking via Processor Multiplier

Manipulating the processor multiplier is the optimal overclocking method, since it neither interrupts nor changes motherboard-level bus speeds. The processor multiplier number that you select in your BIOS Setup menu (see Figure 4-3), or via dipswitches or jumpers on your motherboard, will determine your processor's operating frequency since the processor will multiply the motherboard's front-side-bus frequency by the processor multiplier. Therefore, by increasing the processor multiplier beyond its default setting, you will increase your processor's operating frequency beyond its default as well.

System stability can only be compromised if the maximum operating frequency of the processor's core is exceeded. Maximum performance potential is best realized by combining several overclocking techniques, but multiplier overclocking is a favorite of many enthusiasts because it creates fewer problems.

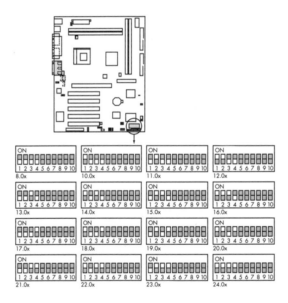

Figure 4-4: Multiplier configuration example

Depending on your system hardware, overclocking through multiplier manipulation alone may be impractical. For example, the most recent Intel processors feature a locked core multiplier, except for the earliest Pentium II-based designs and the occasional unlocked engineering sample that surfaces in the underground market. All current and near-future Intel processors are completely locked, thus forcing owners to rely on front-side bus overclocking techniques.

Knowing your motherboard is critical to assessing the overclocking potential of any current AMD Athlon system. The majority of Athlon-based motherboards lack the features users need to control multiplier values. The required circuitry increases manufacturing costs. Those willing to risk hardware-level modifications can overcome this limitation.

Overclocking via Front-side Bus

Front-side (or processor-to-chipset) overclocking is the best way to maximize system performance, especially when it can be combined with multiplier overclocking. If your system lacks multiplier adjustment capabilities, you must rely solely on bus overclocking at the motherboard level. The difficulty lies in the fact that overclocking the front-side bus can affect the rates of all buses throughout the system.

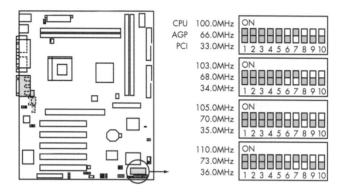

Figure 4-5: Front-side bus configuration example

The front-side bus rate is linked with other bus rates in most x86 systems. The peripheral component interconnect bus, or PCI, the accelerated graphics port bus, or AGP, and the various memory buses, are examples of this design paradigm. Each of the system's interconnect buses serve to connect various devices to the processor, and each operates at a rate fractional to the operating rate of the front-side bus. While not all motherboard chipsets offer identical capabilities, most follow industry design specifications for compatibility reasons.

The Memory Bus

The memory bus can operate in one of two modes, synchronous or asynchronous. Synchronous operation means that the memory bus operates at the same base frequency as the front-side bus. The synchronous memory bus is the simplest architecture to manipulate, though it may not be best for maximizing overclocking potential. Asynchronous operation allows the memory bus to function at a different rate than the front-side bus. Asynchronous designs can be based on incremental frequency changes related to the front-side bus frequency or entirely on independent rates.

Many motherboards are able to operate in either synchronous or asynchronous memory access modes. The ability to change the front-side bus frequency depends on the memory access mode in use. Quality memory, capable of stable operation at extended frequencies, is preferred. As expected, different platforms react differently to memory overclocking.

Old designs using 30- or 72-pin single inline memory modules (SIMMs), like fast-page or extended data out (EDO) memory, tend to become unstable at relatively low operating speeds during overclocking. The older 30-pin designs can rarely scale beyond 40 MHz, while 72-pin designs generally reach their maximum around 83 MHz. The need for asynchronous bus operation with such architectures became evident as processor-to-chipset rates began to outpace memory capabilities.

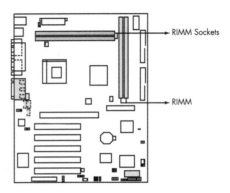

Figure 4-6: RAMBUS memory example

Asynchronous memory operation became even more necessary with the adoption of SDRAM, DDR RAM, and RAMBUS memory technologies. Early PC-66 memory modules were, at best, suspect for overclocking. Later fabrication techniques allowed successful scaling to higher operating speeds, up to 166+ MHz with the PC-166 modules. Asynchronous operation does insert longer latencies in the chipset-to-memory pipeline; however, the benefits of greater bandwidth commonly outweigh such penalties. For this reason most non-Intel-based motherboards allow users to raise or lower the memory bus speed in relation to the front-side bus speed.

Bus	Bus Frequency	Bandwidth	Data Transfer Rate
PCI	33 MHz	33 MHz	133 MB/sec
AGP 1X	66 MHZ	66 MHz	266 MB/sec
AGP 2X	66 MHZ	133 MHz	512 MB/sec
AGP 4X	66 MHZ	266 MHz	0124 MB/sec

Figure 4-7: Common bus rates

The PCI Bus

The PCI bus speed is derived from the front-side bus speed. The PCI 2.x specification defines 33 MHz as the default bus frequency, though most of today's better components can scale to 40 MHz and beyond. In most systems, the PCI bus speed is a fraction of the front-side bus speed. For example, the Pentium IIIe uses a 100-MHz front-side bus. A 1/3 factor is introduced into the PCI timing process to produce the default 33-MHz PCI bus speed.

Certain crossover points in PCI to front-side bus ratios can create stability problems. The most common risky frequencies are those approaching 83 and 124 MHz for the front-side bus. Due to a 1/2 divider limit at the 83-MHz range, the PCI rate is extended to 41.5 MHz, well beyond its 33-MHz default specification. The 124-MHz front-side bus rate leads to a similar scenario, as the 1/3 divider forces a 41.3-MHz PCI rate. Some motherboard designs allow users to refine the divider value, but this feature is not common in production-level boards.

PCI components with the highest risk of failure at 40+ MHz are storage drives, especially early-model IDE drives. SCSI drives do not usually exhibit this problem due to their more exacting specifications. Stability issues can often be resolved by lowering the drive-transfer signaling speed by one level. This results in lower bandwidth, though the performance gains realized through overclocking the processor or the front-side bus may negate any loss. Benchmarking utilities are needed to ascertain performance differences.

The AGP Bus

The AGP bus is similarly limited during front-side bus overclocking. Problems again arise at 83 and 124 MHz for nearly all chipset designs. Some motherboard architectures also suffer instability or high failure rates at 100+ MHz due to limitations in early AGP bus implementations. For example, Intel's popular BX chipset can support proper 133 MHz front-side bus operation for all system buses except the AGP. The BX features only 1/1 and 2/3 AGP divider functions, and thus a 133-MHz front-side bus rate leads to a problematic 88.6-MHz AGP rate.

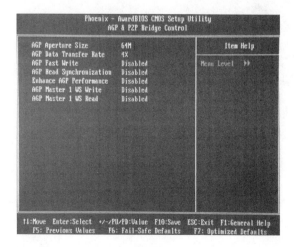

Figure 4-8: AGP bus configuration

Many of the latest AGP graphics accelerators can operate effectively at extended levels, often up to 90 MHz. For maximum stability, it may be necessary to lower AGP transfer speeds by one level (that is, 4x to 2x) or to disable AGP side-band addressing. Those with older AGP video cards or motherboard-level integrated graphics chipsets need to analyze stability closely through long-term testing. Even if an AGP card seems stable, additional frequency loads can damage the graphics accelerator over time. Failure may come after several weeks of operation or problems may never surface. AGP overclocking is a gamble; it requires extreme care, especially when it introduces problematic front-side bus rates into the graphics pipeline.

USB or IEEE 1394 Firewire connections do not usually suffer under front-side bus overclocking. These well-designed implementations can handle the extended operating frequencies involved. Older buses, like ISA, can be problematic. Systems with peripherals based on such architecture would likely see greater benefit from upgrading than from overclocking.

Stability Through Voltage Increase

Achieving stability at extended operating speeds often requires increasing voltage levels, and sustaining faster processor speeds can demand a greater core voltage. Similarly, faster chipset operating speeds can often be sustained through a bump in input/output voltage. Several of the latest DDR memory-based motherboards also allow manipulation of memory bus voltage levels. This feature was originally implemented to preserve compatibility with early DDR modules, but the ability to change memory voltage levels has led to significant improvements in stability. Overclocking enthusiasts have exploited the potential for maximizing operating frequencies in this way.

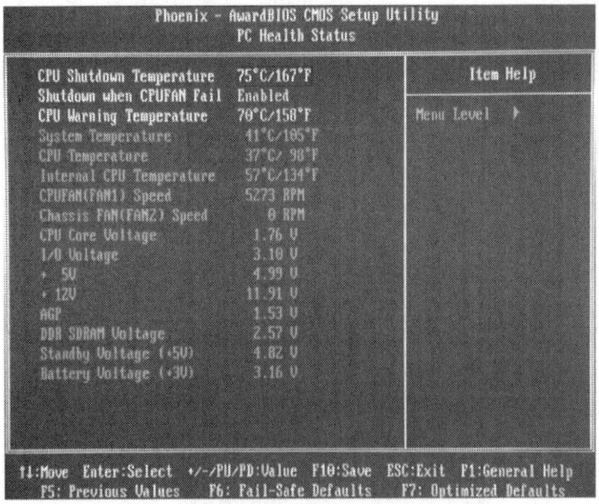

Figure 4-9: Voltage monitoring

Any increases in voltage levels are potentially hazardous. Most current .18- and .25-micron processor core architectures can operate within a 10 percent variance from the default specification, but added stresses require extra measures to protect long-term system stability. Cooling plays an integral role in the voltage manipulation process.

Any increases in voltage levels produce additional heat in the core circuitry. While all circuits can cross certain thermal thresholds, additional cooling is often required to prevent damage from temperature variations. Processor coolers, heat transfer compounds, case fans, and case design can all affect the cooling capabilities of a system. Further discussion of choices in these areas can be found in Chapter 8 dedicated to cooling technologies.

A phenomenon called electron migration can lead to system failure as a result of voltage increases. Electron migration results when moving electrons are displaced across integrated circuit trace routes. As fabrication technologies improve, die size becomes critical in determining maximum voltage tolerances. Smaller die sizes produce narrower trace routes, thus reducing the processor's ability to cope with the stresses of electron migration. As the circuits get smaller, voltage-level tolerances are lowered exponentially. Chapters 6, 7, and 8, detail system-specific information, including information about maximum voltage levels.

5

COOLING

Heatsink Cooling

All electronic circuits discharge heat generated by the movement of electrons. As operating frequencies increase, thermal loads go up (assuming die sizes and fabrication techniques remain constant). Given these facts, a successful overclocker must pay attention to cooling systems and sometimes devise external solutions dedicated to dissipating heat and regulating the processor's temperature.

Figure 5-1: Forced-air heatsink cooler

Most common thermal regulation solutions are built around the concept of forced-air cooling. The standard processor cooler includes a massive metal heatsink and a high revolutions-per-minute (RPM) fan to dissipate heat through convection. Forced-air coolers represent the most cost-effective solution for the widest range of system platforms; the parts are simple in design and readily available. Many solutions are possible, but a heatsink cooler is still the best choice for most overclocking scenarios.

Size, density, shape, and material influence a heatsink's ability to dissipate heat. The best coolers available are often fabricated entirely of copper, with its excellent thermal transfer properties. Copper is also the most expensive option, due to high procurement and manufacturing costs. Aluminum is the most widely used heatsink material. It provides acceptable thermal conductivity at a relatively low cost. At the least expensive end of the heatsink spectrum is cast iron. Iron is a poor thermal conductor, and these coolers should be avoided.

Figure 5-2: All-copper heatsink

Many of today's high-quality heatsink coolers combine two or more metals to maximize thermal conductivity while minimizing cost. The most cost-effective designs use copper as the core material (due to its superior thermal efficiency) and aluminum for the radiating fins (due to its stress-handling properties). This combination provides a good cooling system with improved ruggedness. Copper is not as rigid as aluminum, so you must exercise great care when handling and installing copper coolers.

Cooling fan efficiency is directly proportional to size, RPM, and blade design. The most common fans are 60 millimeters across, with average turning rates in the range of 4500 to 6000 RPM. Fans that operate at high speeds move more air for their size than those with low RPM, though high-speed fans also create more noise. For example, 60-millimeter high-speed fans exceeding 7000 RPM are available for midrange coolers, but prove too noisy for most users.

Figure 5-3: Cooling fan

Large fans 70 to 90 millimeters in size usually move more air than small ones (assuming that the RPM is the same). An adapter mechanism is often required to take advantage of a large fan, however, since most heatsink designs are built around a 60-millimeter fan.

Heatsink Lapping

One popular way to achieve maximum thermal transfer is by lapping the heatsink's base contact surface. The term *lapping* describes the process of sanding the heatsink-to-processor contact surface to eliminate microscopic air pockets caused by machining or extruding in the heatsink fabrication process. In addition, external factors such as rough handling or poor shipping practices can lead to scratches in the contact surface. By smoothing out the surface of the heatsink, you can maximize the surface area that will be in contact with the processor. Even the smallest imperfection can create the opportunity for an air pocket to interfere with contact. This will mean a loss in cooling efficiency, because air is a poor thermal conductor.

The process of lapping can be tedious, especially with poorly machined heatsink coolers. The base surface must be sanded with fine-grit sandpaper to obtain a mirrorlike finish and eliminate as many imperfections as possible. Disassemble the fan cooler from the heatsink before you begin lapping to prevent damage to the fan or electrical connections during the procedure. Clean the heatsink thoroughly to remove any deposits or filings introduced during the lapping process. Alcohol is the best cleaning solution and it won't damage finishes on the heatsink surface.

The best way to begin lapping a heatsink is to start with a low-grit paper (400 to 600), then slowly progress to higher grades until you reach the desired results, usually at the 1200- to 1600-grit level.

The most accurate method for sanding is to move the heatsink's base contact surface across the sandpaper in an alternating circular motion, with the paper firmly affixed to a perfectly flat surface. A small piece of extruded glass, such as a windowpane or mirror, works well as the flat surface. Glass will not scratch the heatsink surface if you make an error. Regular scotch tape or even a mild spray adhesive works best for attaching the sandpaper to the glass. Lapping requires great patience. Some heatsinks can require up to an hour of fine sanding before the desired surface consistency is reached. The procedure is described below.

1. With the sandpaper firmly attached to the glass, move the heatsink across the paper in a figure-eight motion.

2. Apply even pressure throughout the length of the motion to guard against introducing deformed flat spots or upraised regions.

3. Alternate the pattern of movement at regular intervals.

4. Polish and clean the heatsink once its base is sanded to a uniform finish. Cleaning with alcohol will preserve any finishes applied to the surface.

5. Apply a quality metal polish evenly and buff it as specified on the package. A rotary tool with a cloth-polishing wheel operating at a low speed works well for many materials.

6. Once the heatsink is polished, clean it with alcohol again. As with air gaps caused by scratches, polishing materials left on the surface reduce thermal conductivity.

A properly lapped heatsink will result in a processor that runs cooler and with more stability, thus improving your likelihood of achieving overclocking success.

Heat Transfer Compounds

Applying a thermal interface material between the processor core and the heatsink surface will optimize heat transfer, even with a perfectly flat cooler that has undergone the lapping process. Most coolers included with preconfigured OEM systems feature a rubbery synthetic thermal pad in between the heatsink and the processor. Several aftermarket retail coolers also use this thermal pad because it is less expensive than the better solutions.

Thermal paste is preferable to a thermal pad. Remove any existing heatsink pad before you apply the paste. Removal of the rubbery substance should be attempted with a plastic scraper only. The edge of an old plastic credit card usually does the trick, as the card offers a good combination of flexibility and rigidity. Harder scraping implements, such as a razor blade, might scratch the heatsink's base contact surface, no matter how careful you are. Alcohol will remove any remaining deposits.

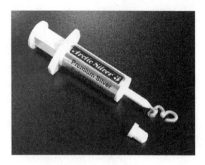

Figure 5-4: Thermal paste

Thermal paste is the preferred thermal interface material because this thin liquidlike substance works well to fill small voids between the processor and heatsink surfaces. Silicon-based and zinc-oxide-based pastes are the most commonly available materials, offering good heat transfer at low cost. Silver-bearing pastes, such as Arctic Silver™ (http://www.arcticsilver.com), are rapidly emerging as the best choice for overclocking because they are efficient for the widest range of processors.

Good-quality silver paste can offer thermal conductivity upwards of 9 watts per meter Kelvin, compared to 0.7 watts per meter Kelvin for traditional pastes. Silver has two negative properties. It can become electrically conductive under extreme pressure, such as that between the processor and heatsink. While this is not normally a concern, you must take great care when applying the paste. Silver-based pastes also cost two or three times as much as standard thermal paste products. Considering that only a small amount of paste is needed for each cooler installation, the cost factor is not a serious barrier.

Application of the thermal paste is a relatively straightforward process, assuming you observe a few simple guidelines:

1. The paste should be applied to the processor core, not the heatsink's base, in a fresh installation.

2. Apply only enough paste to barely obscure the color of the processor core. A thick layer of paste acts as a thermal insulator instead of a thermal capacitor. The paste should be spread as evenly as possible to ensure proper surface contact.

3. Use an edge of plastic or other synthetic material to apply the paste; oils found in human skin can break down or disrupt the polymers in thermal paste.

These instructions can be disregarded if the heatsink comes with the paste already applied.

Case Cooling

Proper case cooling is essential for maximizing the efficiency of the processor cooler. The average cooler fan ranges from 80 to 120 millimeters in size. As with processor cooler fans, large-diameter case fans allow slow blade rotation speeds for low sound-to-noise ratios. Due to increased power current demands, only standard 4-pin Molex pass-through adapters should power large case fans. The common three-wire fan header connectors found on most motherboards cannot supply enough amperage to power most case fan designs. Simple 4-wire to 3-wire adapters are available, at low cost, for case fans with three-prong connecters.

Figure 5-5: ATX power supply

Many modern power supply units are moving to a two-fan design to ensure adequate removal of high-temperature ambient air from both the power transformer and internal case devices. At least one case fan is recommended in addition to any power supply fans already in place. The additional case fan should be mounted to take in air, since most ATX-format power supply fans are mounted to exhaust air from the case.

The goal is to maintain a balance of exhaust air to intake air for consistent flow throughout the case interior. Most cases include predesignated mounting points for fans to enable the best possible airflow regulation. The most common mounting point on a tower is the bottom front side of the case. This placement allows cool air to circulate directly through the devices located in the expansion slots area.

Figure 5-6: Proper fan placement

Air filtration is another concern when installing any additional case cooling fans. Dust deposits that accumulate on system devices can become a serious problem, even in the cleanest operating environments. Microscopic dust particles quickly accumulate on surfaces due to increased airflow inside the case. Basic filtering solutions work best in most scenarios. A piece of low-density foam, sandwiched between two coarse mesh layers and secured between the fan and mounting surface, offers excellent filtration for all but the tiniest of dust particles. The foam filter should be installed in front of the fan's air intake side for maximum efficacy, though either side should work.

Increased noise from multiple case fans can be a real concern, especially for users in a small office or home setting. The best trick to reduce fan noise is to eliminate or dampen vibrations caused by the fans' rotation, which are transferred to the case chassis. A simple rubber washer, installed between each fan and case mount point, usually provides enough cushioning. A thin layer of silicon or nonadhesive RTV sealant can be applied along the fans' edges if you are concerned about possible air leaks in true sealed-case architectures.

Additional cooling components are available to boost the effectiveness of case cooling designs. *Slot coolers* can be installed in an expansion slot to exhaust hot air from warm cards, such as the powerful AGP video cards. *Bay coolers* can be installed to regulate hard-drive temperatures. The intake-style varieties will often direct airflow onto internal system components. *Nidec coolers* are a type of squirrel-cage fan that moves air through an internal slotted wheel. Nidec coolers can move a large amount of air for their low profile. These coolers are best for directing air into the case, and can be secured easily to nearly any internal surface with screws or even double-faced adhesive tape.

Alternative Cooling Technologies

Alternative cooling systems (not based on forced-air technologies) are available, though the associated costs are prohibitive for most enthusiasts. The best of these systems can cool to subzero temperatures, at which electrical circuits can operate quite efficiently. The latest experiments in super-cooling techniques involving liquid helium or nitrogen have revealed unlimited overclocking possibilities.

The predominant concern with subzero cooling is condensation due to the difference between processor temperature and air temperature. Various solutions have been adopted over the years, but most have failed to prove viable. Enthusiasts look toward silicon sealants, Styrofoam blocks, or rubber barriers to seal the processor socket region from outside humidity. These tricks work well for the short term, but tend to break down or fail during long-term use.

The best condensation-blocking solutions are usually the most expensive. Some high-end manufacturers have literally submerged the whole processor, motherboard and all, into a nonconductive liquid to isolate vital system components from variability in air temperature or humidity. Others have opted for a complex processor-to-motherboard socket connector that uses a custom interface to seal the processor completely. While either method works efficiently, implementing such designs can be expensive.

Boot-time problems are also a significant concern. Most technologies lack a real-time response, so the cooling device must reach a certain temperature before the computing system can be booted into operation. Professional products use timing devices and a complex series of electrical relays to shorten the wait. Enthusiasts must often develop homegrown techniques to accomplish the same goal. Responding to the demand for simplified installation and use of alternative cooling technologies, commercial retailers are beginning to stock a number of helpful devices.

Peltier Cooling

Peltier thermoelectric devices are gaining popularity due to their low cost, though many users do not anticipate the secondary costs involved. A Peltier circuit is a thin ceramiclike disk that acts like a heat pump once an electrical current has been applied across its substrate. A nontechnical explanation is that one side of the Peltier disk becomes cooler while the other side becomes warmer.

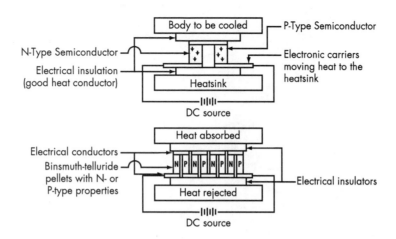

Figure 5-7: Peltier diagram

Cooling the warm side enhances the temperature variance gradient, increasing the circuit's thermal efficiency. This warm-side cooling is usually accomplished by means of a forced-air heatsink, though some use water or vapor-phase cooling to further increase the thermal load coefficient between the warm and cool sides of a Peltier system. A properly designed system can often cool even the hottest of today's processors to near zero temperatures.

Peltier devices require substantial amperage loads to operate at peak efficiency. Average 300-watt power supply units found in today's better computers cannot deal with the demands of a quality Peltier that is 72 watts or higher. An upgrade to a server-grade unit that is 400 watts or higher or adding a second power supply is often required. Wiring an external 12- to 13.8-volt power supply to the Peltier circuit is simple enough, but a relay circuit may be needed to initialize the Peltier at boot time.

Vapor-Phase Cooling

Vapor-phase cooling is active refrigeration technology, similar to the processes involved in heat pumps or air conditioners. A gaseous substance, like freon, is compressed, condensed, and forced through an exchanger device to provide a cooling effect. Vapor-phase coolers are specialized systems, usually tailored to the requirements of a specific computing system.

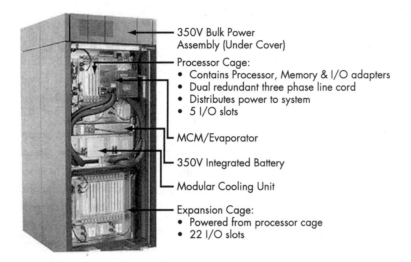

350V Bulk Power
Assembly (Under Cover)

Processor Cage:
• Contains Processor, Memory & I/O adapters
• Dual redundant three phase line cord
• Distributes power to system
• 5 I/O slots

MCM/Evaporator

350V Integrated Battery

Modular Cooling Unit

Expansion Cage:
• Powered from processor cage
• 22 I/O slots

Figure 5-8: KyroTech architecture

Kryotech (http://www.kryotech.com) is a popular manufacturer of vapor-phase refrigerated computing systems. The company provides both pre-configured systems and custom cooling solutions for later system integration. Another popular product is the VapoChill cooler. The VapoChill (http://www.vapochill.com) is a highly coveted aftermarket cooling solution for overclockers. Though its price was previously very high, the VapoChill's North America price was reduced to $469 in October 2002 for their standard edition. The VapoChill is capable of cooling an overclocked processor to less than zero degrees centigrade.

Liquid Cooling

Liquid cooling was once the most popular alternative cooling solution, though the efficiency of today's forced-air systems has decreased demand. In liquid coolers a pump circulates coolant through a holding tank or radiator element and then throughout the system. Fans cool the radiator for maximum thermal efficiency.

Liquid is denser than air and therefore offers greater thermal transference. Adding other cooling technologies, such as a Peltier circuit or vapor-phase system, can further extend the thermal dissipation efficiency of a liquid cooling technique. These options can be introduced, as required, at either the processor or radiator stage of the process.

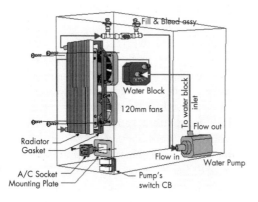

Figure 5-9: Liquid cooler architecture

Many enthusiasts build their own custom liquid cooling systems, but the decreasing cost of aftermarket products tends to encourage purchase over construction. Many quality systems now cost less than $200, making the expenditure of effort and money for a home-built system seem pointless. Moreover, the efficiency of forced-air coolers can reach or even exceed that of most generic liquid coolers. High-end forced-air solutions can cost more than $100, but that is only half the cost of a quality liquid cooler.

Figure 5-10: SwiftTech liquid cooler

Submersion Cooling

Submersion cooling is rapidly gaining favor in hardcore overclocking circles. Submersion implies literally sinking the bulk of a computing system directly into a liquid substance. The liquid can then be chilled to subzero temperatures and with it the computer. The primary advantage of this solution is that no condensation can form on sensitive electronic components. Submersion is a straightforward process: just dip the motherboard into a vat or reservoir of nonconducting liquid. However, you must avoid submerging any drives or power supply units, as these devices will fail, causing system damage.

Submersion cooling is expensive. Fluorinert liquid from the Electronics Manufacturing Division of 3M is the most attractive submersion cooling fluid. However, the cost of acquiring it can be staggering, especially because permits are required to purchase and handle it. Just a few gallons of this material can cost several thousand dollars. (And Fluorinert can evaporate, necessitating the design of a cooling vat system, which prevents evaporation of the liquid, along with your money.)

Enthusiasts have tried other liquids, like pure alcohol, but results vary wildly. Alcohol should never be used, as this material has a very low flash point. The goal is to cool the computer, not set it on fire, or worse, cause it to explode. One alternative is pure mineral oil. *Pure* is the key concept, as most bulk mineral oils on retail shelves have added water and possibly scenting agents. The presence of either impurity will cause the mineral oil to conduct electricity.

6

INTEL OVERCLOCKING

Pentium II Background

The Pentium II processor was Intel's first commercial P6 (also called 686 or 80686) core architecture offered to the general public. The P6 has internal RISC architecture and a CISC-RISC translator. Its design is based on the earlier, moderately successful, Pentium Pro processor. The most significant extension to the original design was the introduction of MMX (multimedia extensions) instruction support. Updates included the introduction of a slot interconnect interface, an integrated 512 KB Level 2 (L2) cache memory mounted directly on the slot circuit board, and various refinements for better cooling and heat dissipation.

The most controversial feature introduced in the Pentium II is full clock-multiplier locking, which severely limits overclocking potential. The earliest Pentium II chips lacked this locked design, but Intel integrated the needed circuitry within a few months. The locked multiplier forced enthusiasts to adopt front-side bus manipulation as a means of overclocking the Pentium II. The disadvantage of this approach is that any changes to the front-side bus speed lead to the subsequent overclocking of nearly all other system and subsystem components, ranging from memory to peripheral component interconnect (PCI) devices and accelerated graphics port (AGP) video cards.

The first Pentium II chips were manufactured with .28-micron circuit pathways. They require a core voltage of 2.8 volts and generate tremendous heat. These factors place intense demands on the power supply and motherboard voltage regulators; therefore, any increase above 3.0 core volts means that a heavy-duty cooling system must first be installed.

The extreme temperatures produced by .28-micron chips, combined with limited bus frequencies in the popular Intel LX motherboard chipset, lowered overclocking potential. The LX chipset was designed for 66 MHz front-side bus (FSB) operation; the maximum unofficial supported frequency is 83 MHz. This frequency can be useful for lower multiplier chips, such as the Pentium II 266 ($83 \times 4.0 = $ ~333 MHz), but the danger of damaging system components becomes significant when other system bus rates change substantially.

The Intel BX chipset became the most popular motherboard choice after the release of 100-MHz front-side bus Pentium II models. Other 100-MHz chipsets, such as VIA's Apollo Pro133, debuted shortly thereafter. These new designs offered improved overclock flexibility, for both 66- and 100-MHz chip owners. The BX and Pro133 both ventured front-side bus support up to 133 MHz. Some companies extended the unofficial specifications to 166 MHz and beyond. The potential for overclocking became clearer as the new 100-MHz Pentium II models incorporated a much cooler and more efficient .25-micron circuit design. The ability to scale successfully above 400 MHz brought the Pentium II to the attention of the overclocking community.

When the .25-micron Pentium II was released, the primary concern became the bus limitations inherent in Intel's popular BX chipset. The BX design could effectively scale to 133 MHz while maintaining the proper FSB-to-PCI ratio, but the AGP bus suffered from a 2/3 divider. It would be overclocked to approximately 88.6 MHz, leading to a high failure rate for most early AGP video cards. (PCI video solutions were unaffected.) Competing chipsets from VIA, SIS, and ALI bypassed this limitation by adding a 1/2 AGP divider, though the early revision of these boards offered other minor compatibility and performance problems compared to Intel's architecture.

Front-side bus speeds near 124 MHz create a problem analogous to the 83-MHz issue. The standard divider of 1/3 generates a PCI bus frequency of approximately 41.3 MHz, thus threatening the stability of various PCI devices, especially hard drives. Some retail motherboards, designed specifically for overclocking, offered the ability to adjust the PCI divider manually at these "problem" frequency ranges. For example, with a 1/4 divider at 124 MHz, the PCI bus reverts to ~31 MHz, a "safe" value, close to the default PCI v2.x specification of 33 MHz.

Restrictions on the processor heatsink's size and orientation also come into play, due to the Slot 1 processor-to-motherboard interface. The heatsink extends parallel to the surface of the motherboard, which imposes a size limit, as the heatsink surface must clear not only the socket, but all other motherboard components as well. Worse yet, many manufacturers have placed the processor slot close enough to the memory slots to block some of them. This factor clearly influences the size and type of heatsink you can use with the Pentium II.

Intel's standard cooling solution proves adequate for default operation, but this small heatsink often fails to deliver the dissipation needed to sustain successful overclocking at extended operating speeds. A more efficient aftermarket cooling solution is needed for any real return. The size of any replacement cooler should be considered carefully. As mentioned, some motherboards simply do not offer enough space for the larger coolers.

Pentium II Klamath Overclocking

Table 6-1: Pentium II Klamath Specifications

Processor Family	Model Name	Intel Pentium II Klamath
	Performance Rating	233 MHz
	Generation	Sixth: 80686 IA-32
Operational Rates	Level 1 Cache Speed	1.0x Core Rate
	Level 2 Cache Speed	0.5x Core Rate
	Front-side Bus Speed	66 MHz
	Multiplier Ratio	3.5x – 4.5x
Physical Design	Interface Packing	242-Pin Slot 1 Cartridge
	Core Die Size	.28 micron, 203 mm^2
	Transistor Count	7.5 Million
	Voltage Interface	Split Core and I/O
	Core Voltage	2.8 volts
	I/O Voltage	3.3 volts
	Level 2 Cache Voltage	3.3 volts
	Power Consumption	23 – 28 watts
	Maximum Power	34.8 – 43 watts
Architectural Design	Core Technology	OOO and Speculative Execution RISC
	Register Support	Integer = 32 bit
		FPU = 80 bit
		MMX = 64 bit
	Execution Units	2 x ALU/MMX
		1 x Pipelined FPU
	Maximum Execution Rate	5 Micro-Ops per Cycle
	Data Bus Width	64 bit
	Maximum Memory Support	Physical = 64 Gigabyte
		Virtual = 64 Terabyte
	Multi-Processor Support	2-way SMP via APIC
	Level 1 Code Cache	16 KB 4-way
	Level 1 Data Cache	16 KB 4-way
	Level 2 Cache	512 KB Unified
	Read Buffer	4 x 32 Byte

(continued on next page)

Table 6-1: Pentium II Klamath Specifications (continued)

Processor Family	Model Name	Intel Pentium II Klamath
	Write Buffer	32 Byte
	Pre-fetch Queue	32 Byte
	Static Branch Prediction	Supported
	Dynamic Branch Prediction	512 Entry 4-way
	RSB Branch Prediction	4 Entry
	Floating-Point Processor	Integrated
	Multimedia Extensions	MMX

Pentium II Klamath 233

Table 6-2: Pentium II Klamath 233 Specifications

Processor Family	Model Name	Intel Pentium II Klamath
	Performance Rating	233 MHz
	Front-side Bus Speed	66 MHz
	Multiplier Ratio	3.5x
Physical Design	Interface Packing	242-Pin Slot 1 Cartridge
	Core Die Size	.28 micron, 203 mm^2
	Transistor Count	7.5 Million
	Voltage Interface	Split Core and I/O
	Core Voltage	2.8 volts
	Power Consumption	23 watts
	Maximum Power	34.8 watts

Table 6-3: Pentium II Klamath 233 Overclocking

Pentium II Klamath	Model Rating	233 MHz
Overclocking Potential	Multiplier Lock Support	Unlocked Multiplier
	Typical Multiplier O/C	Up to 4.0x
	Typical Front-side Bus O/C	Up to 75 MHz
	Typical O/C Potential	266 – 300 MHz
	Maximum O/C Potential	300 – 333 MHz
Overclocking Tolerances	Recommended Cooling Type	Forced-Air Heatsink
	Recommended Heatsink Coolers	Globalwin VEK 16
		Vantec PIID-4535H
	Recommended Peltier Active Cooler	STEP-UP-53X2
	Maximum Core Voltage	3.0 volts with Heatsink Cooler
	Maximum I/O Voltage	3.5 volts with Chipset Cooler
	Maximum Core Temperature	72° Celsius

Strategy

The Pentium II 233 is Intel's first entry in the series. As you might expect, over-clocking potential for this processor is limited. The majority of the P2 233 chips in circulation are not multiplier locked. The lack of multiplier locking with the P2 233 is helpful, as most of early Slot I motherboards lack support for front-side bus speeds above 66 MHz. Overclocking can therefore be accomplished by changing the clock multiplier alone.

The simplest way to overclock the Pentium II 233 is to increase the core multiplier value from the default of 3.5x to 4.0x, and thus achieve 266 MHz. Higher speeds may be possible with some configurations, but limitations in the 0.5x cache architecture will maximize returns at 337.5 MHz (83-MHz front-side bus × 4.5 multiplier). The external Level 2 cache chips found with the P2 233 often fail at speeds above 166 MHz. Some users may be tempted to disable the L2 cache to reach higher core speeds, but removing this important buffer will result in serious performance losses, outweighing any benefits.

Pentium II Klamath 266

Table 6-4: Pentium II Klamath 266 Specifications

Processor Family	Model Name	Intel Pentium II Klamath
	Performance Rating	266 MHz
	Generation	Sixth: 80686 IA-32
Operational Rates	Level 1 Cache Speed	1.0x Core Rate
	Level 2 Cache Speed	0.5x Core Rate
	Front-side Bus Speed	66 MHz
	Multiplier Ratio	4.0x
Physical Design	Interface Packing	242-Pin Slot 1 Cartridge
	Core Die Size	.28 micron, 203 mm^2
	Transistor Count	7.5 Million
	Voltage Interface	Split Core and I/O
	Core Voltage	2.8 volts
	Power Consumption	25 watts
	Maximum Power	38.2 watts

Table 6-5: Pentium II Klamath 266 Overclocking

Pentium II Klamath	Model Rating	266 MHz
Overclocking Potential	Multiplier Lock Support	Unlocked Multiplier
	Typical Multiplier O/C	Up to 4.5x
	Typical Front-side Bus O/C	Up to 75 MHz
	Typical O/C Potential	300 – 333 MHz
	Maximum O/C Potential	333 – 350 MHz
Overclocking Tolerances	Recommended Cooling Type	Forced-Air Heatsink
	Recommended Heatsink Coolers	Globalwin VEK 16
		Vantec PIID-4535H
	Recommended Peltier Active Cooler	STEP-UP-53X2
	Maximum Core Voltage	3.0 volts with Heatsink Cooler
	Maximum I/O Voltage	3.5 volts with Chipset Cooler
	Maximum Core Temperature	73° Celsius

Strategy

The Pentium II Klamath 266 offers overclocking capabilities similar to those of the 233. As the family's second generation, the 266 offers overclocking potential upwards of 350 MHz. Any additional gains are probably attributable to variations in the Level 2 cache memory chips. Intel used various brands and types of these chips in its Klamath series.

Pentium II Klamath 300

Table 6-6: Pentium II Klamath 300 Specifications

Processor Family	Model Name	Intel Pentium II Klamath
	Performance Rating	300 MHz
	Front-side Bus Speed	66 MHz
	Multiplier Ratio	4.5x
Physical Design	Interface Packing	242-Pin Slot 1 Cartridge
	Core Voltage	2.8 volts
	Power Consumption	28 watts
	Maximum Power	43.0 watts

Table 6-7: Pentium II Klamath 300 Overclocking

Pentium II Klamath	Model Rating	300 MHz
Overclocking Potential	Multiplier Lock Support	Potentially Unlocked Multiplier
	Typical Multiplier O/C	Up to 4.5x
	Typical Front-side Bus O/C	Up to 75 MHz
	Typical O/C Potential	333 – 350 MHz
	Maximum O/C Potential	350 MHz
Overclocking Tolerances	Recommended Cooling Type	Forced-Air Heatsink
	Recommended Heatsink Coolers	Globalwin VEK 16
		Vantec PIID-4535H
	Recommended Peltier Active Cooler	STEP-UP-53X2
	Maximum Core Voltage	3.0 volts with Heatsink Cooler
	Maximum I/O Voltage	3.5 volts with Chipset Cooler
	Maximum Core Temperature	75° Celsius

Strategy

The Pentium II 300 MHz offers moderate overclocking potential for those lucky enough to possess a model that is not multiplier locked. Reports have varied over the years since this Klamath model was introduced, but it appears that some units did ship with multiplier-locked cores. Overclocking potential for locked Klamath 300-MHz processors will be limited; increasing the front-side bus beyond 75 MHz is nearly impossible. A front-side bus speed of 83 MHz will result in a core rate of approximately 374 MHz (83 MHz × 4.5), a speed often beyond the capability of the .28-micron Klamath core.

Owners of unlocked Pentium II Klamath 300 processors may benefit if an 83 MHz front-side bus speed is supported by the system's motherboard. Increasing the front-side bus rate to 83 MHz, while decreasing the processor multiplier value to 4.0x, often yields a stable 333 MHz. The increase in front-side bus speed will boost performance significantly: memory and PCI bus rates will also be overclocked. The half-speed Level 2 cache architecture of the P2 limits bandwidth between the processor and memory subsystems. Therefore, additional bandwidth obtained by overclocking the front-side bus can greatly improve memory performance.

Pentium II Deschutes Overclocking

Table 6-8: Pentium II Deschutes Specifications

Processor Family	Model Name	Intel Pentium II Deschutes
	Performance Rating	300 – 450 MHz
	Generation	Sixth: 80686 IA-32
Operational Rates	Level 1 Cache Speed	1.0x Core Rate
	Level 2 Cache Speed	0.5x Core Rate
	Front-side Bus Speed	66 – 100 MHz
	Multiplier Ratio	3.5x – 4.5x
Physical Design	Interface Packing	242-Pin Slot 1 Cartridge
	Core Die Size	.25 micron, 118 mm^2
	Transistor Count	7.5 Million
	Voltage Interface	Split Core and I/O
	Core Voltage	2.0 volts
	I/O Voltage	3.3 volts
	Level 2 Cache Voltage	3.3 volts
	Power Consumption	11 – 24 watts
	Maximum Power	16.8 – 36.4 watts
Architectural Design	Core Technology	OOO and Speculative Execution RISC
	Register Support	Integer = 32 bit
		FPU = 80 bit
		MMX = 64 bit
	Execution Units	2 x ALU/MMX
		1 x Pipelined FPU
	Maximum Execution Rate	5 Micro-Ops per Cycle
	Data Bus Width	64 bit
	Maximum Memory Support	Physical = 64 Gigabyte
		Virtual = 64 Terabyte
	Multi-Processor Support	2-way SMP via APIC
	Level 1 Code Cache	16 KB 4-way
	Level 1 Data Cache	16 KB 4-way
	Level 2 Cache	512 KB Unified
	Read Buffer	4 x 32 Byte
	Write Buffer	32 Byte
	Pre-fetch Queue	32 Byte
	Static Branch Prediction	Supported
	Dynamic Branch Prediction	512 Entry 4-way
	RSB Branch Prediction	4 Entry
	Floating-Point Processor	Integrated
	Multimedia Extensions	MMX

Pentium II Deschutes 266

Table 6-9: Pentium II Deschutes 266 Specifications

Processor Family	Model Name	Intel Pentium II Deschutes
	Performance Rating	266 MHz
	Front-side Bus Speed	66 MHz
	Multiplier Ratio	4.0x
Physical Design	Interface Packing	242-Pin Slot 1 Cartridge
	Core Voltage	2.0 volts
	Power Consumption	11 watts
	Maximum Power	16.8 watts

Table 6-10: Pentium II Deschutes 266 Overclocking

Pentium II Deschutes	Model Rating	266 MHz
Overclocking Potential	Multiplier Lock Support	Locked Multiplier
	Typical Multiplier O/C	N/A
	Typical Front-side Bus O/C	Up to 83 MHz
	Typical O/C Potential	333 – 350 MHz
	Maximum O/C Potential	400 MHz
Overclocking Tolerances	Recommended Cooling Type	Forced-Air Heatsink
	Recommended Heatsink Coolers	Globalwin VEK 16
		Vantec PIID-4535H
	Recommended Peltier Active Cooler	STEP-UP-53X2
	Maximum Core Voltage	2.2 volts with Heatsink Cooler
	Maximum I/O Voltage	3.5 volts with Chipset Cooler
	Maximum Core Temperature	65° Celsius

Strategy

The improved .25-micron Deschutes core arrived for the Pentium II family at the 266-MHz production point. The Deschutes revision offers significantly improved overclocking potential compared to its older Klamath sibling. At 266 MHz, the Deschutes requires substantially less maximum power demand than its Klamath counterpart. Voltage demand is reduced to 2.0 volts, while wattage draw is up to 50% more efficient than previous P2 models.

The Deschutes revision officially introduced full multiplier locking into the majority of Pentium II processors shipped to retail markets. Lack of user-definable multiplier support is a roadblock to overclocking; however, Deschutes' .03-micron core die-size reduction, along with its improved motherboard chipset technology, can boost overclocking potential. Motherboards offering 100+-MHz front-side bus speed appeared along with this updated Pentium II processor.

Overclocking the Pentium II Deschutes 266 falls in the 350-MHz range for most samples. For those with older motherboards, a front-side bus rate of 83 MHz yields a core operating speed near 333 MHz. Systems featuring 100-MHz-capable motherboards can reach 400 MHz (100-MHz front-side bus × 4.0 multiplier) for a few select 266-MHz models. Core voltage rates must rise to 2.2 volts to reach such levels. Good cooling is a must for overclocking this processor; its maximum core rating is 65° Celsius.

Pentium II Deschutes 300

Table 6-11: Pentium II Deschutes 300 Specifications

Processor Family	Model Name	Intel Pentium II Deschutes
	Performance Rating	300 MHz
	Front-side Bus Speed	66 MHz
	Multiplier Ratio	4.5x
Physical Design	Interface Packing	242-Pin Slot 1 Cartridge
	Core Voltage	2.0 volts
	Power Consumption	12 watts
	Maximum Power	18.7 watts

Table 6-12: Pentium II Deschutes 300 Overclocking

Pentium II Deschutes	Model Rating	300 MHz
Overclocking Potential	Multiplier Lock Support	Locked Multiplier
	Typical Multiplier O/C	N/A
	Typical Front-side Bus O/C	Up to 83 MHz
	Typical O/C Potential	338 – 374 MHz
	Maximum O/C Potential	450 MHz
Overclocking Tolerances	Recommended Cooling Type	Forced-Air Heatsink
	Recommended Heatsink Coolers	Globalwin VEK 16
		Vantec PIID-4535H
	Recommended Peltier Active Cooler	STEP-UP-53X2
	Maximum Core Voltage	2.2 volts with Heatsink Cooler
	Maximum I/O Voltage	3.5 volts with Chipset Cooler
	Maximum Core Temperature	65° Celsius

Strategy

The Pentium II Deschutes 300 MHz offers great potential for those with 100-MHz front-side-bus-capable motherboards. The 4.5x multiplier of this processor can overclock to a phenomenal 450 MHz under the right conditions. In any case, 374 MHz should be possible for systems featuring older 83-MHz-capable motherboards.

Successful 450-MHz operation requires substantial cooling. A voltage increase to 2.2 volts (from the core default of 2.0 volts) is needed to attain a stable overclock. A 65° Celsius temperature limitation was imposed by the early Deschutes revisions; thus proper thermal regulation is a dominant concern when pushing core speeds beyond the 400-MHz level. Using radical cooling technologies, like Peltier or forced liquid, in conjunction with increased core voltage levels can produce overclocks of more than 500 MHz for Pentium II Deschutes 300-MHz processors featuring quality Level 2 cache memory.

Pentium II Deschutes 333

Table 6-13: Pentium II Deschutes 333 Specifications

Processor Family	Model Name	Intel Pentium II Deschutes
	Performance Rating	333 MHz
	Front-side Bus Speed	66 MHz
	Multiplier Ratio	5.0x
Physical Design	Interface Packing	242-Pin Slot 1 Cartridge
	Core Voltage	2.0 volts
	I/O Voltage	3.3 volts
	Level 2 Cache Voltage	3.3 volts
	Power Consumption	14 watts
	Maximum Power	20.6 watts

Table 6-14: Pentium II Deschutes 333 Overclocking

Pentium II Deschutes	Model Rating	333 MHz
Overclocking Potential	Multiplier Lock Support	Locked Multiplier
	Typical Multiplier O/C	N/A
	Typical Front-side Bus O/C	Up to 83 MHz
	Typical O/C Potential	375 – 415 MHz
	Maximum O/C Potential	450 – 500 MHz
Overclocking Tolerances	Recommended Cooling Type	Forced-Air Heatsink
	Recommended Heatsink Coolers	Globalwin VEK 16
		Vantec PIID-4535H
	Recommended Peltier Active Cooler	STEP-UP-53X2
	Maximum Core Voltage	2.2 volts with Heatsink Cooler
	Maximum I/O Voltage	3.5 volts with Chipset Cooler
	Maximum Core Temperature	65° Celsius

Strategy

The Pentium II Deschutes 333 MHz is the last of the 66-MHz front-side bus Pentium II processors. With a 5.0x multiplier, the P2 333 is well suited for overclocking upwards of 500 MHz, with the installation of a quality aftermarket cooling solution. Peltier-based cooling presents a good alternative to traditional forced-air heatsink cooling under these conditions.

Systems with older motherboards are generally assured a stable overclock to 375 MHz using the 75-MHz front-side bus rate. The Level 2 cache chips employed in the P2 333-MHz series are often capable of 200+ MHz; thus overclocking beyond 400 MHz is generally successful. Those attempting overclocks upwards of 500 MHz should implement a cooling solution for the Level 2 cache chips in order to ensure stable operation. Some quality Slot 1 coolers feature a special base designed to contact both the processor core and cache SRAM chips to optimize thermal regulation.

Pentium II Deschutes 350

Table 6-15: Pentium II Deschutes 350 Specifications

Processor Family	Model Name	Intel Pentium II Deschutes
	Performance Rating	350 MHz
	Front-side Bus Speed	100 MHz
	Multiplier Ratio	3.5x
Physical Design	Interface Packing	242-Pin Slot 1 Cartridge
	Core Voltage	2.0 volts
	Power Consumption	20 watts
	Maximum Power	29.5 watts

Table 6-16: Pentium II Deschutes 350 Overclocking

Pentium II Deschutes	Model Rating	350 MHz
Overclocking Potential	Multiplier Lock Support	Locked Multiplier
	Typical Multiplier O/C	N/A
	Typical Front-side Bus O/C	Up to 112 MHz
	Typical O/C Potential	392 – 434 MHz
	Maximum O/C Potential	450 – 500 MHz
Overclocking Tolerances	Recommended Cooling Type	Forced-Air Heatsink
	Recommended Heatsink Coolers	Globalwin VEK 16
		Vantec PIID-4535H
	Recommended Peltier Active Cooler	STEP-UP-53X2
	Maximum Core Voltage	2.2 volts with Heatsink Cooler
	Maximum I/O Voltage	3.5 volts with Chipset Cooler
	Maximum Core Temperature	75° Celsius

Strategy

The Pentium II 350 MHz was the first 100-Hz front-side-bus-compatible processor in the Deschutes processor family. Featuring a 3.5x multiplier, the P3 350 is a good candidate for front-side bus overclocking up to 124 MHz, resulting in a core operating speed of 434 MHz. While cooling remains an important concern, the P2 350 offers an improved maximum thermal rating of 75° Celsius.

Remember, take care with system motherboards featuring the popular Intel BX chipset, as this controller lacks support for the highly desirable 1/2 AGP bus divider. Systems featuring PCI video cards should be fine, though systems with AGP graphics accelerators may suffer instability at front-side bus rates exceeding 112 MHz. The majority of Intel-compatible chipsets from ALI, SIS, and VIA do not have this limitation, as they support the 1/2 AGP divider at extended bus frequencies.

Pentium II Deschutes 400

Table 6-17: Pentium II Deschutes 400 Specifications

Processor Family	Model Name	Intel Pentium II Deschutes
	Performance Rating	400 MHz
	Front-side Bus Speed	100 MHz
	Multiplier Ratio	4.0x
Physical Design	Interface Packing	242-Pin Slot 1 Cartridge
	Core Voltage	2.0 volts
	Power Consumption	22 watts
	Maximum Power	32.7 watts

Table 6-18: Pentium II Deschutes 400 Overclocking

Pentium II Deschutes	Model Rating	400 MHz
Overclocking Potential	Multiplier Lock Support	Locked Multiplier
	Typical Multiplier O/C	N/A
	Typical Front-side Bus O/C	Up to 112 MHz
	Typical O/C Potential	448 – 496 MHz
	Maximum O/C Potential	500 – 532 MHz
Overclocking Tolerances	Recommended Cooling Type	Forced-Air Heatsink
	Recommended Heatsink Coolers	Globalwin VEK 16
		Vantec PIID-4535H
	Recommended Peltier Active Cooler	STEP-UP-53X2
	Maximum Core Voltage	2.2 volts with Heatsink Cooler
	Maximum I/O Voltage	3.5 volts with Chipset Cooler
	Maximum Core Temperature	75° Celsius

Strategy

The Pentium II Deschutes 400 MHz offers moderate overclocking potential. Most systems featuring this processor reach their potential around 500 MHz, with good cooling. Those users hoping to reach the 133-MHz front-side bus speed in order to attain 532-MHz operation will likely fail unless extreme cooling is implemented. The .25-micron core die size, combined with the external cache of the Pentium II processor, limits overclocking to the 500 to 550 MHz range for most P2 400 units. Successful overclocking with the P2 400 will most likely require activating the 112-MHz front-side bus speed.

Pentium II Deschutes 450

Table 6-19: Pentium II Deschutes 450 Specifications

Processor Family	Model Name	Intel Pentium II Deschutes
	Performance Rating	450 MHz
	Front-side Bus Speed	100 MHz
	Multiplier Ratio	4.5x
Physical Design	Interface Packing	242-Pin Slot 1 Cartridge
	Core Voltage	2.0 volts
	Power Consumption	24 watts
	Maximum Power	36.4 watts

Table 6-20: Pentium II Deschutes 450 Overclocking

Pentium II Deschutes	Model Rating	450 MHz
Overclocking Potential	Multiplier Lock Support	Locked Multiplier
	Typical Multiplier O/C	N/A
	Typical Front-side Bus O/C	Up to 112 MHz
	Typical O/C Potential	500 – 550 MHz
	Maximum O/C Potential	550 – 575 MHz
Overclocking Tolerances	Recommended Cooling Type	Forced-Air Heatsink
	Recommended Heatsink Coolers	Globalwin VEK 16
		Vantec PIID-4535H
	Recommended Peltier Active Cooler	STEP-UP-53X2
	Maximum Core Voltage	2.2 volts with Heatsink Cooler
	Maximum I/O Voltage	3.5 volts with Chipset Cooler
	Maximum Core Temperature	70° Celsius

Strategy

The Pentium II 450 MHz is the last of the Deschutes line and closes the Pentium II family as a whole. This 4.5x multiplier processor offers little more overclocking potential than its 400 MHz sibling; the average overclock is 504 MHz using the 112-MHz front-side bus speed. Some rare models may reach upwards of 550 MHz, but nearly all P2 450 chips will fail to boot at the 600-MHz level.

Note the lower maximum temperature rating of 70° Celsius for the P2 450, down from 75° for the P2 400. Cooling is a serious concern when overclocking this processor, especially at operating speeds exceeding 500 MHz. The Intel retail heatsink cooler will prove inadequate for any serious attempts; owners should closely examine their system's cooling capabilities before proceeding with overclocking.

Celeron Background

The Celeron processor was originally introduced as a budget variant of the Pentium II, though many overclocking enthusiasts quickly discovered its hidden potential. The .25-micron Celeron is designed for 66-MHz front-side bus operation. The first Celeron models lacked an L2 cache, which means that any increase in clock speeds would affect performance results. The Celeron is available in both 370-pin PGA socket and Slot 1 motherboard interfaces for the broadest range of compatibility.

Of more interest is the Celeron A series. At 100-MHz front-side bus speeds, the 128-KB full-speed on-die L2 cache often allowed this revision to perform better than the more expensive Pentium II with its half-speed 512-KB off-die L2 cache. The average overclock for these Celeron A models extends 50 MHz, and often extends well beyond 200 MHz for some highly desired models.

The Celeron 300 produces the best results due to its low 4.5x multiplier. The most common overclock for this chip is between 450 and 500 MHz with decent cooling and a minimal increase in core voltage. Overclocking the lower range of Celeron speed grades, under more extreme cooling and voltage implementations, can yield results in the 550 to 650 MHz range for most users. Performance results slowly diminish at higher multiplier levels due to the comparative loss in front-side bus speeds, but most Celeron A series processors can reach 500 to 600 MHz with moderate effort.

Celeron Covington Overclocking

Table 6-21: Celeron Covington Specifications

Processor Family	Model Name	Intel Celeron Covington
	Performance Rating	266 – 300 MHz
	Generation	Sixth: 80686 IA-32
Operational Rates	Level 1 Cache Speed	1.0x Core Rate
	Level 2 Cache Speed	N/A
	Front-side Bus Speed	66 MHz
	Multiplier Ratio	4.0 – 4.5x
Physical Design	Interface Packing	242-Pin Slot 1 Cartridge
		370-Pin PPGA Socket
	Core Die Size	.25 micron, 118 mm^2
	Transistor Count	7.5 Million
	Voltage Interface	Split Core and I/O
	Core Voltage	2.0 volts
	I/O Voltage	3.3 volts
	Level 2 Cache Voltage	3.3 volts
	Power Consumption	Slot 1 = 11 – 12 watts
		PPGA = 11 – 12 watts

(continued on next page)

Table 6-21: Celeron Covington Specifications (continued)

Processor Family	Model Name	Intel Celeron Covington
	Maximum Power	Slot 1 = 16.6 – 18.4 watts
		PPGA = 15.6 – 17.5 Watts
Architectural Design	Core Technology	OOO and Speculative Execution RISC
	Register Support	Integer = 32 bit
		FPU = 80 bit
		MMX = 64 bit
	Execution Units	2 x ALU/MMX
		1 x Pipelined FPU
	Maximum Execution Rate	5 Micro-Ops per Cycle
	Data Bus Width	64 bit
	Maximum Memory Support	Physical = 64 Gigabyte
		Virtual = 64 Terabyte
	Multi-Processor Support	2-way SMP via APIC
	Level 1 Code Cache	16 KB 4-way
	Level 1 Data Cache	16 KB 4-way
	Level 2 Cache	N/A
	Read Buffer	4 x 32 Byte
	Write Buffer	32 Byte
	Pre-fetch Queue	32 Byte
	Static Branch Prediction	Supported
	Dynamic Branch Prediction	512 Entry 4-way
	RSB Branch Prediction	4 Entry
	Floating-Point Processor	Integrated
	Multimedia Extensions	MMX

Celeron Covington 266

Table 6-22: Celeron Covington 266 Specifications

Processor Family	Model Name	Intel Celeron Covington
	Performance Rating	266 MHz
	Front-side Bus Speed	66 MHz
	Multiplier Ratio	4.0x
Physical Design	Interface Packing	242-Pin Slot 1 Cartridge
		370-Pin PPGA Socket
	Core Voltage	2.0 volts
	I/O Voltage	3.3 volts
	Power Consumption	Slot 1 = 11 watts
		PPGA = 11 watts
	Maximum Power	Slot 1 = 16.6 watts
		PPGA = 15.6 watts

Table 6-23: Celeron Covington 266 Overclocking

Celeron Covington	Model Rating	266 MHz
Overclocking Potential	Multiplier Lock Support	Locked Multiplier
	Typical Multiplier O/C	N/A
	Typical Front-side Bus O/C	Up to 100 MHz
	Typical O/C Potential	300 – 333 MHz
	Maximum O/C Potential	400+ MHz
Overclocking Tolerances	Recommended Cooling Type	Forced-Air Heatsink
	Recommended Heatsink Coolers	Globalwin VEK 16
		Vantec PIID-4535H
		Globalwin CAK-38
	Recommended Peltier Active Cooler	STEP-UP-53X2
	Maximum Core Voltage	2.2 volts with Heatsink Cooler
	Maximum I/O Voltage	3.5 volts with Chipset Cooler
	Maximum Core Temperature	85° Celsius

Strategy

The Covington series in the Intel Celeron family debuted at 266 MHz. The Covington lacks a Level 2 cache memory, and thus it was marketed as an entry-level processor. The Covington also introduced the 370-pin socket PPGA format (PGA 370) in hopes of lowering production costs. Being a socketed processor, the Celeron does not require the expensive Slot 1 interface board as does the Pentium II. A traditional Slot 1 design was retained to ensure legacy support among Intel's OEM partners.

The internal core matches the Pentium II, so this chip retains the powerful processing capabilities of its larger brother. All but the earliest Celeron models feature locked multipliers. Front-side bus overclocking offers the best performance return for the Covington: the increase in memory bandwidth can compensate, to some extent, for the absence of an L2 cache.

The Celeron Covington generally offers better overclocking potential than the Pentium II. The lack of a Level 2 cache eliminates the possibility of cache memory chips failing due to extended overclocking attempts. The Celeron C266 offers great potential for front-side bus overclocking at 100 MHz, yielding a 400-MHz core operating speed. Systems with motherboards lacking 100-MHz support will be limited to 333 MHz, though any increase in front-side bus speed will improve the Covington's performance.

The Intel retail series heatsink cooler should prove acceptable for moderate overclocking in the 300 to 333 MHz range. All Covington models up to 433 MHz feature a maximum thermal rating of 85° Celsius; thus, extra cooling is only required when overclocking is above 400 MHz.

Celeron Covington 300

Table 6-24: Celeron Covington 300 Specifications

Processor Family	Model Name	Intel Celeron Covington
	Performance Rating	300 MHz
	Front-side Bus Speed	66 MHz
	Multiplier Ratio	4.5x
Physical Design	Interface Packing	242-Pin Slot 1 Cartridge
		370-Pin PPGA Socket
	Core Voltage	2.0 volts
	I/O Voltage	3.3 volts
	Level 2 Cache Voltage	3.3 volts
	Power Consumption	Slot 1 = 12 watts
		PPGA = 12 watts
	Maximum Power	Slot 1 = 18.4 watts
		PPGA = 17.5 watts

Table 6-25: Celeron Covington 300 Overclocking

Celeron Covington	Model Rating	300 MHz
Overclocking Potential	Multiplier Lock Support	Locked Multiplier
	Typical Multiplier O/C	N/A
	Typical Front-side Bus O/C	Up to 100 MHz
	Typical O/C Potential	338 – 374 MHz
	Maximum O/C Potential	450+ MHz
Overclocking Tolerances	Recommended Cooling Type	Forced-Air Heatsink
	Recommended Heatsink Coolers	Globalwin VEK 16
		Vantec PIID-4535H
		Globalwin CAK-38
	Recommended Peltier Active Cooler	STEP-UP-53X2
	Maximum Core Voltage	2.2 volts with Heatsink Cooler
	Maximum I/O Voltage	3.5 volts with Chipset Cooler
	Maximum Core Temperature	85° Celsius

Strategy

The Celeron Covington 300 MHz offers great potential for systems featuring 100-MHz front-side-bus-capable motherboards. The C300 features a 4.5x multiplier that corresponds well to the 100 MHz-bus speed, yielding 450-MHz overclocking. Most systems will require an increase in core voltage levels to 2.2 volts in order to maintain stability at 450 MHz and beyond. A small percentage of Celeron C300 processors have been known to attain operating speeds in excess of 500 MHz, though only by risking dangerous core voltage increases, which are often mitigated by alternative cooling methods, such as Peltier or forced liquid.

Celeron Mendocino Overclocking

Table 6-26: Celeron Mendocino Specifications

Processor Family	Model Name	Intel Celeron Mendocino
	Performance Rating	300 – 533 MHz
	Generation	Sixth: 80686 IA-32
Operational Rates	Level 1 Cache Speed	1.0x Core Rate
	Level 2 Cache Speed	1.0x Core Rate
	Front-side Bus Speed	66 MHz
	Multiplier Ratio	4.5 – 8.0x
Physical Design	Interface Packing	242-Pin Slot 1 Cartridge
		370-Pin PPGA Socket
	Core Die Size	.25 micron, 154 mm^2
	Transistor Count	19 Million
	Voltage Interface	Split Core and I/O
	Core Voltage	2.0 volts
	I/O Voltage	3.3 volts
	Level 2 Cache Voltage	3.3 volts
	Power Consumption	12 – 19 watts
	Maximum Power	18.4 – 28.3 watts
Architectural Design	Core Technology	OOO and Speculative Execution RISC
	Register Support	Integer = 32 bit
		FPU = 80 bit
		MMX = 64 bit
	Execution Units	2 x ALU/MMX
		1 x Pipelined FPU
	Maximum Execution Rate	5 Micro-Ops per Cycle
	Data Bus Width	64 bit
	Maximum Memory Support	Physical = 64 Gigabyte
		Virtual = 64 Terabyte
	Multi-Processor Support	2-way SMP via APIC
	Level 1 Code Cache	16 KB 4-way
	Level 1 Data Cache	16 KB 4-way
	Level 2 Cache	128 KB Unified
	Read Buffer	4 x 32 Byte
	Write Buffer	32 Byte
	Pre-fetch Queue	32 Byte
	Static Branch Prediction	Supported
	Dynamic Branch Prediction	512 Entry 4-way
	RSB Branch Prediction	4 Entry
	Floating-Point Processor	Integrated
	Multimedia Extensions	MMX

Celeron Mendocino 300

Table 6-27: Celeron Mendocino 300 Specifications

Processor Family	Model Name	Intel Celeron Mendocino
	Performance Rating	300 MHz
	Front-side Bus Speed	66 MHz
	Multiplier Ratio	4.5x
Physical Design	Interface Packing	242-Pin Slot 1 Cartridge
		370-Pin PPGA Socket
	Core Voltage	2.0 volts
	Power Consumption	12 watts
	Maximum Power	18.4 watts

Table 6-28: Celeron Mendocino 300 Overclocking

Celeron Mendocino	Model Rating	300 MHz
Overclocking Potential	Multiplier Lock Support	Locked Multiplier
	Typical Multiplier O/C	N/A
	Typical Front-side Bus O/C	Up to 100 MHz
	Typical O/C Potential	338 – 374 MHz
	Maximum O/C Potential	450+ MHz
Overclocking Tolerances	Recommended Cooling Type	Forced-Air Heatsink
	Recommended Heatsink Coolers	Globalwin VEK 16
		Vantec PIID-4535H
		Thermalright SK6
		Globalwin CAK-38
	Recommended Peltier Active Cooler	STEP-UP-53X2
	Maximum Core Voltage	2.2 volts with Heatsink Cooler
	Maximum I/O Voltage	3.5 volts with Chipset Cooler
	Maximum Core Temperature	85° Celsius

Strategy

The Celeron Mendocino introduced a 128-KB Level 2 cache embedded directly in the processor core. The earlier cacheless Celeron Covington series could not compete in desktop application performance, even for the entry-level market. The addition of the Level 2 cache boosted the performance of nearly all software running on the Celeron Mendocino.

This performance increase actually bumped the Mendocino into a competitive position against Intel's own flagship desktop processor, the Pentium II Deschutes. While featuring only one-quarter the Level 2 cache of the P2, the Celeron Mendocino, with its full-speed cache architecture, offered nearly equivalent performance. Intel quickly transitioned the Pentium II to a 100-MHz front-side bus speed, leaving the Celeron dependant on the older 66-MHz standard. This generated a marketable performance difference between the two processor families.

The overclocking community quickly took notice of the performance potential of the new Celeron A series. By overclocking the front-side bus to 100 MHz, users could make the inexpensive Celeron A perform within a few percentage points of the costly Pentium II in nearly all benchmark tests. The embedded cache architecture also removed the limitation of external cache memory chips, thus allowing the internal P2-derived core to excel.

The Celeron 300A offers an 80+% success rate when overclocking to 450 MHz with a 100-MHz front-side bus. Many chips will require an increase in core voltage to 2.2 volts to maintain stability, but a small percentage of the best chips can scale beyond 450 MHz without voltage or cooling modifications. As usual, any increase in voltage levels will require the addition of a cooling system, though the retail Intel heatsink should be adequate for overclocking in the 338 to 374 MHz ranges.

Celeron Mendocino 333

Table 6-29: Celeron Mendocino 333 Specifications

Processor Family	Model Name	Intel Celeron Mendocino
	Performance Rating	333 MHz
	Front-side Bus Speed	66 MHz
	Multiplier Ratio	5.0x
Physical Design	Interface Packing	242-Pin Slot 1 Cartridge
		370-Pin PPGA Socket
	Core Voltage	2.0 volts
	Power Consumption	14 watts
	Maximum Power	20.2 watts

Table 6-30: Celeron Mendocino 333 Overclocking

Celeron Mendocino	Model Rating	333 MHz
Overclocking Potential	Multiplier Lock Support	Locked Multiplier
	Typical Multiplier O/C	N/A
	Typical Front-side Bus O/C	Up to 100 MHz
	Typical O/C Potential	375 – 415 MHz
	Maximum O/C Potential	450 – 500+ MHz
Overclocking Tolerances	Recommended Cooling Type	Forced-Air Heatsink
	Recommended Heatsink Coolers	Globalwin VEK 16
		Vantec PIID-4535H
		Thermalright SK6
		Globalwin CAK-38
	Recommended Peltier Active Cooler	STEP-UP-53X2
	Maximum Core Voltage	2.2 volts with Heatsink Cooler
	Maximum I/O Voltage	3.5 volts with Chipset Cooler
	Maximum Core Temperature	85° Celsius

Strategy

The Celeron 333A is able to scale overclocking speeds upwards of 500 MHz, with little more than a quality aftermarket cooler and a slight 0.1 to 0.2-volt bump in the core voltage rating. Otherwise, the Celeron 333A resembles the 300A in most aspects. For those with 100-MHz-capable motherboards, the 333A offers great overclocking potential and minimal effort. Overclocks in the 375 or 415 MHz range often require nothing more than increasing the front-side bus rate to 75 or 83 MHz, respectively.

Celeron Mendocino 366

Table 6-31: Celeron Mendocino 366 Specifications

Processor Family	Model Name	Intel Celeron Mendocino
	Performance Rating	366 MHz
	Front-side Bus Speed	66 MHz
	Multiplier Ratio	5.5x
Physical Design	Interface Packing	242-Pin Slot 1 Cartridge
		370-Pin PPGA Socket
	Core Voltage	2.0 volts
	Power Consumption	14 watts
	Maximum Power	22.2 watts

Table 6-32: Celeron Mendocino 366 Overclocking

Celeron Mendocino	Model Rating	366 MHz
Overclocking Potential	Multiplier Lock Support	Locked Multiplier
	Typical Multiplier O/C	N/A
	Typical Front-side Bus O/C	Up to 100 MHz
	Typical O/C Potential	413 – 457 MHz
	Maximum O/C Potential	550 + MHz
Overclocking Tolerances	Recommended Cooling Type	Forced-Air Heatsink
	Recommended Heatsink Coolers	Globalwin VEK 16
		Vantec PIID-4535H
		Thermalright SK6
		Globalwin CAK-38
	Recommended Peltier Active Cooler	STEP-UP-53X2
	Maximum Core Voltage	2.2 volts with Heatsink Cooler
	Maximum I/O Voltage	3.5 volts with Chipset Cooler
	Maximum Core Temperature	85° Celsius

Strategy

The Celeron 366A is perhaps the most popular Mendocino processor model for overclocking enthusiasts. This chip features a 5.5x multiplier that responds well to 100-MHz front-side bus overclocking, yielding an impressive 550-MHz core operating speed. With this third model in the Mendocino family, Intel had nearly perfected the Celeron core for high-frequency operation in hopes of extending the Celeron line beyond 500 MHz.

The Celeron 366A is so well crafted that many units can scale easily beyond 600 MHz with the help of a quality cooling solution. The 366A attracted the attention of many professional users, as this chip was often used to build over-clockable dual processor systems. According to most surveys, more than 90% of all Celeron 366A units can attain a stable overclock to 550 MHz with minimal intervention.

Celeron Mendocino 400

Table 6-33: Celeron Mendocino 400 Specifications

Processor Family	Model Name	Intel Celeron Mendocino
	Performance Rating	400 MHz
	Front-side Bus Speed	66 MHz
	Multiplier Ratio	6.0x
Physical Design	Interface Packing	242-Pin Slot 1 Cartridge
		370-Pin PPGA Socket
	Core Voltage	2.0 volts
	Power Consumption	15 watts
	Maximum Power	23.4 watts

Table 6-34: Celeron Mendocino 400 Overclocking

Celeron Mendocino	Model Rating	400 MHz
Overclocking Potential	Multiplier Lock Support	Locked Multiplier
	Typical Multiplier O/C	N/A
	Typical Front-side Bus O/C	Up to 100 MHz
	Typical O/C Potential	450 – 498 MHz
	Maximum O/C Potential	600 MHz
Overclocking Tolerances	Recommended Cooling Type	Forced-Air Heatsink
	Recommended Heatsink Coolers	Globalwin VEK 16
		Vantec PIID-4535H
		Thermalright SK6
		Globalwin CAK-38
	Recommended Peltier Active Cooler	STEP-UP-53X2
	Maximum Core Voltage	2.2 volts with Heatsink Cooler
	Maximum I/O Voltage	3.5 volts with Chipset Cooler
	Maximum Core Temperature	85° Celsius

Strategy

The Celeron 400A is the last of the highly overclockable processors in the Mendocino family. The 400A operates with a 6x multiplier; thus overclocking the 100-MHz front-side bus speed yields a core operational speed of 600 MHz. A .25-micron design, the Celeron A cannot scale successfully beyond 550 or 600 MHz without using radical cooling technologies.

The majority of Celeron 400A processors will reach their maximum over-clocked speed near 500 MHz. Only a small number of these chips will ever be stable at 600 MHz. Those who successfully overclock to this extended frequency will need to monitor core temperatures closely, as the .25-micron core of the Celeron A can reach damaging thermal loads in seconds. Quality forced-air heatsink coolers should prove adequate, but overclocking beyond 500 MHz with the retail Intel cooler should not be attempted.

Celeron Mendocino 433

Table 6-35: Celeron Mendocino 433 Specifications

Processor Family	Model Name	Intel Celeron Mendocino
	Performance Rating	433 MHz
	Front-side Bus Speed	66 MHz
	Multiplier Ratio	6.5x
Physical Design	Interface Packing	242-Pin Slot 1 Cartridge
		370-Pin PPGA Socket
	Core Voltage	2.0 volts
	Power Consumption	16 watts
	Maximum Power	24.6 watts

Table 6-36: Celeron Mendocino 433 Overclocking

Celeron Mendocino	Model Rating	433 MHz
Overclocking Potential	Multiplier Lock Support	Locked Multiplier
	Typical Multiplier O/C	N/A
	Typical Front-side Bus O/C	Up to 83 MHz
	Typical O/C Potential	488 – 540 MHz
	Maximum O/C Potential	550 – 600 MHz
Overclocking Tolerances	Recommended Cooling Type	Forced-Air Heatsink
	Recommended Heatsink Coolers	Globalwin VEK 16
		Vantec PIID-4535H
		Thermalright SK6
		Globalwin CAK-38
	Recommended Peltier Active Cooler	STEP-UP-53X2
	Maximum Core Voltage	2.2 volts with Heatsink Cooler
	Maximum I/O Voltage	3.5 volts with Chipset Cooler
	Maximum Core Temperature	85° Celsius

Strategy

The Celeron 433A allows little headroom for successful scaling beyond 540 MHz. Its 6.5x core multiplier will limit successful overclocks near 500 MHz with traditional heatsink cooling. Considering the lack of effective frequency scaling, the retail Intel heatsink should prove more than adequate for overclocking at speeds approaching 500 MHz. Otherwise, the Celeron 433A offers only moderate overclocking returns, because the 100-MHz front-side bus speed cannot be realized with this processor.

Celeron Mendocino 466

Table 6-37: Celeron Mendocino 466 Specifications

Processor Family	Model Name	Intel Celeron Mendocino
	Performance Rating	466 MHz
	Front-side Bus Speed	66 MHz
	Multiplier Ratio	7.0x
Physical Design	Interface Packing	242-Pin Slot 1 Cartridge
		370-Pin PPGA Socket
	Core Voltage	2.0 volts
	Power Consumption	17 watts
	Maximum Power	25.6 watts

Table 6-38: Celeron Mendocino 466 Overclocking

Celeron Mendocino	Model Rating	466 MHz
Overclocking Potential	Multiplier Lock Support	Locked Multiplier
	Typical Multiplier O/C	N/A
	Typical Front-side Bus O/C	Up to 75 MHz
	Typical O/C Potential	525 – 550 MHz
	Maximum O/C Potential	581 – 600 MHz
Overclocking Tolerances	Recommended Cooling Type	Forced-Air Heatsink
	Recommended Heatsink Coolers	Globalwin VEK 16
		Vantec PIID-4535H
		Thermalright SK6
		Globalwin CAK-38
	Recommended Peltier Active Cooler	STEP-UP-53X2
	Maximum Core Voltage	2.2 volts with Heatsink Cooler
	Maximum I/O Voltage	3.5 volts with Chipset Cooler
	Maximum Core Temperature	70° Celsius

Strategy

The Celeron 466A offers limited overclocking support. The internal 7.0x core multiplier, combined with an aging .25-micron core design, max out at 525 MHz (75-MHz front-side bus) for most of these chips. Even reaching an 83-MHz front-side bus speed will prove difficult, as the 466A model carries a maximum thermal rating of 70° Celsius. Any increase in the core voltage rate will require an aftermarket cooling solution.

Celeron Mendocino 500

Table 6-39: Celeron Mendocino 500 Specifications

Processor Family	Model Name	Intel Celeron Mendocino
	Performance Rating	500 MHz
	Front-side Bus Speed	66 MHz
	Multiplier Ratio	7.5x
Physical Design	Interface Packing	242-Pin Slot 1 Cartridge
		370-Pin PPGA Socket
	Core Voltage	2.0 volts
	Power Consumption	18 watts
	Maximum Power	27 watts

Table 6-40: Celeron Mendocino 500 Overclocking

Celeron Mendocino	Model Rating	500 MHz
Overclocking Potential	Multiplier Lock Support	Locked Multiplier
	Typical Multiplier O/C	N/A
	Typical Front-side Bus O/C	Up to 75 MHz
	Typical O/C Potential	563 – 575 MHz
	Maximum O/C Potential	~ 600 MHz
Overclocking Tolerances	Recommended Cooling Type	Forced-Air Heatsink
	Recommended Heatsink Coolers	Globalwin VEK 16
		Vantec PIID-4535H
		Thermalright SK6
		Globalwin CAK-38
	Recommended Peltier Active Cooler	STEP-UP-53X2
	Maximum Core Voltage	2.2 volts with Heatsink Cooler
	Maximum I/O Voltage	3.5 volts with Chipset Cooler
	Maximum Core Temperature	70° Celsius

Strategy

The Celeron 500A is a minimal overclocking model in most configurations. The 7.5x multiplier restricts successful overclocking to a 75-MHz front-side bus speed. In addition, a poor thermal rating for the 25-micron core will void most overclocking attempts beyond 550 MHz.

Celeron Mendocino 533

Table 6-41: Celeron Mendocino 533 Specifications

Processor Family	Model Name	Intel Celeron Mendocino
	Performance Rating	533 MHz
	Front-side Bus Speed	66 MHz
	Multiplier Ratio	8.0x
	Core Voltage	2.0 volts
	Power Consumption	19 watts
	Maximum Power	28.3 watts

Table 6-42: Celeron Mendocino 533 Overclocking

Celeron Mendocino	Model Rating	533 MHz
Overclocking Potential	Multiplier Lock Support	Locked Multiplier
	Typical Multiplier O/C	N/A
	Typical Front-side Bus O/C	Up to 66 – 75 MHz
	Typical O/C Potential	550 – 575 MHz
	Maximum O/C Potential	~ 600 MHz
Overclocking Tolerances	Recommended Cooling Type	Forced-Air Heatsink
	Recommended Heatsink Coolers	Globalwin VEK 16
		Vantec PIID-4535H
		Thermalright SK6
		Globalwin CAK-38
	Recommended Peltier Active Cooler	STEP-UP-53X2
	Maximum Core Voltage	2.2 volts with Heatsink Cooler
	Maximum I/O Voltage	3.5 volts with Chipset Cooler
	Maximum Core Temperature	70° Celsius

Strategy

The Mendocino 533-MHz model is the final generation in the .25-micron Celeron family. Featuring an 8.0x multiplier, this processor is not well suited to overclocking. A few 533A units may reach 600 MHz with a 75-MHz front-side bus, but attempts at higher returns will usually result in a processor unable to boot the system. Considering this limitation, the retail Intel heatsink should prove efficient enough for stable operation at 600 MHz if proper case cooling is applied.

Pentium III Katmai Background

The Pentium III Katmai represents an evolutionary step for the Pentium II design. The design includes the SSE multimedia instruction set, which differentiates Katmai from its earlier cousins. Increased efficiency in Intel's design allowed the Katmai to scale up to 600 MHz; thus the demand for these chips was quite high during the early stages of Intel's P3 marketing initiative.

The most promising Katmai overclock lies in the Pentium III 450-MHz processor. A 100-MHz front-side bus chip with a 4.5x multiplier, this processor was well suited to the 133+-MHz front-side bus capabilities of many popular motherboards. Overclocks to 600 MHz are usually stable with only a slight increase in the core voltage and the use of a quality cooling solution.

Early overclocking returns were so positive that Intel quickly introduced a Pentium III 600b MHz Katmai. The b identifier signifies 133-MHz front-side bus support. Even so, do not expect much overclocking potential beyond 600 MHz with the Katmai cooled by traditional forced-air techniques. The Katmai was Intel's last processor to be built atop the .25-micron fabrication process, which limits MHz scalability.

Pentium III Katmai Overclocking

Table 6-43: Pentium III Katmai Specifications

Processor Family	Model Name	Intel Pentium III Katmai
	Performance Rating	600 MHz
	Generation	Sixth: 80686 IA-32
Operational Rates	Level 1 Cache Speed	1.0x Core Rate
	Level 2 Cache Speed	0.5x Core Rate
	Front-side Bus Speed	100 – 133 MHz
	Multiplier Ratio	4.5x – 6.0x
Physical Design	Interface Packing	242-Pin Slot 1 Cartridge
	Core Die Size	.25 micron, 128mm^2
	Transistor Count	~ 9.5 Million
	Voltage Interface	Split Core and I/O
	Core Voltage	2.00 – 2.05 volts
	I/O Voltage	3.3 volts
	Level 2 Cache Voltage	3.3 volts
	Power Consumption	17 – 23 watts
	Maximum Power	25.3 – 34.5 watts
Architectural Design	Core Technology	OOO and Speculative Execution RISC
	Register Support	Integer = 32 bit
		FPU = 80 bit
		MMX = 64 bit
		SSE = 128 bit
	Execution Units	2 x ALU/MMX/SSE
		1 x Pipelined FPU
	Maximum Execution Rate	5 Micro-Ops per Cycle
	Data Bus Width	64 bit
	Maximum Memory Support	Physical = 64 Gigabyte
		Virtual = 64 Terabyte
	Multi-Processor Support	2-way SMP via APIC

(continued on next page)

Table 6-43: Pentium III Katmai Specifications (continued)

Processor Family	Model Name	Intel Pentium III Katmai
	Level 1 Code Cache	16 KB 4-way
	Level 1 Data Cache	16 KB 4-way
	Level 2 Cache	512 KB Unified
	Read Buffer	4 x 32 Byte
	Write Buffer	32 Byte
	Pre-fetch Queue	32 Byte
	Static Branch Prediction	Supported
	Dynamic Branch Prediction	512 Entry 4-way
	RSB Branch Prediction	4 Entry
	Floating-Point Processor	Integrated
	Multimedia Extensions	MMX, SSE

Pentium III Katmai 450

Table 6-44: Pentium III Katmai 450 Specifications

Processor Family	Model Name	Intel Pentium III Katmai
	Performance Rating	450 MHz
	Front-side Bus Speed	100 MHz
	Multiplier Ratio	4.5x
Physical Design	Interface Packing	242-Pin Slot 1 Cartridge
	Core Voltage	2.0 volts
	Power Consumption	17 watts
	Maximum Power	25.3 watts

Table 6-45: Pentium III Katmai 450 Overclocking

Pentium III Katmai	Model Rating	450 MHz
Overclocking Potential	Multiplier Lock Support	Locked Multiplier
	Typical Multiplier O/C	N/A
	Typical Front-side Bus O/C	Up to 112 – 124 MHz
	Typical O/C Potential	504 – 558 MHz
	Maximum O/C Potential	600+ MHz
Overclocking Tolerances	Recommended Cooling Type	Forced-Air Heatsink
	Recommended Heatsink Coolers	Globalwin VES20
		Alpha P3125
	Recommended Peltier Active Cooler	Swiftech MC1000
		PC-10a Cooler
	Maximum Core Voltage	2.2 volts with Heatsink Cooler
	Maximum I/O Voltage	3.5 volts with Chipset Cooler
	Maximum Core Temperature	80 – 85° Celsius

Strategy

The Katmai 450 MHz introduced the new Pentium III core. This chip is solid for overclocking due to its highly refined .25-micron core, coupled with a low 4.5x multiplier and 100-MHz front-side bus support. The Katmai shares many attributes with its Pentium II sibling, though the higher-quality cache memory chips allow the Katmai 450 to scale up to 600 MHz efficiently, given sufficient cooling.

The 4.5x multiplier is well suited for 124-MHz front-side bus overclocking, yielding a respectable 558 MHz. A small number of these chips will reach 600 MHz with quality cooling, but be prepared to bump the core voltage to 2.2 volts for stability. The Katmai does demand power; alternative cooling methods based on Peltier or liquid technologies are desirable.

Pentium III Katmai 500

Table 6-46: Pentium III Katmai 500 Specifications

Processor Family	Model Name	Intel Pentium III Katmai
	Performance Rating	500 MHz
	Front-side Bus Speed	100 MHz
	Multiplier Ratio	5.0x
Physical Design	Interface Packing	242-Pin Slot 1 Cartridge
	Core Voltage	2.0 voltage
	Power Consumption	19 watts
	Maximum Power	28 watts

Table 6-47: Pentium III Katmai 500 Overclocking

Pentium III Katmai	Model Rating	500 MHz
Overclocking Potential	Multiplier Lock Support	Locked Multiplier
	Typical Multiplier O/C	N/A
	Typical Front-side Bus O/C	Up to 112 – 124 MHz
	Typical O/C Potential	560 – 600 MHz
	Maximum O/C Potential	600+ MHz
Overclocking Tolerances	Recommended Cooling Type	Forced-Air Heatsink
	Recommended Heatsink Coolers	Globalwin VES20
		Alpha P3125
	Recommended Peltier Active Cooler	Swiftech MC1000
		PC-10a Cooler
	Maximum Core Voltage	2.2 volts with Heatsink Cooler
	Maximum I/O Voltage	3.5 volts with Chipset Cooler
	Maximum Core Temperature	80 – 85° Celsius

Strategy

Overclocking the Pentium III Katmai 500 MHz works best with the 112-MHz front-side bus rate. Unlike the Katmai 450, this model is not suitable for 133-MHz bus overclocking due to its higher 5.0x internal multiplier. Most Katmai 500 processors will reach maximum overclocking potential around 600 MHz, though many units will never see returns beyond the 560-MHz level.

Pentium III Katmai 550

Table 6-48: Pentium III Katmai 550 Specifications

Processor Family	Model Name	Intel Pentium III Katmai
	Performance Rating	550 MHz
	Front-side Bus Speed	100 MHz
	Multiplier Ratio	5.5x
	Core Voltage	2.0 volts
	Power Consumption	21 watts
	Maximum Power	30.8 watts

Table 6-49: Pentium III Katmai 550 Overclocking

Pentium III Katmai	Model Rating	550 MHz
Overclocking Potential	Multiplier Lock Support	Locked Multiplier
	Typical Multiplier O/C	N/A
	Typical Front-side Bus O/C	Up to 112 MHz
	Typical O/C Potential	575 – 616 MHz
	Maximum O/C Potential	~ 650 MHz
Overclocking Tolerances	Recommended Cooling Type	Forced-Air Heatsink
	Recommended Heatsink Coolers	Globalwin VES20
		Alpha P3125
	Recommended Peltier Active Cooler	Swiftech MC1000
		PC-10a Cooler
	Maximum Core Voltage	2.2 volts with Heatsink Cooler
	Maximum I/O Voltage	3.5 volts with Chipset Cooler
	Maximum Core Temperature	80 – 85° Celsius

Strategy

The Katmai 550-MHz processor also offers minimal overclocking potential due to its 5.5x internal multiplier. Most Katmai 550 models will reach their maximum overclocking rate around 575 MHz, just beyond the default core rate of this chip. Accordingly, the retail Intel heatsink cooler should prove adequate for overclocking this processor.

Pentium III Katmai 600

Table 6-50: Pentium III Katmai 600 Specifications

Processor Family	Model Name	Intel Pentium III Katmai
	Performance Rating	600 MHz
	Front-side Bus Speed	100 MHz
	Multiplier Ratio	6.0x
Physical Design	Interface Packing	242-Pin Slot 1 Cartridge
	Core Voltage	2.0 volts
	Power Consumption	23 watts
	Maximum Power	34.5 watts

Table 6-51: Pentium III Katmai 600 Overclocking

Pentium III Katmai	Model Rating	600 MHz
Overclocking Potential	Multiplier Lock Support	Locked Multiplier
	Typical Multiplier O/C	N/A
	Typical Front-side Bus O/C	105 – 112 MHz
	Typical O/C Potential	630 – 672 MHz
	Maximum O/C Potential	~ 700 MHz
Overclocking Tolerances	Recommended Cooling Type	Forced-Air Heatsink
	Recommended Heatsink Coolers	Globalwin VES20
		Alpha P3125
	Recommended Peltier Active Cooler	Swiftech MC1000
		PC-10a Cooler
	Maximum Core Voltage	2.2 volts with Heatsink Cooler
	Maximum I/O Voltage	3.5 volts with Chipset Cooler
	Maximum Core Temperature	80 – 85° Celsius

Strategy

The Pentium III 600 brought an end to the 100-MHz front-side-bus-compatible Katmai series of processors. The final model in this series, the Katmai 600, lacks overclocking potential beyond the 112-MHz front-side bus rate, leading to a theoretical maximum near 672 MHz. Earlier Katmai models offer better performance; lower ranges of the Katmai series can often overclock to a speedier 133-MHz front-side bus rate.

Pentium III Katmai 533B

Table 6-52: Pentium III Katmai 533B Specifications

Processor Family	Model Name	Intel Pentium III Katmai
	Performance Rating	533 MHz
	Front-side Bus Speed	133 MHz
	Multiplier Ratio	4.0x
Physical Design	Interface Packing	242-Pin Slot 1 Cartridge
	Core Voltage	2.0 volts
	Power Consumption	20 watts
	Maximum Power	29.7 watts

Table 6-53: Pentium III Katmai 533B Overclocking

Pentium III Katmai	Model Rating	533 MHz
Overclocking Potential	Multiplier Lock Support	Locked Multiplier
	Typical Multiplier O/C	N/A
	Typical Front-side Bus O/C	140 MHz
	Typical O/C Potential	~ 560 MHz
	Maximum O/C Potential	600+ MHz
Overclocking Tolerances	Recommended Cooling Type	Forced-Air Heatsink
	Recommended Heatsink Coolers	Globalwin VES20
		Alpha P3125
	Recommended Peltier Active Cooler	Swiftech MC1000
		PC-10a Cooler
	Maximum Core Voltage	2.2 volts with Heatsink Cooler
	Maximum I/O Voltage	3.5 volts with Chipset Cooler
	Maximum Core Temperature	80 – 85° Celsius

Strategy

The Katmai 600 finished the 100-MHz front-side bus series. Taking a cue from the overclocking community, Intel slid the Katmai to a 133-MHz front-side bus rating. This new series is marked by the addition of a B modifier to each model's speed rating.

Still suffering from the .25-micron core design, the Katmai 533B provides modest overclocking potential. Perhaps worse than the processor's core limitation is the lack of support for extended front-side bus speeds in the popular 133-MHz-capable Slot 1 boards. After VIA introduced its Apollo Pro133A chipset, support for motherboard rates beyond 133 MHz began to appear in the mainstream markets. Intel released its own i815 and i820 chipsets and the latter of these offered RAMBUS memory support.

Most Katmai 533B chips can successfully overclock to 560 MHz. The retail Intel heatsink should be adequate; a core voltage increase of 0.1 volts is usually all that is required. Any increase in the front-side bus rate can offer significant performance returns through increased memory bandwidth when the memory subsystem is operating at or above the processor bus rate. The popular VIA Pro133A chipset introduced support for down-clocking memory, using asynchronous signaling. Benchmarking will measure the performance gains, assuming memory down-clocking is employed to attain a higher front-side bus speed.

Pentium III Katmai 600B

Table 6-54: Pentium III Katmai 450 Specifications

Processor Family	Model Name	Intel Pentium III Katmai
	Performance Rating	600 MHz
	Front-side Bus Speed	133 MHz
	Multiplier Ratio	4.5x
Physical Design	Interface Packing	242-Pin Slot 1 Cartridge
	Core Voltage	2.05 volts
	Power Consumption	23 watts
	Maximum Power	34.5 watts

Table 6-55: Pentium III Katmai 450 Overclocking

Pentium III Katmai	Model Rating	600 MHz
Overclocking Potential	Multiplier Lock Support	Locked Multiplier
	Typical Multiplier O/C	N/A
	Typical Front-side Bus O/C	~ 140 MHz
	Typical O/C Potential	630 – 650 MHz
	Maximum O/C Potential	675+ MHz
Overclocking Tolerances	Recommended Cooling Type	Forced-Air Heatsink
	Recommended Heatsink Coolers	Globalwin VES20
		Alpha P3125
	Recommended Peltier Active Cooler	Swiftech MC1000
		PC-10a Cooler
	Maximum Core Voltage	2.2 volts with Heatsink Cooler
	Maximum I/O Voltage	3.5 volts with Chipset Cooler
	Maximum Core Temperature	80 – 85° Celsius

Strategy

The Pentium III Katmai 600B offers overclocking potential similar to its 533-MHz counterpart. Notice the increase to 2.05 volts for the core voltage rating compared to 2.0 volts for older Katmai models. Intel must have recognized the limitations of its .25-micron fabrication process. A 0.05 volt increase appears minimal, but the reality is that Intel needed the bump in voltage to sustain its sales model at this higher frequency.

The Katmai 600B marked the end of a generation. It was the last .25-micron processor offered by Intel's desktop computing division. Overclocking this model proves difficult beyond 650 MHz; many chips never reach beyond the factory default of 600 MHz at a 2.05 volts core. Due to a peak power demand of 34.5 watts, the Katmai 600B will require massive cooling if overclocking returns exceeding 650 MHz are to be attained. Peltier cooling is a popular solution for this model, but the costs can be prohibitive given the small potential performance gains.

Pentium III Coppermine Background

After noting the limits of its .25-micron fabrication process, Intel shifted to a new .18-micron core for the Pentium III Coppermine. Intel also made its Level 2 cache internal to the core die, thus improving performance compared to the Katmai's external cache architecture. The "Coppermine" name created confusion, however, and many users upgraded to this architecture believing that its internal circuitry featured a copper interconnect design. In truth, the Coppermine still used the aluminum standard. Even so, upon its release the Coppermine became the best overclocking option available.

The desktop Coppermine is available in two distinct forms. Overclocking techniques remained consistent for the Slot 1 interface (a long, skinny card-edge socket) for Coppermine. The newer model, featuring a 370-pin FCPGA socket (a flat, square socket), extended overclocking potential by allowing the use of vertical heatsink coolers for greater thermal dissipation and efficiency. Combined with a new .18-micron core and lower operating voltage, the Coppermine allows overclocks in the hundreds of MHz, some even exceeding default operating frequencies by more than 50%!

Those possessing type eb processors will have less headroom for overclocking. The 133-MHz front-side bus of this series, combined with motherboard chipset limitations, prevents achieving higher speeds. A higher multiplier value is desirable in this series, especially for those interested in overclocking to 1+ GHz for maximum performance.

The most promising models are in the e series. These chips feature a base 100-MHz front-side bus design. The lower multiplier ranges (5.5x to 7.5x) offer overclocking returns of 200 to 300 MHz, requiring only a slight bump in core voltage levels and the addition of an aftermarket cooler. Even the retail cooler provided by Intel can often provide satisfactory cooling for overclocking by 100 to 150 MHz.

Pentium III Coppermine Overclocking

Table 6-56: Pentium III Coppermine Specifications

Processor Family	Model Name	Intel Pentium III Coppermine
	Performance Rating	500 – 1133 MHz
	Generation	Sixth: 80686 IA-32
Operational Rates	Level 1 Cache Speed	1.0x Core Rate
	Level 2 Cache Speed	1.0x Core Rate
	Front-side Bus Speed	100 – 133 MHz
	Multiplier Ratio	5.0x – 8.5x
Physical Design	Interface Packing	242-Pin Slot 1 Cartridge
		370-Pin FCPGA Socket
	Core Die Size	.18 micron
	Core Size by Stepping	A2 = 106 mm^2
		B0 = 104 mm^2
		CO = 90 mm^2
		D0 = 95 mm^2
	Transistor Count	28.1 Million
	Voltage Interface	Split Core and I/O
	Core Voltage	1.65 – 1.75 volts
	I/O Voltage	3.3 volts
	Level 2 Cache Voltage	3.3 volts
	Power Consumption	11 – 22 watts
	Maximum Power	16 – 33 watts
Architectural Design	Core Technology	OOO and Speculative Execution RISC
	Register Support	Integer = 32 bit
		FPU = 80 bit
		MMX = 64 bit
		SSE = 128 bit
	Execution Units	2 x ALU/MMX/SSE
		1 x Pipelined FPU
	Maximum Execution Rate	5 Micro-Ops per Cycle
	Data Bus Width	64 bit
	Maximum Memory Support	Physical = 64 Gigabyte
		Virtual = 64 Terabyte
	Multi-Processor Support	2-way SMP via APIC
	Level 1 Code Cache	16 KB 4-way
	Level 1 Data Cache	16 KB 4-way
	Level 2 Cache	256 KB Unified
	Read Buffer	4 x 32 Byte
	Write Buffer	32 Byte
	Pre-fetch Queue	32 Byte
	Static Branch Prediction	Supported

(continued on next page)

Table 6-56: Pentium III Coppermine Specifications (continued)

Processor Family	Model Name	Intel Pentium III Coppermine
	Dynamic Branch Prediction	512 Entry 4-way
	RSB Branch Prediction	4 Entry
	Floating-Point Processor	Integrated
	Multimedia Extensions	MMX, SSE

Pentium III Coppermine 500E

Table 6-57: Pentium III Coppermine 500E Specifications

Processor Family	Model Name	Intel Pentium III Coppermine
	Performance Rating	500 MHz
	Front-side Bus Speed	100 MHz
	Multiplier Ratio	5.0x
Physical Design	Interface Packing	370-Pin FCPGA Socket
		242-Pin Slot 1 Cartridge
	Core Voltage	1.65 volts
	Power Consumption	11 watts
	Maximum Power	16 watts

Table 6-58: Pentium III Coppermine 500E Overclocking

Pentium III Coppermine	Model Rating	500 MHz
Overclocking Potential	Multiplier Lock Support	Locked Multiplier
	Typical Multiplier O/C	N/A
	Typical Front-side Bus O/C	124 – 133 MHz
	Typical O/C Potential	620 – 665 MHz
	Maximum O/C Potential	700+ MHz
Overclocking Tolerances	Recommended Cooling Type	Forced-Air Heatsink
	Recommended Heatsink Coolers	Swiftech MCX370
		Alpha PAL8045
		Globalwin VOS32
	Recommended Peltier Active Cooler	MCX370 Peltier
		MC1000 Peltier
	Maximum Core Voltage	1.85 volts with Heatsink Cooler
	Maximum I/O Voltage	3.5 volts with Chipset Cooler
	Maximum Core Temperature	80° Celsius

Strategy

The E series Pentium III Coppermine offers great overclocking potential for systems featuring chips with low multiplier values. Being a 100-MHz front-side-compatible processor, the 500E is a superb candidate for overclocking to 665 MHz, with its 5x internal multiplier, via a jump to the 133-MHz front-side bus rate. Relatively low wattage demands, combined with a high thermal tolerance, often allow overclocking of this processor using the retail Intel heatsink cooler. Systems offering 133 MHz motherboard bus support require little user intervention because core voltage values increase only 5 to 10%.

Pentium III Coppermine 550E

Table 6-59: Pentium III Coppermine 550E Specifications

Processor Family	Model Name	Intel Pentium III Coppermine
	Performance Rating	550 MHz
	Front-side Bus Speed	100 MHz
	Multiplier Ratio	5.5x
Physical Design	Interface Packing	370-Pin FCPGA Socket
		242-Pin Slot 1 Cartridge
	Core Voltage	1.65 volts
	Power Consumption	12 watts
	Maximum Power	17.6 watts

Table 6-60: Pentium III Coppermine 550E Overclocking

Pentium III Coppermine	Model Rating	550 MHz
Overclocking Potential	Multiplier Lock Support	Locked Multiplier
	Typical Multiplier O/C	N/A
	Typical Front-side Bus O/C	124 – 133 MHz
	Typical O/C Potential	682 – 732 MHz
	Maximum O/C Potential	800+ MHz
Overclocking Tolerances	Recommended Cooling Type	Forced-Air Heatsink
	Recommended Heatsink Coolers	Swiftech MCX370
		Alpha PAL8045
		Globalwin VOS32
	Recommended Peltier Active Cooler	MCX370 Peltier
		MC1000 Peltier
	Maximum Core Voltage	1.85 volts with Heatsink Cooler
	Maximum I/O Voltage	3.5 volts with Chipset Cooler
	Maximum Core Temperature	80° Celsius

Strategy

The Pentium III Coppermine 550E MHz processor offers superb overclocking potential. The vast majority of these processors can overclock upwards of 700 MHz with no additional cooling or increase in core voltage. Factoring in a high thermal tolerance rating and a low failure rate, the 550E represented Intel's first quality overclocking solution since the original Celeron series. For hardcore overclockers, the P3 550E offers immense possibilities; a significant number of processors of this type can scale toward 900 MHz, assuming that quality cooling is properly applied.

Pentium III Coppermine 600E

Table 6-61: Pentium III Coppermine 600E Specifications

Processor Family	Model Name	Intel Pentium III Coppermine
	Performance Rating	600 MHz
	Front-side Bus Speed	100 MHz
	Multiplier Ratio	6.0x
Physical Design	Interface Packing	370-Pin FCPGA Socket
		242-Pin Slot 1 Cartridge
	Core Voltage	1.65 volts
	Power Consumption	13 watts
	Maximum Power	19.8 watts

Table 6-62: Pentium III Coppermine 600E Overclocking

Pentium III Coppermine	Model Rating	600 MHz
Overclocking Potential	Multiplier Lock Support	Locked Multiplier
	Typical Multiplier O/C	N/A
	Typical Front-side Bus O/C	124 – 133 MHz
	Typical O/C Potential	744 – 798 MHz
	Maximum O/C Potential	800+ MHz
Overclocking Tolerances	Recommended Cooling Type	Forced-Air Heatsink
	Recommended Heatsink Coolers	Swiftech MCX370
		Alpha PAL8045
		Globalwin VOS32
	Recommended Peltier Active Cooler	MCX370 Peltier
		MC1000 Peltier
	Maximum Core Voltage	1.85 volts with Heatsink Cooler
	Maximum I/O Voltage	3.5 volts with Chipset Cooler
	Maximum Core Temperature	80° Celsius

While not as popular as its 550 MHz counterpart, the Pentium III Coppermine 600E does offer a respectable overclocking return. Most 600E chips can effectively scale to frequencies above 750 MHz with nothing more than a modest increase in the motherboard front-side bus speed. A slight increase in core voltage will often net a positive overclocking return beyond 800 MHz, using only the retail Intel heatsink.

Pentium III Coppermine 650E

Table 6-63: Pentium III Coppermine 650E Specifications

Processor Family	Model Name	Intel Pentium III Coppermine
	Performance Rating	650 MHz
	Front-side Bus Speed	100 MHz
	Multiplier Ratio	6.5x
Physical Design	Interface Packing	370-Pin FCPGA Socket
		242-Pin Slot 1 Cartridge
	Core Voltage	1.65 volts
	Power Consumption	14 watts
	Maximum Power	21.5 watts

Table 6-64: Pentium III Coppermine 650E Overclocking

Pentium III Coppermine	Model Rating	650 MHz
Overclocking Potential	Multiplier Lock Support	Locked Multiplier
	Typical Multiplier O/C	N/A
	Typical Front-side Bus O/C	112 – 124 MHz
	Typical O/C Potential	728 – 806 MHz
	Maximum O/C Potential	850+ MHz
Overclocking Tolerances	Recommended Cooling Type	Forced-Air Heatsink
	Recommended Heatsink Coolers	Swiftech MCX370
		Alpha PAL8045
		Globalwin VOS32
	Recommended Peltier Active Cooler	MCX370 Peltier
		MC1000 Peltier
	Maximum Core Voltage	1.85 volts with Heatsink Cooler
	Maximum I/O Voltage	3.5 volts with Chipset Cooler
	Maximum Core Temperature	80° Celsius

Strategy

The Pentium III 650E represents a good option for systems with motherboards lacking official 133-MHz front-side bus support. Even when operating with the limited Intel BX chipset, the 650E can offer easy scalability to 800 MHz with only a moderate increase in core voltage rates. The comparatively high 6.5x internal multiplier of this processor presents real potential for scaling up to 865 MHz with boards supporting the 133-MHz front-side bus rate. Considering the increased electrical demand of the 650E, additional cooling will usually be required when increasing core voltage values beyond a marginal 5% threshold.

Pentium III Coppermine 700E

Table 6-65: Pentium III Coppermine 700E Specifications

Processor Family	Model Name	Intel Pentium III Coppermine
	Performance Rating	700 MHz
	Front-side Bus Speed	100 MHz
	Multiplier Ratio	7.0x
Physical Design	Interface Packing	370-Pin FCPGA Socket
		242-Pin Slot 1 Cartridge
	Core Voltage	1.65 volts
	Power Consumption	15 watts
	Maximum Power	23.1 watts

Table 6-66: Pentium III Coppermine 700E Overclocking

Pentium III Coppermine	Model Rating	700 MHz
Overclocking Potential	Multiplier Lock Support	Locked Multiplier
	Typical Multiplier O/C	N/A
	Typical Front-side Bus O/C	112 – 120 MHz
	Typical O/C Potential	784 – 840 MHz
	Maximum O/C Potential	850 – 900+ MHz
Overclocking Tolerances	Recommended Cooling Type	Forced-Air Heatsink
	Recommended Heatsink Coolers	Swiftech MCX370
		Alpha PAL8045
		Globalwin VOS32
	Recommended Peltier Active Cooler	MCX370 Peltier
		MC1000 Peltier
	Maximum Core Voltage	1.85 volts with Heatsink Cooler
	Maximum I/O Voltage	3.5 volts with Chipset Cooler
	Maximum Core Temperature	80° Celsius

Strategy

Given increasing multiplier values in the E series of Coppermine processors, the P3 700E represents the point at which 133-MHz front-side bus overclocking will prove limited for most system configurations. A 931-MHz core frequency can be attained from such an overclock, but be prepared to upgrade to a quality aftermarket forced-air heatsink cooler in order to maintain stability. The cooler bundled with most 700E models is insufficient for overclocking at 900+ MHz. It cannot cope with increased temperatures at the 1.85 core voltage level.

Pentium III Coppermine 750E

Table 6-67: Pentium III Coppermine 750E Specifications

Processor Family	Model Name	Intel Pentium III Coppermine
	Performance Rating	750 MHz
	Front-side Bus Speed	100 MHz
	Multiplier Ratio	7.5x
Physical Design	Interface Packing	370-Pin FCPGA Socket
		242-Pin Slot 1 Cartridge
	Core Voltage	1.65 volts
	Power Consumption	16 watts
	Maximum Power	24.7 watts

Table 6-68: Pentium III Coppermine 750E Overclocking

Pentium III Coppermine	Model Rating	750 MHz
Overclocking Potential	Multiplier Lock Support	Locked Multiplier
	Typical Multiplier O/C	N/A
	Typical Front-side Bus O/C	112 – 115 MHz
	Typical O/C Potential	840 – 863 MHz
	Maximum O/C Potential	900+ MHz
Overclocking Tolerances	Recommended Cooling Type	Forced-Air Heatsink
	Recommended Heatsink Coolers	Swiftech MCX370
		Alpha PAL8045
		Globalwin VOS32
	Recommended Peltier Active Cooler	MCX370 Peltier
		MC1000 Peltier
	Maximum Core Voltage	1.85 volts with Heatsink Cooler
	Maximum I/O Voltage	3.5 volts with Chipset Cooler
	Maximum Core Temperature	80° Celsius

Strategy

The Pentium III Coppermine 750E MHz processor offers marginal scalability, due to its relatively high 7.0x internal multiplier. Overclocking via the 133-MHz front-side bus rate will prove limited in most tweaking scenarios. The resulting 1000 MHz clock rate will often fail, assuming that the processor does boot at all, due to the massive increase in core voltage required to sustain such an overclock. A quality Peltier cooler, or something equally powerful, is definitely required if you hope to push the performance envelope.

Pentium III Coppermine 800E

Table 6-69: Pentium III Coppermine 800E Specifications

Processor Family	Model Name	Intel Pentium III Coppermine
	Performance Rating	800 MHz
	Front-side Bus Speed	100 MHz
	Multiplier Ratio	8.0x
Physical Design	Interface Packing	370-Pin FCPGA Socket
		242-Pin Slot 1 Cartridge
	Core Voltage	1.65 volts
	Power Consumption	18 watts
	Maximum Power	26.4 watts

Table 6-70: Pentium III Coppermine 800E Overclocking

Pentium III Coppermine	Model Rating	800 MHz
Overclocking Potential	Multiplier Lock Support	Locked Multiplier
	Typical Multiplier O/C	N/A
	Typical Front-side Bus O/C	112 – 115 MHz
	Typical O/C Potential	896 – 920 MHz
	Maximum O/C Potential	950+ MHz
Overclocking Tolerances	Recommended Cooling Type	Forced-Air Heatsink
	Recommended Heatsink Coolers	Swiftech MCX370
		Alpha PAL8045
		Globalwin VOS32
	Recommended Peltier Active Cooler	MCX370 Peltier
		MC1000 Peltier
	Maximum Core Voltage	1.85 volts with Heatsink Cooler
	Maximum I/O Voltage	3.5 volts with Chipset Cooler
	Maximum Core Temperature	80° Celsius

Strategy

The 800E MHz model of the Pentium III Coppermine series lacks the overclocking potential of its siblings. Attempts to reach the 133-MHz front-side bus rate will generally fail. Only the rare processor will offer scalability to the 1064-MHz range. Even then, expect to use the largest heatsink or Peltier cooler to properly dissipate the excessive thermal loads produced with core voltages approaching 1.85 volts.

Pentium III Coppermine 850E

Table 6-71: Pentium III Coppermine 850E Specifications

Processor Family	Model Name	Intel Pentium III Coppermine
	Performance Rating	850 MHz
	Front-side Bus Speed	100 MHz
	Multiplier Ratio	8.5x
Physical Design	Interface Packing	370-Pin FCPGA Socket
		242-Pin Slot 1 Cartridge
	Core Voltage	1.65 volts
	Power Consumption	18 watts
	Maximum Power	26.7 watts

Table 6-72: Pentium III Coppermine 850E Overclocking

Pentium III Coppermine	Model Rating	850 MHz
Overclocking Potential	Multiplier Lock Support	Locked Multiplier
	Typical Multiplier O/C	N/A
	Typical Front-side Bus O/C	105 – 112 MHz
	Typical O/C Potential	893 – 952 MHz
	Maximum O/C Potential	975 – 1000+ MHz
Overclocking Tolerances	Recommended Cooling Type	Forced-Air Heatsink
	Recommended Heatsink Coolers	Swiftech MCX370
		Alpha PAL8045
		Globalwin VOS32
	Recommended Peltier Active Cooler	MCX370 Peltier
		MC1000 Peltier
	Maximum Core Voltage	1.85 volts with Heatsink Cooler
	Maximum I/O Voltage	3.5 volts with Chipset Cooler
	Maximum Core Temperature	80° Celsius

Strategy

The Pentium III 850E MHz is best suited for moderate overclocking via the 112 MHz front-side bus rate. The resulting 952 MHz core operating speed is generally in the range of the 850E's overclocking capabilities. Attempts at higher frequency ranges approaching 1000 MHz will be difficult, even for the best system configurations. The increased efficiency offered by a Peltier or liquid cooling solution will be important if you hope to push your 850E system into the 1 GHz arena.

Pentium III Coppermine 533EB

Table 6-73: Pentium III Coppermine 533EB Specifications

Processor Family	Model Name	Intel Pentium III Coppermine
	Performance Rating	533 MHz
	Front-side Bus Speed	133 MHz
	Multiplier Ratio	4.0x
Physical Design	Interface Packing	370-Pin FCPGA Socket
		242-Pin Slot 1 Cartridge
	Core Voltage	1.65 volts
	Power Consumption	9 watts
	Maximum Power	17.5 watts

Table 6-74: Pentium III Coppermine 533EB Overclocking

Pentium III Coppermine	Model Rating	533 MHz
Overclocking Potential	Multiplier Lock Support	Locked Multiplier
	Typical Multiplier O/C	N/A
	Typical Front-side Bus O/C	140 MHz
	Typical O/C Potential	560 MHz
	Maximum O/C Potential	~ 600 MHz
Overclocking Tolerances	Recommended Cooling Type	Forced-Air Heatsink
	Recommended Heatsink Coolers	Swiftech MCX370
		Alpha PAL8045
		Globalwin VOS32
	Recommended Peltier Active Cooler	MCX370 Peltier
		MC1000 Peltier
	Maximum Core Voltage	1.85 volts with Heatsink Cooler
	Maximum I/O Voltage	3.5 volts with Chipset Cooler
	Maximum Core Temperature	80° Celsius

Strategy

In stark contrast to the E series of Coppermine processors, the 133-MHz front-side bus Pentium III EB offers poor overclocking potential. The internal multiplier value of the processor decreases in the series. Even the best Pentium III motherboards commonly lack the ability for stable operation beyond the 150-MHz front-side bus speed. Some boards claim support exceeding 166 MHz, though this is more a selling feature than a practical solution for Pentium III overclocking.

Even at the 140-MHz front-side bus speed, the 533EB allows processor overclocking to only 560 MHz. Even under the best conditions, the 533EB will prove troublesome at core operating speeds exceeding 600 MHz. Cooling and voltage will be minimal concerns. The motherboard will present a greater challenge than will the processor.

Pentium III Coppermine 600EB

Table 6-75: Pentium III Coppermine 600EB Specifications

Processor Family	Model Name	Intel Pentium III Coppermine
	Performance Rating	600 MHz
	Front-side Bus Speed	133 MHz
	Multiplier Ratio	4.5x
Physical Design	Interface Packing	370-Pin FCPGA Socket
		242-Pin Slot 1 Cartridge
	Core Voltage	1.65 volts
	Power Consumption	11 watts
	Maximum Power	19.8 watts

Table 6-76: Pentium III Coppermine 600EB Overclocking

Pentium III Coppermine	Model Rating	600 MHz
Overclocking Potential	Multiplier Lock Support	Locked Multiplier
	Typical Multiplier O/C	N/A
	Typical Front-side Bus O/C	140 MHz
	Typical O/C Potential	630 MHz
	Maximum O/C Potential	~ 675 MHz
Overclocking Tolerances	Recommended Cooling Type	Forced-Air Heatsink
	Recommended Heatsink Coolers	Swiftech MCX370
		Alpha PAL8045
		Globalwin VOS32
	Recommended Peltier Active Cooler	MCX370 Peltier
		MC1000 Peltier
	Maximum Core Voltage	1.85 volts with Heatsink Cooler
	Maximum I/O Voltage	3.5 volts with Chipset Cooler
	Maximum Core Temperature	80° Celsius

Strategy

Overclocking potential of the Pentium III EB series improves as core multiplier values increase, though most 600EB systems will never realize returns beyond 675 MHz. The lower-spectrum EB models bar successful overclocking, even at modest frequency ranges. Both the 533EB and the 600EB are poor choices for overclocking enthusiasts.

Pentium III Coppermine 667EB

Table 6-77: Pentium III Coppermine 667EB Specifications

Processor Family	Model Name	Intel Pentium III Coppermine
	Performance Rating	667 MHz
	Front-side Bus Speed	133 MHz
	Multiplier Ratio	5.0x
Physical Design	Interface Packing	370-Pin FCPGA Socket
		242-Pin Slot 1 Cartridge
	Core Voltage	1.65 volts
	Power Consumption	15 watts
	Maximum Power	22 watts

Table 6-78: Pentium III Coppermine 667EB Overclocking

Pentium III Coppermine	Model Rating	667 MHz
Overclocking Potential	Multiplier Lock Support	Locked Multiplier
	Typical Multiplier O/C	N/A
	Typical Front-side Bus O/C	140 MHz
	Typical O/C Potential	700 MHz
	Maximum O/C Potential	~ 750 MHz
Overclocking Tolerances	Recommended Cooling Type	Forced-Air Heatsink
	Recommended Heatsink Coolers	Swiftech MCX370
		Alpha PAL8045
		Globalwin VOS32
	Recommended Peltier Active Cooler	MCX370 Peltier
		MC1000 Peltier
	Maximum Core Voltage	1.85 volts with Heatsink Cooler
	Maximum I/O Voltage	3.5 volts with Chipset Cooler
	Maximum Core Temperature	80° Celsius

Strategy

Assuming overclocking via a 150-MHz front-side bus rate, a significant portion of Pentium III 667EB chips can effectively scale to 750 MHz. Otherwise, expect overclocking returns under 700 MHz, as this chip still suffers from a low multiplier. One note of interest is the change in Intel's model designation scheme to avoid any public relations fallout from marketing a 666 processor (the biblical "number of the beast").

Pentium III Coppermine 733EB

Table 6-79: Pentium III Coppermine 733EB Specifications

Processor Family	Model Name	Intel Pentium III Coppermine
	Performance Rating	733 MHz
	Front-side Bus Speed	133 MHz
	Multiplier Ratio	5.5x
Physical Design	Interface Packing	370-Pin FCPGA Socket
		242-Pin Slot 1 Cartridge
	Core Voltage	1.65 volts
	Power Consumption	16 watts
	Maximum Power	24.1 watts

Table 6-80: Pentium III Coppermine 733EB Overclocking

Pentium III Coppermine	Model Rating	733 MHz
Overclocking Potential	Multiplier Lock Support	Locked Multiplier
	Typical Multiplier O/C	N/A
	Typical Front-side Bus O/C	140 MHz
	Typical O/C Potential	770 MHz
	Maximum O/C Potential	~ 825 MHz
Overclocking Tolerances	Recommended Cooling Type	Forced-Air Heatsink
	Recommended Heatsink Coolers	Swiftech MCX370
		Alpha PAL8045
		Globalwin VOS32
	Recommended Peltier Active Cooler	MCX370 Peltier
		MC1000 Peltier
	Maximum Core Voltage	1.85 volts with Heatsink Cooler
	Maximum I/O Voltage	3.5 volts with Chipset Cooler
	Maximum Core Temperature	80° Celsius

Strategy

The Pentium III 733EB MHz is the first EB series processor to feature an internal multiplier value capable of sustaining overclocked operation beyond the 800-MHz range. As with previous EB processors, cooling and voltage levels will require little user intervention for most configurations. The Pentium III core is well suited to maximize overclocking potential for this model. Even so, a 5.5x multiplier limits its appeal in the overclocking community.

Pentium III Coppermine 800EB

Table 6-81: Pentium III Coppermine 800EB Specifications

Processor Family	Model Name	Intel Pentium III Coppermine
	Performance Rating	800 MHz
	Front-side Bus Speed	133 MHz
	Multiplier Ratio	6.0x
Physical Design	Interface Packing	370-Pin FCPGA Socket
		242-Pin Slot 1 Cartridge
	Core Voltage	1.65 volts
	Power Consumption	18 watts
	Maximum Power	24.5 watts

Table 6-82: Pentium III Coppermine 800EB Overclocking

Pentium III Coppermine	Model Rating	800 MHz
Overclocking Potential	Multiplier Lock Support	Locked Multiplier
	Typical Multiplier O/C	N/A
	Typical Front-side Bus O/C	140 MHz
	Typical O/C Potential	850 MHz
	Maximum O/C Potential	900+ MHz
Overclocking Tolerances	Recommended Cooling Type	Forced-Air Heatsink
	Recommended Heatsink Coolers	Swiftech MCX370
		Alpha PAL8045
		Globalwin VOS32
	Recommended Peltier Active Cooler	MCX370 Peltier
		MC1000 Peltier
	Maximum Core Voltage	1.85 volts with Heatsink Cooler
	Maximum I/O Voltage	3.5 volts with Chipset Cooler
	Maximum Core Temperature	80° Celsius

Strategy

The Pentium III 800EB MHz processor marks a shift in the EB series toward overclocking potential. Designed atop a 6.0x core multiplier, the 800EB is a good candidate for overclocking at 900 MHz and beyond. Unlike its earlier siblings, it requires a moderate increase in core voltage for successful operation beyond 900 MHz. Install an aftermarket cooling system to maintain stability.

Pentium III Coppermine 866EB

Table 6-83: Pentium III Coppermine 866EB Specifications

Processor Family	Model Name	Intel Pentium III Coppermine
	Performance Rating	866 MHz
	Front-side Bus Speed	133 MHz
	Multiplier Ratio	6.5x
Physical Design	Interface Packing	370-Pin FCPGA Socket
		242-Pin Slot 1 Cartridge
	Core Voltage	1.65 volts
	Power Consumption	18 watts
	Maximum Power	26.9 watts

Table 6-84: Pentium III Coppermine 866EB Overclocking

Pentium III Coppermine	Model Rating	866 MHz
Overclocking Potential	Multiplier Lock Support	Locked Multiplier
	Typical Multiplier O/C	N/A
	Typical Front-side Bus O/C	140 – 150 MHz
	Typical O/C Potential	910 – 975 MHz
	Maximum O/C Potential	1000+ MHz
Overclocking Tolerances	Recommended Cooling Type	Forced-Air Heatsink
	Recommended Heatsink Coolers	Swiftech MCX370
		Alpha PAL8045
		Globalwin VOS32
	Recommended Peltier Active Cooler	MCX370 Peltier
		MC1000 Peltier
	Maximum Core Voltage	1.85 volts with Heatsink Cooler
	Maximum I/O Voltage	3.5 volts with Chipset Cooler
	Maximum Core Temperature	80° Celsius

Strategy

Equipped with its 6.5x multiplier, the Pentium III Coppermine 866EB MHz is a contender for successful 1000+-MHz overclocking when paired with a quality motherboard. The 866EB demands a serious supply of wattage, so overclocking will require a massive forced-air heatsink cooler. The retail Intel heatsink will offer a minimal return at best; most configurations will reach 910 MHz before the system fails to boot.

Pentium III Coppermine 933EB

Table 6-85: Pentium III Coppermine 933EB Specifications

Processor Family	Model Name	Intel Pentium III Coppermine
	Performance Rating	933 MHz
	Front-side Bus Speed	133 MHz
	Multiplier Ratio	7.0x
Physical Design	Interface Packing	370-Pin FCPGA Socket
		242-Pin Slot 1 Cartridge
	Core Voltage	1.65 volts
	Power Consumption	19 watts
	Maximum Power	27.5 watts

Table 6-86: Pentium III Coppermine 933EB Overclocking

Pentium III Coppermine	Model Rating	933 MHz
Overclocking Potential	Multiplier Lock Support	Locked Multiplier
	Typical Multiplier O/C	N/A
	Typical Front-side Bus O/C	140 MHz
	Typical O/C Potential	980 MHz
	Maximum O/C Potential	1000+ MHz
Overclocking Tolerances	Recommended Cooling Type	Forced-Air Heatsink
	Recommended Heatsink Coolers	Swiftech MCX370
		Alpha PAL8045
		Globalwin VOS32
	Recommended Peltier Active Cooler	MCX370 Peltier
		MC1000 Peltier
	Maximum Core Voltage	1.75 volts with Heatsink Cooler
	Maximum I/O Voltage	3.5 volts with Chipset Cooler
	Maximum Core Temperature	60 – 70° Celsius

Strategy

The Pentium III 933EB MHz processor is available in two different models, each featuring a slightly different core design. The earliest 933EB chips reach a maximum thermal load of 60° Celsius before core failure, while some later models can scale upwards to the 70 to 75° range due to improved core stepping. Older models will be of the 0686h family, while the latest chips show a 068Ah designator. All the models produce serious thermal loads that require massive cooling for any overclocking potential beyond 1000 MHz.

Pentium III Coppermine 1000EB

Table 6-87: Pentium III Coppermine 1000EB Specifications

Processor Family	Model Name	Intel Pentium III Coppermine
	Performance Rating	1000 MHz
	Front-side Bus Speed	133 MHz
	Multiplier Ratio	7.5x
Physical Design	Interface Packing	370-Pin FCPGA Socket
		242-Pin Slot 1 Cartridge
	Core Voltage	1.65 – 1.75 volts
	Power Consumption	20 watts
	Maximum Power	29.8 watts

Table 6-88: Pentium III Coppermine 1000EB Overclocking

Pentium III Coppermine	Model Rating	1000 MHz
Overclocking Potential	Multiplier Lock Support	Locked Multiplier
	Typical Multiplier O/C	N/A
	Typical Front-side Bus O/C	140 MHz
	Typical O/C Potential	1050 MHz
	Maximum O/C Potential	1100+ MHz
Overclocking Tolerances	Recommended Cooling Type	Forced-Air Heatsink
	Recommended Heatsink Coolers	Swiftech MCX370
		Alpha PAL8045
		Globalwin VOS32
	Recommended Peltier Active Cooler	MCX370 Peltier
		MC1000 Peltier
	Maximum Core Voltage	1.85 volts with Heatsink Cooler
	Maximum I/O Voltage	3.5 volts with Chipset Cooler
	Maximum Core Temperature	60 – 70° Celsius

Strategy

As with the 933EB, the Pentium III 1000EB MHz processor shipped in several architectural configurations during its lifespan. The earliest chips featured a maximum thermal load of 60° Celsius, while later processors were rated at 70°. Voltage ratings also varied across different revisions of the processor; units shipped at the 1.65, 1.7, and 1.75 volt levels. The .18-micron Pentium III design was nearing the end of its viability with the 1000EB. As a result, overclocking the 1000EB beyond 1100 MHz will prove difficult.

Pentium III Coppermine 1130EB

Table 6-89: Pentium III Coppermine 1130EB Specifications

Processor Family	Model Name	Intel Pentium III Coppermine
	Performance Rating	1130 MHz
	Front-side Bus Speed	133 MHz
	Multiplier Ratio	8.5x
Physical Design	Interface Packing	370-Pin FCPGA Socket
		242-Pin Slot 1 Cartridge
	Core Voltage	1.65 volts
	Power Consumption	25 watts
	Maximum Power	37.5 watts

Table 6-90: Pentium III Coppermine 1130EB Overclocking

Pentium III Coppermine	Model Rating	1130 MHz
Overclocking Potential	Multiplier Lock Support	Locked Multiplier
	Typical Multiplier O/C	N/A
	Typical Front-side Bus O/C	Minimal
	Typical O/C Potential	Minimal
	Maximum O/C Potential	~ 1200 MHz
Overclocking Tolerances	Recommended Cooling Type	Forced-Air Heatsink
	Recommended Heatsink Coolers	Swiftech MCX370
		Alpha PAL8045
		Globalwin VOS32
	Recommended Peltier Active Cooler	MCX370 Peltier
		MC1000 Peltier
	Maximum Core Voltage	1.85 volts with Heatsink Cooler
	Maximum I/O Voltage	3.5 volts with Chipset Cooler
	Maximum Core Temperature	70° Celsius

Strategy

The Pentium III Coppermine 1130EB actually appeared, disappeared, and then reappeared in limited qualities during its ill-fated lifespan. Some of the earliest versions suffered stability and compatibility problems, resulting in suspended production. After a long delay, the 1130EB experienced a short renaissance before Intel released its next flagship production, the Pentium 4.

Issues surrounding the P3 1130EB likely resulted from its enormous peak power demand—37.5 watts at full load (almost 8 watts more than its 1000EB sibling). The 1130EB requires serious cooling to dissipate such a thermal load; overclocking is limited to a few MHz for most configurations. Increasing the core voltage to 1.85 volts should only be attempted with an active cooling solution, such as a Peltier-based heatsink or radical vapor-phase technology.

Celeron II Background

The .18-micron Celeron II is basically the Pentium III Coppermine upgrade to the Celeron marketing strategy. Most users simply discard the II designation; even Intel marketing refers to this processor simply as Celeron. The Level 2 cache is scaled back to 128 KB, though all other Pentium III features are supported. The newer FCPGA socket format is also carried over, as is the 100-MHz bus speed for upper frequency ranges of the product line. Overclocking returns parallel those of the Coppermine family, with higher-end chips approaching their limits at 800 to 1100 MHz.

Celeron II Overclocking

Table 6-91: Celeron II Specifications

Processor Family	Model Name	Intel Celeron II
	Performance Rating	533 – 1300+ MHz
	Generation	Sixth: 80686 IA-32
Operational Rates	Level 1 Cache Speed	1.0x Core Rate
	Level 2 Cache Speed	1.0x Core Rate
	Front-side Bus Speed	66 – 100 MHz
	Multiplier Ratio	5.0x – 13.0+x
Physical Design	Interface Packing	370-Pin FCPGA Socket
	Core Die Size	.18 micron
	Core Size by Stepping	A2 = 106 mm^2
		B0 = 104 mm^2
		C0 = 90 mm^2
		D0 = 95 mm^2
	Transistor Count	28.1 Million Total
		1/2 Cache Disabled
	Voltage Interface	Split Core and I/O
	Core Voltage	1.5 volts
	I/O Voltage	3.3 volts
	Level 2 Cache Voltage	3.3 volts
	Power Consumption	9 – 22 watts
	Maximum Power	14 – 33 watts
Architectural Design	Core Technology	OOO and Speculative Execution RISC
	Register Support	Integer = 32 bit
		FPU = 80 bit
		MMX = 64 bit
		SSE = 128 bit
	Execution Units	2 x ALU/MMX/SSE
		1 x Pipelined FPU
	Maximum Execution Rate	5 Micro-Ops per Cycle

(continued on next page)

Table 6-91: Celeron II Specifications (continued)

Processor Family	Model Name	Intel Celeron II
	Data Bus Width	64 bit
	Maximum Memory Support	Physical = 64 Gigabyte
		Virtual = 64 Terabyte
	Multi-Processor Support	2-way SMP via APIC
	Level 1 Code Cache	16 KB 4-way
	Level 1 Data Cache	16 KB 4-way
	Level 2 Cache	128 KB Unified
	Read Buffer	4 x 32 Byte
	Write Buffer	32 Byte
	Pre-fetch Queue	32 Byte
	Static Branch Prediction	Supported
	Dynamic Branch Prediction	512 Entry 4-way
	RSB Branch Prediction	4 Entry
	Floating-Point Processor	Integrated
	Multimedia Extensions	MMX, SSE

Celeron II 533

Table 6-92: Celeron II 533 Specifications

Processor Family	Model Name	Intel Celeron II
	Performance Rating	533 MHz
	Front-side Bus Speed	66 MHz
	Multiplier Ratio	8.0x
Physical Design	Interface Packing	370-Pin FCPGA Socket
	Core Voltage	1.5 volts
	Power Consumption	9 watts
	Maximum Power	14 watts

Table 6-93: Celeron II 533 Overclocking

Celeron II	Model Rating	533 MHz
Overclocking Potential	Multiplier Lock Support	Locked Multiplier
	Typical Multiplier O/C	N/A
	Typical Front-side Bus O/C	83 – 100 MHz
	Typical O/C Potential	664 – 800 MHz
	Maximum O/C Potential	800+ MHz
Overclocking Tolerances	Recommended Cooling Type	Forced-Air Heatsink
	Recommended Heatsink Coolers	Swiftech MCX370
		Alpha PAL8045
	Recommended Peltier Active Cooler	MCX370 Peltier
	Maximum Core Voltage	1.85 volts with Heatsink Cooler
	Maximum I/O Voltage	3.5 volts with Chipset Cooler
	Maximum Core Temperature	90° Celsius

Strategy

The Celeron II 533-MHz processor can be confused with its older Celeron 533 counterpart due to the similarity in model name. However, the newer .18-micron Celeron II 533-MHz processor offers overclocking potential unparalleled by any model in the original Celeron family. Most chips from this particular speed grade will overclock easily upwards of 700 MHz, with no changes in voltage or cooling requirements. The best chips can scale beyond 800 MHz.

Celeron II 566

Table 6-94: Celeron II 566 Specifications

Processor Family	Model Name	Intel Celeron II
	Performance Rating	566 MHz
	Front-side Bus Speed	66 MHz
	Multiplier Ratio	8.5x
Physical Design	Interface Packing	370-Pin FCPGA Socket
	Core Voltage	1.5 volts
	Power Consumption	10 watts
	Maximum Power	14.9 watts

Table 6-95: Celeron II 566 Overclocking

Celeron II	Model Rating	566 MHz
Overclocking Potential	Multiplier Lock Support	Locked Multiplier
	Typical Multiplier O/C	N/A
	Typical Front-side Bus O/C	83 – 100 MHz
	Typical O/C Potential	706 – 850 MHz
	Maximum O/C Potential	900+ MHz
Overclocking Tolerances	Recommended Cooling Type	Forced-Air Heatsink
	Recommended Heatsink Coolers	Swiftech MCX370
		Alpha PAL8045
	Recommended Peltier Active Cooler	MCX370 Peltier
	Maximum Core Voltage	1.85 volts with Heatsink Cooler
	Maximum I/O Voltage	3.5 volts with Chipset Cooler
	Maximum Core Temperature	90° Celsius

Strategy

The Celeron II 566 is a popular choice among overclockers due to its 8.5x internal multiplier. With a 100-MHz front-side bus rate, this chip offers an appealing overclock to 850 MHz with little effort outside the addition of a good-quality heatsink cooler. Some users have reported overclocking returns beyond 900 MHz with active Peltier or liquid cooling, thus rivaling the performance of the best Pentium III Coppermine models.

Celeron II 600

Table 6-96: Celeron II 600 Specifications

Processor Family	Model Name	Intel Celeron II
	Performance Rating	600 MHz
	Front-side Bus Speed	66 MHz
	Multiplier Ratio	9.0x
Physical Design	Interface Packing	370-Pin FCPGA Socket
	Core Voltage	1.5 volts
	Power Consumption	12 watts
	Maximum Power	19.6 watts

Table 6-97: Celeron II 600 Overclocking

Celeron II	Model Rating	600 MHz
Overclocking Potential	Multiplier Lock Support	Locked Multiplier
	Typical Multiplier O/C	N/A
	Typical Front-side Bus O/C	83 – 100 MHz
	Typical O/C Potential	747 – 900 MHz
	Maximum O/C Potential	900 – 950 MHz
Overclocking Tolerances	Recommended Cooling Type	Forced-Air Heatsink
	Recommended Heatsink Coolers	Swiftech MCX370
		Alpha PAL8045
	Recommended Peltier Active Cooler	MCX370 Peltier
	Maximum Core Voltage	1.85 volts with Heatsink Cooler
	Maximum I/O Voltage	3.5 volts with Chipset Cooler
	Maximum Core Temperature	90° Celsius

Strategy

A successful overclocker, the Celeron II 600-MHz processor never quite reached the acclaim awarded to its 566-MHz counterpart. The slightly higher 9.0x internal multiplier can prove limiting for chips not capable of sustaining 900-MHz. Many popular motherboards lack front-side bus speeds between 83 and 100 MHz; thus overclocking enthusiasts are shut down at 747 MHz.

Celeron II 633

Table 6-98: Celeron II 633 Specifications

Processor Family	Model Name	Intel Celeron II
	Performance Rating	633 MHz
	Front-side Bus Speed	66 MHz
	Multiplier Ratio	9.5x
Physical Design	Interface Packing	370-Pin FCPGA Socket
	Core Voltage	1.5 volts
	Power Consumption	13 watts
	Maximum Power	20.2 watts

Table 6-99: Celeron II 633 Overclocking

Celeron II	Model Rating	633 MHz
Overclocking Potential	Multiplier Lock Support	Locked Multiplier
	Typical Multiplier O/C	N/A
	Typical Front-side Bus O/C	83 – 100 MHz
	Typical O/C Potential	789 – 950 MHz
	Maximum O/C Potential	~ 950 MHz
Overclocking Tolerances	Recommended Cooling Type	Forced-Air Heatsink
	Recommended Heatsink Coolers	Swiftech MCX370
		Alpha PAL8045
	Recommended Peltier Active Cooler	MCX370 Peltier
	Maximum Core Voltage	1.85 volts with Heatsink Cooler
	Maximum I/O Voltage	3.5 volts with Chipset Cooler
	Maximum Core Temperature	82° Celsius

Strategy

The Celeron II 633-MHz processor carries the same faults as its 600-MHz sibling. While a small percentage of these units can successfully operate at 100 MHz, many users are forced into operating at 789 MHz due to the 83 MHz front-side bus limitation. Also note the lower thermal threshold for this chip: Intel decreased the maximum core temperature fail rate to 82° Celsius, compared to 90° Celsius for the earlier Celeron II models. Overclocking the 633 will require improved cooling to achieve significant returns.

Celeron II 667

Table 6-100: Celeron II 667 Specifications

Processor Family	Model Name	Intel Celeron II
	Performance Rating	667 MHz
	Front-side Bus Speed	66 MHz
	Multiplier Ratio	10.0x
Physical Design	Interface Packing	370-Pin FCPGA Socket
	Core Voltage	1.5 volts
	Power Consumption	14 watts
	Maximum Power	21.1 watts

Table 6-101: Celeron II 667 Overclocking

Celeron II	Model Rating	667 MHz
Overclocking Potential	Multiplier Lock Support	Locked Multiplier
	Typical Multiplier O/C	N/A
	Typical Front-side Bus O/C	75 – 83 MHz
	Typical O/C Potential	750 – 830 MHz
	Maximum O/C Potential	850 – 950 MHz
Overclocking Tolerances	Recommended Cooling Type	Forced-Air Heatsink
	Recommended Heatsink Coolers	Swiftech MCX370
		Alpha PAL8045
	Recommended Peltier Active Cooler	MCX370 Peltier
	Maximum Core Voltage	1.85 volts with Heatsink Cooler
	Maximum I/O Voltage	3.5 volts with Chipset Cooler
	Maximum Core Temperature	82° Celsius

Strategy

The Celeron II 667 shares the naming quirk of its Pentium III counterpart. Once again, Intel avoided marketing a processor numbered 666. Sadly, the C2 667 also brought an end to successful 100-MHz front-side motherboard overclocking, due to its high 10.0x multiplier. Average overclocking for this unit falls in the 750 to 850 MHz range.

Celeron II 700

Table 6-102: Celeron II 700 Specifications

Processor Family	Model Name	Intel Celeron II
	Performance Rating	700 MHz
	Front-side Bus Speed	66 MHz
	Multiplier Ratio	10.5x
Physical Design	Interface Packing	370-Pin FCPGA Socket
	Core Voltage	1.5 volts
	Power Consumption	12 watts
	Maximum Power	21.9 watts

Table 6-103: Celeron II 700 Overclocking

Celeron II	Model Rating	700 MHz
Overclocking Potential	Multiplier Lock Support	Locked Multiplier
	Typical Multiplier O/C	N/A
	Typical Front-side Bus O/C	75 – 83 MHz
	Typical O/C Potential	788 – 872 MHz
	Maximum O/C Potential	900+ MHz
Overclocking Tolerances	Recommended Cooling Type	Forced-Air Heatsink
	Recommended Heatsink Coolers	Swiftech MCX370
		Alpha PAL8045
	Recommended Peltier Active Cooler	MCX370 Peltier
	Maximum Core Voltage	1.5 volts with Heatsink Cooler
	Maximum I/O Voltage	3.5 volts with Chipset Cooler
	Maximum Core Temperature	80° Celsius

Strategy

The Celeron II 700-MHz processor brought a definitive end to 100-MHz front-side bus overclocking. Only a few rare units of this speed grade can successfully operate at 1050 MHz, due to the 10.5x multiplier. Also note the ever-decreasing maximum core temperature rating of this speed grade compared to earlier Celeron II models. Any overclocking of this processor will usually require the addition of an aftermarket cooling solution. At a minimum, real-time active thermal monitoring is recommended for overclocking attempts.

Celeron II 733

Table 6-104: Celeron II 733 Specifications

Processor Family	Model Name	Intel Celeron II
	Performance Rating	733 MHz
	Front-side Bus Speed	66 MHz
	Multiplier Ratio	11.0x
Physical Design	Interface Packing	370-Pin FCPGA Socket
	Core Voltage	1.5 volts
	Power Consumption	15 watts
	Maximum Power	22.8 watts

Table 6-105: Celeron II 733 Overclocking

Celeron II	Model Rating	733 MHz
Overclocking Potential	Multiplier Lock Support	Locked Multiplier
	Typical Multiplier O/C	N/A
	Typical Front-side Bus O/C	75 – 83 MHz
	Typical O/C Potential	825 – 913 MHz
	Maximum O/C Potential	~ 950 MHz
Overclocking Tolerances	Recommended Cooling Type	Forced-Air Heatsink
	Recommended Heatsink Coolers	Swiftech MCX370
		Alpha PAL8045
	Recommended Peltier Active Cooler	MCX370 Peltier
	Maximum Core Voltage	1.85 volts with Heatsink Cooler
	Maximum I/O Voltage	3.5 volts with Chipset Cooler
	Maximum Core Temperature	80° Celsius

Strategy

The Celeron II 733 is the last truly overclockable 66-MHz bus-based processor in the family. Even the best models in this speed grade will reach their maximum overclocking potential around 950 MHz without the addition of nontraditional cooling technologies. This model signaled the end of overclocking attempts beyond the 83-MHz front-side bus rate for this family.

Celeron II 766

Table 6-106: Celeron II 766 Specifications

Processor Family	Model Name	Intel Celeron II
	Performance Rating	766 MHz
	Front-side Bus Speed	66 MHz
	Multiplier Ratio	11.50x
Physical Design	Interface Packing	370-Pin FCPGA Socket
	Core Voltage	1.5 volts
	Power Consumption	16 watts
	Maximum Power	23.6 watts

Table 6-107: Celeron II 766 Overclocking

Celeron II	Model Rating	766 MHz
Overclocking Potential	Multiplier Lock Support	Locked Multiplier
	Typical Multiplier O/C	N/A
	Typical Front-side Bus O/C	70 – 75 MHz
	Typical O/C Potential	805 – 863 MHz
	Maximum O/C Potential	~ 950 MHz
Overclocking Tolerances	Recommended Cooling Type	Forced-Air Heatsink
	Recommended Heatsink Coolers	Swiftech MCX370
		Alpha PAL8045
	Recommended Peltier Active Cooler	MCX370 Peltier
	Maximum Core Voltage	1.85 volts with Heatsink Cooler
	Maximum I/O Voltage	3.5 volts with Chipset Cooler
	Maximum Core Temperature	80° Celsius

Strategy

Overclocking with the Celeron II 766 will be limited beyond the 75-MHz front-side bus rate. Some rare samples may reach 83 MHz, but the success rate for such overclocks is extremely low compared to those on lower-clocked Celeron II models. The C2 766 is not a good choice for overclocking enthusiasts, due to its debilitating 11.5x multiplier.

Celeron II 800E

Table 6-108: Celeron II 800E Specifications

Processor Family	Model Name	Intel Celeron II
	Performance Rating	800 MHz
	Front-side Bus Speed	100 MHz
	Multiplier Ratio	8.0x
Physical Design	Interface Packing	370-Pin FCPGA Socket
	Core Voltage	1.5 volts
	Power Consumption	16 watts
	Maximum Power	24.5 watts

Table 6-109: Celeron II 800E Overclocking

Celeron II	Model Rating	800 MHz
Overclocking Potential	Multiplier Lock Support	Locked Multiplier
	Typical Multiplier O/C	N/A
	Typical Front-side Bus O/C	105 – 112 MHz
	Typical O/C Potential	840 – 896 MHz
	Maximum O/C Potential	950+ MHz
Overclocking Tolerances	Recommended Cooling Type	Forced-Air Heatsink
	Recommended Heatsink Coolers	Swiftech MCX370
		Alpha PAL8045
	Recommended Peltier Active Cooler	MCX370 Peltier
	Maximum Core Voltage	1.85 volts with Heatsink Cooler
	Maximum I/O Voltage	3.5 volts with Chipset Cooler
	Maximum Core Temperature	85° Celsius

Strategy

The Celeron II 800 marked the debut of the E series designation in the C2 family. As with the Pentium III Coppermine, any unit bearing the E modifier is a 100-MHz front-side-bus-compatible processor. Overclocking these chips is moderately successful; most samples offer returns similar to their P3E counterparts. Note the increase in maximum core thermal ratings, a clear indication of Intel's introduction of new core stepping for the C2 architecture.

Celeron II 850E

Table 6-110: Celeron II 850E Specifications

Processor Family	Model Name	Intel Celeron II
	Performance Rating	850 MHz
	Front-side Bus Speed	100 MHz
	Multiplier Ratio	8.5x
Physical Design	Interface Packing	370-Pin FCPGA Socket
	Core Voltage	1.5 volts
	Power Consumption	17 watts
	Maximum Power	25.7 watts

Table 6-111: Celeron II 850E Overclocking

Celeron II	Model Rating	850 MHz
Overclocking Potential	Multiplier Lock Support	Locked Multiplier
	Typical Multiplier O/C	N/A
	Typical Front-side Bus O/C	105 – 112 MHz
	Typical O/C Potential	893 – 952 MHz
	Maximum O/C Potential	1000+ MHz
Overclocking Tolerances	Recommended Cooling Type	Forced-Air Heatsink
	Recommended Heatsink Coolers	Swiftech MCX370
		Alpha PAL8045
	Recommended Peltier Active Cooler	MCX370 Peltier
	Maximum Core Voltage	1.85 volts with Heatsink Cooler
	Maximum I/O Voltage	3.5 volts with Chipset Cooler
	Maximum Core Temperature	85° Celsius

Strategy

Due to its 8.5x internal multiplier, the Celeron II 850 MHz processor is a great candidate for overclocking via the 112-MHz front-side bus. Given the improved thermal efficiency of the C2E core, the 850E can offer scalability beyond 1000 MHz for many configurations.

Celeron II 900E

Table 6-112: Celeron II 900E Specifications

Processor Family	Model Name	Intel Celeron II
	Performance Rating	900 MHz
	Front-side Bus Speed	66 MHz
	Multiplier Ratio	9.5x
Physical Design	Interface Packing	370-Pin FCPGA Socket
	Core Voltage	1.5 volts
	Power Consumption	18 watts
	Maximum Power	26.7 watts

Table 6-113: Celeron II 900E Overclocking

Celeron II	Model Rating	900 MHz
Overclocking Potential	Multiplier Lock Support	Locked Multiplier
	Typical Multiplier O/C	N/A
	Typical Front-side Bus O/C	105 – 112 MHz
	Typical O/C Potential	945 – 1008 MHz
	Maximum O/C Potential	1025 – 1100 MHz
Overclocking Tolerances	Recommended Cooling Type	Forced-Air Heatsink
	Recommended Heatsink Coolers	Swiftech MCX370
		Alpha PAL8045
	Recommended Peltier Active Cooler	MCX370 Peltier
	Maximum Core Voltage	1.85 volts with Heatsink Cooler
	Maximum I/O Voltage	3.5 volts with Chipset Cooler
	Maximum Core Temperature	85° Celsius

Strategy

The Celeron II 900E offers modest overclocking potential in the 945 to 1008 MHz range. At this point in its evolution, this processor family was limited to its .18-micron core architecture. Most configurations featuring this processor will reach a maximum overclock of around 1050 MHz. Only two additional speed grades were released after the 900E, as Intel moved rapidly to new core architecture.

Celeron II 1000E

Table 6-114: Celeron II 1000E Specifications

Processor Family	Model Name	Intel Celeron II
	Performance Rating	1000 MHz
	Front-side Bus Speed	100 MHz
	Multiplier Ratio	10.0x
Physical Design	Interface Packing	370-Pin FCPGA Socket
	Core Voltage	1.5 volts
	Power Consumption	20 watts
	Maximum Power	29 watts

Table 6-115: Celeron II 1000E Overclocking

Celeron II	Model Rating	1000 MHz
Overclocking Potential	Multiplier Lock Support	Locked Multiplier
	Typical Multiplier O/C	N/A
	Typical Front-side Bus O/C	105 – 110 MHz
	Typical O/C Potential	1050 – 1100 MHz
	Maximum O/C Potential	1100+ MHz
Overclocking Tolerances	Recommended Cooling Type	Forced-Air Heatsink
	Recommended Heatsink Coolers	Swiftech MCX370
		Alpha PAL8045
	Recommended Peltier Active Cooler	MCX370 Peltier
	Maximum Core Voltage	1.85 volts with Heatsink Cooler
	Maximum I/O Voltage	3.5 volts with Chipset Cooler
	Maximum Core Temperature	80° Celsius

Strategy

The specifications of the Celeron II 1000E indicate a decrease in maximum core temperature ratings. Accordingly, overclocking this processor will prove limited beyond 1100 MHz. Worse yet, most chips from this speed grade will fail to operate successfully at speeds beyond 1050 MHz, only a 5% increase for the risk.

Celeron II 1100E

Table 6-116: Celeron II 1100E Specifications

Processor Family	Model Name	Intel Celeron II
	Performance Rating	1100 MHz
	Front-side Bus Speed	100 MHz
	Multiplier Ratio	11.0x
Physical Design	Interface Packing	370-Pin FCPGA Socket
	Core Voltage	1.5 volts
	Power Consumption	22 watts
	Maximum Power	33 watts

Table 6-117: Celeron II 1100E Overclocking

Celeron II	Model Rating	1100 MHz
Overclocking Potential	Multiplier Lock Support	Locked Multiplier
	Typical Multiplier O/C	N/A
	Typical Front-side Bus O/C	103 – 105 MHz
	Typical O/C Potential	1133 – 1155 MHz
	Maximum O/C Potential	1175 – 1200 MHz
Overclocking Tolerances	Recommended Cooling Type	Forced-Air Heatsink
	Recommended Heatsink Coolers	Swiftech MCX370
		Alpha PAL8045
	Recommended Peltier Active Cooler	MCX370 Peltier
	Maximum Core Voltage	1.85 volts with Heatsink Cooler
	Maximum I/O Voltage	3.5 volts with Chipset Cooler
	Maximum Core Temperature	80° Celsius

Strategy

At 1100 MHz the Celeron II family came to an end. The 1100E model offers minimal overclocking return for most configurations, though a few underground reports have indicated marginal scalability beyond 1200 MHz with high core voltages and the application of quality cooling. However, most Celeron II 1100E systems will fail to boot around 1150 MHz, due to limitations built in by the .18-micron fabrication.

Pentium III/Celeron Tualatin Background

The Tualatin was a stopgap in Intel's midrange product line. This rather unusual processor appeared after the release of the Pentium 4 flagship product series. The Tualatin built on the Coppermine design by introducing a streamlined .13-micron core architecture and adding a hardware data prefetch mechanism to maximize efficient instructions per clock. Intel also chose to adapt its socket interface with the Tualatin by introducing a new socket standard called

FCPGA2, which is incompatible with the huge number of traditional Socket 370 FCPGA motherboards still in use around the world. While the different socket standards may start to get a bit confusing, you should simply keep in mind which socket type you have on your motherboard and which processors work with that particular socket type, rather than trying to understand why Intel chose to complicate our lives with so many socket standards.

The latest 1.2+-GHz Celeron features a core-die reduction to .13 micron, plus a migration to Intel's new FCPGA2 socket format. Its base design closely resembles the Tualatin, though the feature set has been scaled back to a 128-KB Level 2 cache, 100-MHz front-side bus support, and no advanced hardware data prefetch mechanism. This new breed of Celeron T series chips offers overclocking results similar to the Tualatin chips. Most will reach 1400+ MHz with good cooling and a minor bump in core voltage.

Pentium III Tualatin Overclocking

While the Tualatin requires a new socket format, it represents the most overclockable Pentium III design to date. Many users report overclocks upwards of 2 GHz with radical cooling. Traditional forced-air heatsink cooling techniques usually peak between 1400 and 1600 MHz. Unlike previous designs, the new .13-micron architecture is not tolerant of changes in core voltages. Take great care when pushing the safety limit of 10% beyond default specifications.

Table 6-118: Pentium III Tualatin Specifications

Processor Family	Model Name	Intel Tualatin
	Performance Rating	1130 – 1260+ MHz
	Generation	Sixth: 80686 IA-32
Operational Rates	Level 1 Cache Speed	1.0x Core Rate
	Level 2 Cache Speed	1.0x Core Rate
	Front-side Bus Speed	100 – 133 MHz
	Multiplier Ratio	8.5x – 13+x
Physical Design	Interface Packing	370-Pin FCPGA2 Socket
	Core Die Size	.13 micron
	Core Size by Stepping	80 mm^2
	Transistor Count	256 KB = 28.1 Million
		512 KB = 44 Million
	Voltage Interface	Split Core and I/O
	Core Voltage	1.45 – 1.475 volts
	I/O Voltage	3.3 volts
	Level 2 Cache Voltage	3.3 volts
	Power Consumption	15 – 21 watts
	Maximum Power	23.8 – 31.2 watts

(continued on next page)

Table 6-118: Pentium III Tualatin Specifications (continued)

Processor Family	Model Name	Intel Tualatin
Architectural Design	Core Technology	OOO and Speculative Execution RISC
	Register Support	Integer = 32 bit
		FPU = 80 bit
		MMX = 64 bit
		SSE = 128 bit
	Execution Units	2 x ALU/MMX/SSE
		1 x Pipelined FPU
	Maximum Execution Rate	5 Micro-Ops per Cycle
	Data Bus Width	64 bit
	Maximum Memory Support	Physical = 64 Gigabyte
		Virtual = 64 Terabyte
	Multi-Processor Support	2-way SMP via APIC
	Level 1 Code Cache	16 KB 4-way
	Level 1 Data Cache	16 KB 4-way
	Level 2 Cache	256 – 512 KB Unified
	Read Buffer	4 x 32 Byte
	Write Buffer	32 Byte
	Pre-fetch Queue	32 Byte
	Static Branch Prediction	Supported
	Dynamic Branch Prediction	512 Entry 4-way
	RSB Branch Prediction	4 Entry
	Floating-Point Processor	Integrated
	Multimedia Extensions	MMX, SSE

Disassembling Slot 1 Processors

1. You must disassemble the factory-installed casing in order to install aftermarket cooling devices in Slot 1 processors. The case is secured in place with four interlocking pins. Begin by laying the processor on its side, with the thermal plate facing up. Eight pins will be visible, but only the four pins near the outer edge of the casing require manipulation.

2. Insert a flathead screwdriver into the region between the thermal plate and the casing's edge. You may wish to cover the head of the screwdriver with a thin cloth to avoid scratching the case. Simply rotate the screwdriver until you hear a clicking sound. This click signifies release of the upper pins. Use the same method for removing the two lower pins, but take care not to insert the screwdriver tip too far into the processor assembly, as this could damage the internal circuit board.

3. You must also disassemble the inner thermal plate once the casing has been removed. First flip the processor over so that the thermal plate is facing away. A series of small teeth embedded in a spring system, secured against four interconnecting pins, holds the thermal plate in position. Using a small

punch or jeweler's screwdriver, carefully apply pressure around the toothed regions until the catches bend away.

4. The processing unit can now be removed from the casing by gently lifting the printed circuit board away from the four interconnecting pins. Installation of the aftermarket heatsink, waterblock, or Peltier cooler varies according to model, though most coolers are secured by plastic strips or other simple mounting techniques. The best solutions use dual heatsinks for each side of the printed circuit board. Mounting screws secure the cooler to the circuit board by applying pressure from both sides of the processing unit.

Take care to note the shape of the Intel thermal plate, as some Pentium II models feature a specialized plate designed to contact both the processor core and the cache memory chips. If a comparable heatsink design is not available, installing a shim between the chips and heatsink can achieve the cooling needed for proper operation. Alternatively, a fan can be mounted to blow across the cache chips.

Socket to Slot Converters

Socket 370 to Slot 1 "Slotket" converter cards offer a popular upgrade path to move from older Slot 1-based systems to the latest Socket 370-based Pentium III Coppermine and Celeron II processors. The best of these Slotket cards offer great overclocking support. Many models allow users to configure the values for core voltage and front-side bus speeds directly on the Slotket card itself, assuming the motherboard supports custom values.

Figure 6-1: Iwill Slotket II

The Slot 1 interface uses certain pins for automatic configuration of front-side bus and voltage levels. A Slot 1 motherboard equipped with a quality Slotket converter (Abit or Iwill recommended) and a highly overclockable Pentium III Coppermine processor can offer superb overclocking potential. A Slotket also allows installation of 370-pin socket cooling solutions, thus increasing the efficiency of the thermal exchange while decreasing overall user effort.

Hacking the Slot 1 Interface

Using the same techniques discussed for a Slotket converter card, a true Slot 1 processor can be modified by altering the electrical states of various pins along the printed circuit board interface's connection to the motherboard. Blocking electrical inputs on certain pins can facilitate overclocking for motherboards with limited configuration support.

Many methods have been developed for the isolation of pins from an electrical connector. The most extreme process involves actually severing the pin with a sharp razor blade. This action is irreversible without intricate knowledge of advanced soldering techniques. The simplest process is to use dielectric paint to insulate the pin. The risk is that these paints can be abrasive to the motherboard connector and may decompose under extended thermal load.

The best solution comes in the form of Teflon electrical tape. The basic idea is to prevent the pin from making an electrical connection to the motherboard by covering it with the Teflon tape. A standard 2-millimeter-thick tape possesses dielectric properties upwards of 8000 volts, thus ensuring no electron migration across the insulating material. Teflon is also extremely resilient. It can withstand great temperatures and stress loads. The tape can easily be cut with a razor blade to fit across the desired pin(s). Take care to ensure that the tape covers the entire lower region of the pin, with no overlapping onto surrounding pin or circuit junctions.

The most popular hardware hack is found with pin B21. When you isolate this pin, a Slot 1 processor designed for 66-MHz front-side bus operation can be forced to identify itself to the motherboard as a 100-MHz bus chip. Remember that locked chips will implement the same multiplier, regardless of the front-side bus rate; thus any bus speed increases will overclock the core processing unit. Systems featuring unlocked chips can implement a lower multiplier, if overclocking the processor core is not desired, while retaining the performance advantage of the 100-MHz bus speed.

Pin B21 can be located by placing the processor on its side, with the longest row of connecting pins oriented to the right-hand side. The position of pin B21 can now be found by counting 21 pins from the right-hand side of the processor.

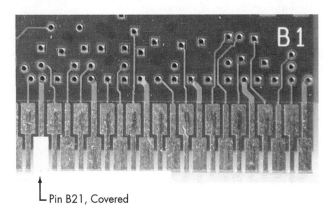

Pin B21, Covered

Figure 6-2: Slot 1 processor (back side, bottom right) pin B21, covered

Core voltage modifications are also possible for most Slot 1 models. Again, this assumes that the system's motherboard actually supports the values assigned after the pins are modified. A motherboard without proper voltage support might give erroneous voltage values, thus damaging the processor core circuitry. Any voltage hacking techniques require extreme care and patience.

Covering pins A121, A119, and B119 will set the core voltage to 2.2 volts for .25-micron processor models. Be careful to examine all connection points closely with a magnifying glass before proceeding to install the processor. If the junction point at A119 allows any connection, the chip will be autodetected as requiring a core voltage of 2.6 volts, a level that will destroy nearly all .25-micron Intel processors.

Newer .18-micron Slot 1 models can be modified to 1.85 volts using a similar technique. Only pin A119 needs to be covered to force the autodetection of 1.85 volts for the core processor voltage. Any increases in core voltage values can lead to processor failure due to increased thermal loads, so be sure to install a cooling system capable of dissipating the increased temperatures caused by these techniques.

Pentium 4 Willamette Background

With the P6 core reaching its final days of mass production, Intel ushered in the redesigned Pentium 4 as its new midrange flagship product. The Pentium 4 is an entirely new core built atop technologies never before implemented for an x86 class processor, such as a double-speed integer execution unit, SSE2 streaming multimedia instructions, and a trace cache architecture. These new features yielded the highest performance processor available for most multimedia applications.

Despite these advanced technologies, the Pentium 4 platform has its shortcomings, due to its extremely long pipeline. The older Pentium 3 and AMD Athlon designs achieve better results for the broadest range of applications, at least as measured in per-MHz efficiency. The Pentium 4 must run at 2 GHz before it can outperform its competitors; even then, the difference is negligible for most desktop applications and games.

Considering this lack of per-MHz effectiveness, overclocking the Pentium 4 will help maximize performance. As with previous Intel designs, the P4 is multiplier locked. Worse, the Willamette is fabricated through a .18-micron process, which does not respond well to overclocking at the default core voltage. A 10% core voltage increase, combined with a massive cooling unit, can usually offer improvements in the 200 to 400 MHz range.

Actual performance returns across a variety of applications and benchmarks also need to be examined when overclocking the Pentium 4. Intel introduced a clock-throttling mechanism that can effectively power down segments of the processor's core during times of intense thermal load. This new feature is engineered to ensure stability for OEM systems that lack quality cooling configurations, though it can adversely affect overclocking performance for systems with inadequate cooling properties.

It should be noted that the Pentium 4 uses the 100-MHz Quad Data Rate bus, or QDR, which results in a 400-MHz FSB speed.

Pentium 4 Willamette Overclocking

Table 6-119: Pentium 4 Willamette Specifications

Processor Family	Model Name	Intel Pentium 4 Willamette
	Performance Rating	1300 – 2000 MHz
	Generation	Seventh: 80786 IA-32
Operational Rates	Level 1 Cache Speed	1.0x Core Rate
	Level 2 Cache Speed	1.0x Core Rate
	Front-side Bus Speed	400 MHz (4 x 100 MHz)
	Multiplier Ratio	13.0x – 20.0x
Physical Design	Interface Packing	423-Pin PGA
		478-Pin PGA
	Core Die Size	.18 micron
	Core Size by Stepping	217 mm^2
	Transistor Count	42 Million
	Voltage Interface	Split Core and I/O
	Core Voltage	1.7 – 1.75 volts
	I/O Voltage	3.3 volts
	Level 2 Cache Voltage	3.3 volts
	Power Consumption	51.8 – 75.3 watts
	Maximum Power	71 – 100 watts
Architectural Design	Core Technology	OOO and Speculative Execution RISC
	Register Support	Integer = 32 bit
		FPU = 80 bit
		MMX = 64 bit
		SSE/SSE2 = 128 bit
	Maximum Execution Rate	6 Micro-Ops per Cycle
	Data Bus Width	64 bit
	Maximum Memory Support	Physical = 64 Gigabyte
		Virtual = 64 Terabyte
	Level 2 Cache	256 KB Unified
	Pre-fetch Queue	256 Byte
	Static Branch Prediction	Supported
	Dynamic Branch Prediction	4,096 Entry
	RSB Branch Prediction	16 Entry
	Floating-Point Processor	Integrated
	Multimedia Extensions	MMX, SSE, SSE2

Pentium 4 Willamette 1300

Table 6-120: Pentium 4 Willamette 1300 Specifications

Processor Family	Model Name	Intel Pentium 4 Willamette
	Performance Rating	1300 MHz
	Front-side Bus Speed	400 QDR (4 x 100 MHz)
	Multiplier Ratio	13.0x
Physical Design	Interface Packing	423-Pin PGA
		478-Pin PGA
	Core Voltage	1.7 – 1.75 volts
	Power Consumption	51.6 watts
	Maximum Power	74 watts

Table 6-121: Pentium 4 Willamette 1300 Overclocking

Pentium 4 Willamette	Model Rating	1300 MHz
Overclocking Potential	Multiplier Lock Support	Locked Multiplier
	Typical Multiplier O/C	N/A
	Typical Front-side Bus O/C	440 – 460 QDR
		(110 – 115 MHz)
	Typical O/C Potential	1430 – 1495 MHz
	Maximum O/C Potential	1500 – 1600 MHz
Overclocking Tolerances	Recommended Cooling Type	Forced-Air Heatsink
	Recommended Heatsink Coolers	Zalman CNPS-5000
		Swiftech MCX-478
	Maximum Core Voltage	1.85 volts
	Maximum I/O Voltage	3.5 volts with Chipset Cooler
	Maximum Core Temperature	80° Celsius

Strategy

The Willamette 1300-MHz processor marked Intel's entry-level push into the Pentium 4 marketing campaign. One of the first P4-derived chips available to consumers, the P4 1300 lacks the performance to compete with older Pentium III and Athlon designs. As a result, this chip realized only marginal success with overclocking; many units failed to overclock successfully past 1500 MHz in testing with prerelease P3 1300 processors.

Pentium 4 Willamette 1400

Table 6-122: Pentium 4 Willamette 1400 Specifications

Processor Family	Model Name	Intel Pentium 4 Willamette
	Performance Rating	1400 MHz
	Front-side Bus Speed	400 QDR (4 x 100 MHz)
	Multiplier Ratio	14.0x
Physical Design	Interface Packing	423-Pin PGA
		478-Pin PGA
	Core Voltage	1.7 – 1.75 volts
	Power Consumption	55.3 watts
	Maximum Power	74 watts

Table 6-123: Pentium 4 Willamette 1400 Overclocking

Pentium 4 Willamette	Model Rating	1400 MHz
Overclocking Potential	Multiplier Lock Support	Locked Multiplier
	Typical Multiplier O/C	N/A
	Typical Front-side Bus O/C	440 – 480 QDR
		(110 – 120 MHz)
	Typical O/C Potential	1540 – 1680 MHz
	Maximum O/C Potential	1700 – 1800 MHz
Overclocking Tolerances	Recommended Cooling Type	Forced-Air Heatsink
	Recommended Heatsink Coolers	Zalman CNPS-5000
		Swiftech MCX-478
	Maximum Core Voltage	2.1 volts with Extreme Cooling
	Maximum I/O Voltage	3.5 volts with Chipset Cooler
	Maximum Core Temperature	70° Celsius

Strategy

The Pentium 4 1400-MHz processor suffered a fate similar to its 1300-MHz sibling in the overclocking community. Again, Intel failed to deliver significant performance gains over existing Pentium III and Athlon models in most consumer-oriented software performance testing. Overclocking returns did improve, but the imposed thermal limitation of 70° Celsius mandates installation of a quality cooling solution for those seeking returns in excess of 1700 MHz.

Pentium 4 Willamette 1500

Table 6-124: Pentium 4 Willamette 1500 Specifications

Processor Family	Model Name	Intel Pentium 4 Willamette
	Performance Rating	1500 MHz
	Front-side Bus Speed	400 QDR (4 x 100 MHz)
	Multiplier Ratio	15.0x
Physical Design	Interface Packing	423-Pin PGA
		478-Pin PGA
	Core Voltage	1.7 – 1.75 volts
	Power Consumption	57.9 watts
	Maximum Power	79 watts

Table 6-125: Pentium 4 Willamette 1500 Overclocking

Pentium 4 Willamette	Model Rating	1500 MHz
Overclocking Potential	Multiplier Lock Support	Locked Multiplier
	Typical Multiplier O/C	N/A
	Typical Front-side Bus O/C	440 – 480 QDR
		(110 – 120 MHz)
	Typical O/C Potential	1650 – 1800 MHz
	Maximum O/C Potential	2000+ MHz
Overclocking Tolerances	Recommended Cooling Type	Forced-Air Heatsink
	Recommended Heatsink Coolers	Zalman CNPS-5000
		Swiftech MCX-478
	Maximum Core Voltage	2.1 volts with Extreme Cooling
	Maximum I/O Voltage	3.5 volts with Chipset Cooler
	Maximum Core Temperature	72° Celsius

Strategy

The Willamette 1500 MHz was the best-selling Intel processor in the early months of the P4 marketing initiative, due to its impressive performance-to-price ratio. Most units in this speed grade can attain stable overclocks exceeding 1700 MHz with installation of a decent heatsink cooler and a slight core voltage increase. As the P4 1500 design imposes a relatively low thermal limit of 72° Celsius, any attempts at overclocking beyond 1900 MHz should include high-quality forced-air heatsink cooling.

Pentium 4 Willamette 1600

Table 6-126: Pentium 4 Willamette 1600 Specifications

Processor Family	Model Name	Intel Pentium 4 Willamette
	Performance Rating	1600 MHz
	Front-side Bus Speed	400 QDR (4 x 100 MHz)
	Multiplier Ratio	16.0x
Physical Design	Interface Packing	423-Pin PGA
		478-Pin PGA
	Core Voltage	1.7 – 1.75 volts
	Power Consumption	61 watts
	Maximum Power	83 watts

Table 6-127: Pentium 4 Willamette 1600 Overclocking

Pentium 4 Willamette	Model Rating	1600 MHz
Overclocking Potential	Multiplier Lock Support	Locked Multiplier
	Typical Multiplier O/C	N/A
	Typical Front-side Bus O/C	440 – 480 QDR
		(110 – 120 MHz)
	Typical O/C Potential	1760 – 1920 MHz
	Maximum O/C Potential	2100+ MHz
Overclocking Tolerances	Recommended Cooling Type	Forced-Air Heatsink
	Recommended Heatsink Coolers	Zalman CNPS-5000
		Swiftech MCX-478
	Maximum Core Voltage	2.1 volts with Extreme Cooling
	Maximum I/O Voltage	3.5 volts with Chipset Cooler
	Maximum Core Temperature	75° Celsius

Strategy

The Pentium 4 Willamette 1600-MHz processor offers great overclocking potential with minimal concern for system instability. Nearly all P4 1600 models can reach 1900 MHz straight from the retail box, without any significant increases in core voltage rates. However, cooling becomes a dominant concern beyond 2000 MHz, as this chip features a maximum core temperature threshold of 75° Celsius.

Pentium 4 Willamette 1700

Table 6-128: Pentium 4 Willamette 1700 Specifications

Processor Family	Model Name	Intel Pentium 4 Willamette
	Performance Rating	1700 MHz
	Front-side Bus Speed	400 QDR (4 x 100 MHz)
	Multiplier Ratio	17.0x
Physical Design	Interface Packing	423-Pin PGA
		478-Pin PGA
	Core Voltage	1.7 – 1.75 volts
	Power Consumption	64 watts
	Maximum Power	87 watts

Table 6-129: Pentium 4 Willamette 1700 Overclocking

Pentium 4 Willamette	Model Rating	1700 MHz
Overclocking Potential	Multiplier Lock Support	Locked Multiplier
	Typical Multiplier O/C	N/A
	Typical Front-side Bus O/C	440 – 480 QDR
		(110 – 120 MHz)
	Typical O/C Potential	1870 – 2040 MHz
	Maximum O/C Potential	2100+ MHz
Overclocking Tolerances	Recommended Cooling Type	Forced-Air Heatsink
	Recommended Heatsink Coolers	Zalman CNPS-5000
		Swiftech MCX-478
	Maximum Core Voltage	2.1 volts with Extreme Cooling
	Maximum I/O Voltage	3.5 volts with Chipset Cooler
	Maximum Core Temperature	76° Celsius

Strategy

The Pentium 4 Willamette 1700-MHz processor is well respected in the over-clocking community. The internal 17x multiplier is well suited to operation with processor speeds in excess of 120 MHz (480 QDR). Given a quality cooling solution, most P4 1700 units should scale up to 2100 MHz with minimal fuss and no major concerns.

Pentium 4 Willamette 1800

Table 6-130: Pentium 4 Willamette 1800 Specifications

Processor Family	Model Name	Intel Pentium 4 Willamette
	Performance Rating	1800 MHz
	Front-side Bus Speed	400 QDR (4 x 100 MHz)
	Multiplier Ratio	18.0x
Physical Design	Interface Packing	423-Pin PGA
		478-Pin PGA
	Core Voltage	1.7 – 1.75 volts
	Power Consumption	66.7 watts
	Maximum Power	88 watts

Table 6-131: Pentium 4 Willamette 1800 Overclocking

Pentium 4 Willamette	Model Rating	1800 MHz
Overclocking Potential	Multiplier Lock Support	Locked Multiplier
	Typical Multiplier O/C	N/A
	Typical Front-side Bus O/C	440 – 460 QDR
		(110 – 115 MHz)
	Typical O/C Potential	1980 – 2070 MHz
	Maximum O/C Potential	2100+ MHz
Overclocking Tolerances	Recommended Cooling Type	Forced-Air Heatsink
	Recommended Heatsink Coolers	Zalman CNPS-5000
		Swiftech MCX-478
	Maximum Core Voltage	2.1 volts with Extreme Cooling
	Maximum I/O Voltage	3.5 volts with Chipset Cooler
	Maximum Core Temperature	77° Celsius

Strategy

The Pentium 4 Willamette 1800-MHz processor offers a good balance in its 18x core-to-processor bus multiplier ratio. Overclocking returns approaching 2100 MHz should be realized with minimal effort. However, the P4 1800 represents a transition phase in the Willamette architecture for overclocking enthusiasts; models featuring higher multipliers will offer less performance return, due to restrictions in processor bus speeds. The P4 1800 displays evidence of this shift when speed grades of the Willamette design are closely compared.

Pentium 4 Willamette 1900

Table 6-132: Pentium 4 Willamette 1900 Specifications

Processor Family	Model Name	Intel Pentium 4 Willamette
	Performance Rating	1900 MHz
	Front-side Bus Speed	400 QDR (4 × 100 MHz)
	Multiplier Ratio	19.0x
Physical Design	Interface Packing	423-Pin PGA
		478-Pin PGA
	Core Voltage	1.7 – 1.75 volts
	Power Consumption	72.8 watts
	Maximum Power	92 watts

Table 6-133: Pentium 4 Willamette 1900 Overclocking

Pentium 4 Willamette	Model Rating	1900 MHz
Overclocking Potential	Multiplier Lock Support	Locked Multiplier
	Typical Multiplier O/C	N/A
	Typical Front-side Bus O/C	440 – 460 QDR
		(110 – 115MHz)
	Typical O/C Potential	2090 – 2185MHz
	Maximum O/C Potential	2200+ MHz
Overclocking Tolerances	Recommended Cooling Type	Forced-Air Heatsink
	Recommended Heatsink Coolers	Zalman CNPS-5000
		Swiftech MCX-478
	Maximum Core Voltage	2.1 volts with Extreme Cooling
	Maximum I/O Voltage	3.5 volts with Chipset Cooler
	Maximum Core Temperature	73° Celsius

Strategy

The Pentium 4 Willamette 1900-MHz processor will offer moderate scalability upwards to the 2100 to 2200 MHz range for most system configurations. The .18-micron design of this chip stifles successful overclocking beyond 2200 MHz, regardless of the cooling or voltage levels involved.

Pentium 4 Willamette 2000

Table 6-134: Pentium 4 Willamette 2000 Specifications

Processor Family	Model Name	Intel Pentium 4 Willamette
	Performance Rating	2000 MHz
	Front-side Bus Speed	400 QDR (4 x 100 MHz)
	Multiplier Ratio	20.0x
Physical Design	Interface Packing	423-Pin PGA
		478-Pin PGA
	Core Voltage	1.70 –1.75 volts
	Power Consumption	71.8 Watts
	Maximum Power	96 Watts

Table 6-135: Pentium 4 Willamette 2000 Overclocking

Pentium 4 Willamette	Model Rating	2000 MHz
Overclocking Potential	Multiplier Lock Support	Locked Multiplier
	Typical Multiplier O/C	N/A
	Typical Front-side Bus O/C	420 – 440 QDR
		(105 – 110 MHz)
	Typical O/C Potential	2100 – 2200 MHz
	Maximum O/C Potential	2200+ MHz
Overclocking Tolerances	Recommended Cooling Type	Forced-Air Heatsink
	Recommended Heatsink Coolers	Zalman CNPS-5000
		Swiftech MCX-478
	Maximum Core Voltage	2.1 volts with Extreme Cooling
	Maximum I/O Voltage	3.5 volts with Chipset Cooler
	Maximum Core Temperature	74° Celsius

Strategy

The Pentium 4 Willamette family of processors saw its supposedly final incarnation with the release of the P4 2000. This chip offers marginal overclocking capabilities, with most users realizing maximum return in the 2100 to 2200 MHz range. Improved cooling or increases in core voltage will do little to push the Willamette any further; the .18-micron design hinders overclocking beyond 2200 MHz for most traditional system configurations.

Pentium 4 Northwood Background

The Pentium 4 Northwood is the latest commercial offering in the P4 architecture for desktop users. The Northwood extends the base Willamette architecture by adding a 256-KB Level 2 cache, bringing the total to an impressive 512 KB. Design enhancements include a .13-micron core fabrication process. This smaller die size, combined with additional production revisions, allows the Pentium 4 Northwood to attain impressive overclocking results compared to its Willamette siblings.

Overclocking potential for the P4 Northwood can extend above 500 to 800 MHz with traditional forced-air heatsink cooling and a minimal increase in core voltage levels. Those willing to undertake extreme cooling measures will witness the greatest returns. Recent liquid gas cooling experiments have yielded short-term overclocking results above the 4-GHz range for the latest Northwood revisions. Otherwise, less radical Peltier or vapor-phase cooling technologies should allow operation near the 3-GHz level for most higher-clocked Northwood models.

Intel demonstrated an impressive 3.5-GHz Pentium 4 system in 2001, thus revealing the potential for real P4 overclocking.

Pentium 4 Northwood Overclocking

Table 6-136: Pentium 4 Northwood Specifications

Processor Family	Model Name	Intel Pentium 4 Northwood
	Performance Rating	1600 – 3000+ MHz
	Generation	Seventh: 80786 IA-32
Operational Rates	Level 1 Cache Speed	1.0x Core Rate
	Level 2 Cache Speed	1.0x Core Rate
	Front-side Bus Speed	400 MHz (4 x 100 MHz)
	Multiplier Ratio	16.0x – 30.0+x
Physical Design	Interface Packing	478-Pin PGA
	Core Die Size	.13 micron
	Core Size by Stepping	131 – 146 mm^2
	Transistor Count	55 Million
	Voltage Interface	Split Core and I/O
	Core Voltage	1.50 volts
	I/O Voltage	3.3 volts
	Level 2 Cache Voltage	3.3 volts
	Power Consumption	52.4 – 57.8 watts
	Maximum Power	66 – 74 watts

(continued on next page)

Table 6-136: Pentium 4 Northwood Specifications (continued)

Processor Family	Model Name	Intel Pentium 4 Northwood
Architectural Design	Core Technology	OOO and Speculative Execution RISC
	Register Support	Integer = 32 bit
		FPU = 80 bit
		MMX = 64 bit
		SSE/SSE2 = 128 bit
	Maximum Execution Rate	6 Micro-Ops per Cycle
	Data Bus Width	64 bit
	Maximum Memory Support	Physical = 64 Gigabyte
		Virtual = 64 Terabyte
	Level 2 Cache	512 KB Unified
	Pre-fetch Queue	256 Byte
	Static Branch Prediction	Supported
	Dynamic Branch Prediction	4,096 Entry
	RSB Branch Prediction	16 Entry
	Floating-Point Processor	Integrated
	Multimedia Extensions	MMX, SSE, SSE2

Pentium 4 Northwood 1600A

Table 6-137: Pentium 4 Northwood 1600A Specifications

Processor Family	Model Name	Intel Pentium 4 Northwood
	Performance Rating	1600 MHz
	Front-side Bus Speed	400 QDR (4 x 100 MHz)
	Multiplier Ratio	16.0x
Physical Design	Interface Packing	478 Pin PGA
	Core Voltage	1.5v
	Power Consumption	38.7 watts
	Maximum Power	49 watts

Table 6-138: Pentium 4 Northwood 1600A Overclocking

Pentium 4 Northwood	Model Rating	2000 MHz
Overclocking Potential	Multiplier Lock Support	Locked Multiplier
	Typical Multiplier O/C	N/A
	Typical FSB O/C	532-600 QDR (133-150 MHz)
	Typical O/C Potential	2128-2400 MHz
	Maximum O/C Potential	2800+ MHz
Overclocking Tolerances	Recommended Cooling Type	Forced-Air Heatsink
	Recommended Heatsink Coolers	Swiftech MCX-478
	Maximum Core Voltage	1.75v with Extreme Cooling
	Maximum I/O Voltage	3.5v with Chipset Cooler
	Maximum Core Temperature	66° Celsius

Strategy

The P4 1600A offers incredible overclocking potential due to its highly refined .13-micron copper core fabrication process. Most units can attain stable operation at 2400 MHz (that's an 800-MHz overclock) with nothing more than an increase in bus speed, though you may need to increase to 1.60v or 1.65v for improved stability. The P4 1600A is one of the most often overclocked processors out there. With a whopping 275 entries in the Overclockers.com CPU database, the P4 1600A is often compared to the old Celeron 300A for its overclocking potential to price ratio.

Pentium 4 Northwood 1800A

Table 6-139: Pentium 4 Northwood 1800A Specifications

Processor Family	Model Name	Intel Pentium 4 Northwood
	Performance Rating	1800 MHz
	Front-side Bus Speed	400 QDR (4 x 100 MHz)
	Multiplier Ratio	18.0x
Physical Design	Interface Packing	478 Pin PGA
	Core Voltage	1.5v
	Power Consumption	41.6 watts
	Maximum Power	54 watts

Table 6-140: Pentium 4 Northwood 1800A Overclocking

Pentium 4 Northwood	Model Rating	1800 MHz
Overclocking Potential	Multiplier Lock Support	Locked Multiplier
	Typical Multiplier O/C	N/A
	Typical FSB O/C	532 QDR (133 MHz)
	Typical O/C Potential	2400 MHz
	Maximum O/C Potential	2800+ MHz
Overclocking Tolerances	Recommended Cooling Type	Forced-Air Heatsink
	Recommended Heatsink Coolers	Swiftech MCX-478
	Maximum Core Voltage	1.75v with Extreme Cooling
	Maximum I/O Voltage	3.5v with Chipset Cooler
	Maximum Core Temperature	67° Celsius

Strategy

The P4 1800A tends to be less popular than the 1600A (157 overclocking submissions at Overclockers.com, for comparison sake) since it is slightly more expensive than the 1600A without offering many additional advantages. Stock cooling and the default 1.50v voltage will likely get you to 2400 MHz with a 133-MHz bus speed, though once again you may need 1.60v or 1.65v to improve stability. There is one advantage that the 1800A offers over the 1600A: you can run at 2400 MHz with a lower 133-MHz bus rather than a 150-MHz bus, thanks to the 18.0x multiplier on the 1800A.

Pentium 4 Northwood 2000A

Table 6-141: Pentium 4 Northwood 2000A Specifications

Processor Family	Model Name	Intel Pentium 4 Northwood
	Performance Rating	2000 MHz
	Front-side Bus Speed	400 QDR (4 x 100 MHz)
	Multiplier Ratio	20.0x
Physical Design	Interface Packing	478-Pin PGA
	Core Voltage	1.5 volts
	Power Consumption	52.4 watts
	Maximum Power	66 watts

Table 6-142: Pentium 4 Northwood 2000A Overclocking

Pentium 4 Northwood	Model Rating	2000 MHz
Overclocking Potential	Multiplier Lock Support	Locked Multiplier
	Typical Multiplier O/C	N/A
	Typical Front-side Bus O/C	440 – 480 QDR (110 – 120 MHz)
	Typical O/C Potential	2200 – 2400 MHz
	Maximum O/C Potential	2400+ MHz
Overclocking Tolerances	Recommended Cooling Type	Forced-Air Heatsink
	Recommended Heatsink Coolers	Swiftech MCX-478
	Maximum Core Voltage	1.75 volts with Extreme
Cooling		
	Maximum I/O Voltage	3.5 volts with Chipset Cooler
	Maximum Core Temperature	68° Celsius

Strategy

The P4 2000A features a 20.0x multiplier, once again enabling a higher core operating speed with a lower front side bus. That's good if you're trying to push the core speed to the max, without stressing subsystems that are driven by the FSB, but it may offer lower overall system performance as compared to using a slightly higher FSB and a slightly lower processor core operating speed. If you're aiming for 2400 MHz, the 1600A or 1800A will therefore yield greater overall performance due to their higher FSBs, along with comparable stability, depending on voltage, cooling, and your particular processor sample.

Pentium 4 Northwood 2200A

Table 6-143: Pentium 4 Northwood 2200A Specifications

Processor Family	Model Name	Intel Pentium 4 Northwood
	Performance Rating	2200 MHz
	Front-side Bus Speed	400 QDR (4 x 100 MHz)
	Multiplier Ratio	22.0x
Physical Design	Interface Packing	478-Pin PGA
	Core Voltage	1.5 volts
	Power Consumption	55.1 watts
	Maximum Power	71 watts

Table 6-144: Pentium 4 Northwood 2200A Overclocking

Pentium 4 Northwood	Model Rating	2200 MHz
Overclocking Potential	Multiplier Lock Support	Locked Multiplier
	Typical Multiplier O/C	N/A
	Typical Front-side Bus O/C	423 – 440 QDR (105 – 110 MHz)
	Typical O/C Potential	2310 – 2420 MHz
	Maximum O/C Potential	2500+ MHz
Overclocking Tolerances	Recommended Cooling Type	Forced-Air Heatsink
	Recommended Heatsink Coolers	Swiftech MCX-478
	Maximum Core Voltage	1.85 volts
	Maximum I/O Voltage	3.5 volts with Chipset Cooler
	Maximum Core Temperature	69° Celsius

Strategy

The Pentium 4 Northwood 2200 processor extends good overclocking balance by means of its 22.0x multiplier-to-processor bus ratio. Many chips in this speed grade can effectively scale past 2500 MHz with a minimal increase in core voltage levels. Otherwise, nearly all P4 2200A processors should attain a stable overclock near the 2400-MHz frequency level with little more than a quick adjustment to the motherboard's processor bus speed.

Pentium 4 Northwood 2400A

Table 6-145: Pentium 4 Northwood 2400A Specifications

Processor Family	Model Name	Intel Pentium 4 Northwood
	Performance Rating	2400 MHz
	Front-side Bus Speed	400 QDR (4 x 100 MHz)
	Multiplier Ratio	24.0x
Physical Design	Interface Packing	478-Pin PGA
	Core Voltage	1.5 volts
	Power Consumption	55.1 watts
	Maximum Power	74 watts

Table 6-146: Pentium 4 Northwood 2400A Overclocking

Pentium 4 Northwood	Model Rating	2400 MHz
Overclocking Potential	Multiplier Lock Support	Locked Multiplier
	Typical Multiplier O/C	N/A
	Typical Front-side Bus O/C	420 – 440 QDR (105 – 110 MHz)
	Typical O/C Potential	2520 – 2640 MHz
	Maximum O/C Potential	2700+ MHz
Overclocking Tolerances	Recommended Cooling Type	Forced-Air Heatsink
	Recommended Heatsink Coolers	Swiftech MCX-478
	Maximum Core Voltage	1.75 volts with Extreme Cooling
	Maximum I/O Voltage	3.5 volts with Chipset Cooler
	Maximum Core Temperature	70° Celsius

Strategy

In terms of raw MHz scalability, the Pentium 4 Northwood 2400-MHz processor represents the pinnacle of current overclocking potential. Early reports with the chip have indicated overclocking returns in the 2700 to 2800 MHz range, with standard forced-air heatsink cooling. Subzero active cooling technologies have produced yields exceeding 3000 MHz with this impressive processor. The .13-micron P4 core is in its infancy, so expect future designs to offer scalability approaching 4000 MHz in real-world configurations.

Pentium 4 Northwood "B"

In mid-2002, Intel released a 133 MHz FSB (533 QDR) version of the Pentium 4 Northwood, designated as "B." It is available in speeds ranging from 2.26 GHz to 2.80+ GHz. If you have no interest in overclocking (which may make reading this book somewhat counterproductive), the Northwood "B" is an attractive chip given its ability to offer higher overall system performance due to its higher FSB. But for overclocking, the Northwood "B" offers a lower price to performance ratio than the cheaper Northwood "A," and is therefore not recommended for overclockers.

Pentium Xeon Series

The Xeon series of Pentium processors is the server and workstation variant of the Intel line. Most models can be overclocked using techniques similar to the ones that work with their desktop cousins, though motherboard manufacturers do not always support the options required for success. Xeon parts are designed for maximum stability and reliability, which minimizes the need for multiplier or bus manipulation beyond the standard autodetect routines.

All Pentium II and many Pentium III Xeon chips are based on Intel's Slot 2 processor-to-motherboard interconnect. The comparative advantages of the Slot 2 Xeon over the Slot 1 desktop offerings include better support for multiple processor configurations and the presence of massive Level 2 caches for increased symmetric multiprocessing performance. Most Slot 2 motherboards are designed to accommodate only the Intel retail heatsink cooler; problems can be caused by the introduction of aftermarket cooling solutions. Some Slot 1 coolers can be used, as long as modifications are made so that components mounted near the motherboard-to-processor interface can clear properly.

Later Pentium III Xeon chips adopted the 370-pin FCPGA socket interface for compatibility across the widest range of motherboard designs. In single- or dual-processor systems, these chips exhibit the same overclocking characteristics as the standard Pentium III Coppermine. Demand for Pentium III Xeons in the desktop sector is minimal. The majority of PC users are not willing to pay more to obtain the extended reliability and stability these chips can offer.

The Pentium 4 Xeon is Intel's current flagship x86 processor, though its high price, combined with the need to pair it with a costly motherboard design, does little to attract the overclocking crowd. Symmetric multithreading (SMT), recently added in 2+-GHz models, allows the P4 Xeon to emulate a dual-core processor, thus maximizing performance in multithreaded operating systems like Windows XP Professional. Even so, overclocking potential is generally considered to be limited, due to Intel's rigorous design specifications for its i860 motherboard chipset. Such specifications ensure maximum reliability for critical applications, but also limit flexibility for enthusiasts.

7

AMD OVERCLOCKING

AMD Background

AMD is one of the longest-lived manufacturers of x86 computing technology. The company's market share increased rapidly after the release of its K5 core architecture. Some iterations of AMD designs were almost indistinguishable from the products of Intel or Cyrix. In the early days, nearly all x86 products resembled each other closely, as manufacturers worked to establish a common PC standard. The success of AMD's current Athlon platform shows that the company has learned to harness the power of market diversification that began with the original K5.

With the K5 series, AMD first diverged from its competitors in design, engineering, and production. The K5 contained one of the most efficient integer execution units ever made, though its lack of a full-pipelined floating-point unit essentially relegated K5 architecture to the budget realm. Gaming and multimedia interests drove the high-end market toward performance platforms, like Intel's redesigned Pentium processor, and away from architectures like the K5, which was closely related to the 486 design.

The AMD K5 compared favorably to the Pentium running a wide range of desktop applications. While the underpowered floating-point unit raised questions, performance was still acceptable for most users of the day. The real stumbling block for the K5 was not its engineering as much as the way it was sold to consumers.

AMD used integer benchmarking results compared to the Pentium to name, rate, and market each model in the K5 series. The choice to compare benchmark numbers instead of clock frequencies caused some analysts to accuse AMD of deception. While the K5 could outperform the Pentium "clock for clock" in integer applications, multimedia programs lagged. Many vendors decided to market the K5 under its operating frequency, while retaining the performance rating (PR) number for general comparisons.

The K6 was an evolutionary step for AMD. It offered minimal core improvements over the K5. The main architectural differences included MMX (multimedia) instruction set enhancements and adaptations to the core that supported a split-voltage interface to maintain motherboard compatibility with Intel's Pentium MMX. AMD's marketing strategy for the K6 was, however, dramatically different than it had been for the K5.

AMD chose to develop, market, and name the K6 processors by their operating frequencies, dropping the questionable PR-naming convention. Further core refinements, combined with additional MMX improvements, brought the K6 series a loyal following in the budget market segments. Intel retained the lead in multimedia performance. The rather dismal floating-point unit persisted in the K6 processors, limiting AMD to the entry-level realm.

Eventually, AMD recognized the need for an architecture revision and a new multimedia solution, especially after Intel released the powerful Pentium II platform. While the K6 could compete with the Pentium MMX, it could not compete with the P2 core architecture.

Lacking the resources to develop a completely new platform, AMD looked toward a new multimedia instruction set to compete with Intel's superior floating-point execution. The company adopted a streaming multimedia instruction set for its new K6-2. The K6-2 introduced key upgrades to the K6 design. The 3DNow! instruction set extended the floating-point capabilities of the K6, and an increase to 100 MHz in front-side bus speed improved memory and subsystem performance. The core die size also decreased to .25 micron, allowing the K6-2 to scale toward 550 MHz.

3DNow! was a forward-looking technology developed along the same lines as Intel's MMX instruction set. MMX allows for more efficient processing of integer mathematical computations; 3DNow! allows efficient combination of multiple floating-point operations in specialized instructions. 3DNow! also required many software optimizations at the programming code level, so AMD moved quickly to acquire and maintain development contracts.

When running properly optimized software applications using 3DNow! technology, instead of pure floating-point mathematics, the K6-2 could compete and even surpass the Intel architecture's performance. Game and hardware driver developers quickly adopted the new standard, and the K6-2 infiltrated all desktop markets. Even without 3DNow!, the K6-2 offered adequate floating-point performance through sheer increases in MHz (compared to the K5). Given low retail prices and compatibility with existing Socket 7 motherboards, the K6-2 rapidly emerged as the first real competitor to Intel's Pentium II and Celeron product lines.

Once the K6-2 found acceptance in the desktop market, AMD saw the need to develop a workstation and server-grade processor. The primary limitation of the K6-2 is memory bandwidth performance, but AMD could do little about motherboard chipset design. Manufacturers like VIA and SIS had failed to improve memory bandwidth or latency since the inception of Socket 7. ALI did improve the architecture related to memory access, but its chipsets suffered compatibility and stability problems when used with the newly popular AGP graphics accelerators.

AMD recognized the deficiency in bandwidth and opted for a solution at the processor level. The K6-2 implements a one-tier internal cache memory buffer, with the second-level buffer surface mounted on the motherboard. The Level 2 cache is accessed at the front-side bus rate because the chipset handles the transactions.

AMD's K6-3 took a page from Intel's playbook by introducing a Level 2 cache embedded inside the processor core. This internal L2 operates at the same rate as the core, increasing the cache memory latency and bandwidth exponentially compared to the K6-2. The cache memory mounted on the motherboard became a third-tier cache acting as an intermediary between the fast processor and slow system memory.

The K6-3 was marketed primarily as a server. Its new three-level cache architecture encouraged integer performance exceeding that of Intel's Pentium II at similar core clock rates. Curiously, the K6-3 450 could often exceed the integer performance of the more expensive Pentium III 450. Server environments have little need for floating-point multimedia performance; thus the K6-3 captured a significant slice of the higher-end processor market due to its superb performance and low-cost implementation. AMD could finally compete with Intel at all levels of the x86 market.

The plus series (marked with the + symbol) of K6 processors was a stopgap to maintain market visibility for AMD in the mobile computing segment. Both the K6-2 and K6-3 product lines featured a plus series variation. Core die size was reduced to .18 micron, which improved thermal efficiency. Architectural improvements include AMD's new 3DNow! DSP standards. The K6-3+ core remained basically the same, while the K6-2+ was upgraded to include an on-die 128 KB Level 2 cache memory architecture.

AMD Athlon Architecture

AMD recognized the need for a new architecture upon the release of Intel's Pentium III platform. The K6-2 had remained the mainstay for AMD throughout the reign of the Pentium II, but it could not rise to P3 standards. Instead of developing another K6-based revision, AMD undertook the arduous task of engineering a completely new design. Upon its release, the Athlon (K7) rapidly became the new choice for performance computing. The Athlon product series performs by raw power, featuring parallel execution for improved efficiency.

The transition to a new motherboard bus architecture paved the way for the Athlon's impressive success. The K7 interface is based on Digital Equipment Corporation's Alpha EV6 architecture. The Alpha processor is actually a 64-bit reduced instruction set computer (RISC), while the Athlon is a traditional 32-bit x86 offering. Using an off-the-shelf motherboard allowed AMD to concentrate its engineering efforts on the processor core itself. The resulting K7 Athlon core still lies at the heart of AMD's desktop computers, despite revisions to integrate on-die cache and extension set improvements.

The EV6 motherboard architecture eliminates the standard front-side bus approach by separating each relevant system bus. Buses are still interlinked through a base timing configuration for deriving transfer rates. The processor bus operates in a double-data-rate (DDR) mode that transfers information on both the rising and falling edges of the clock signal. Other buses can operate as usual, though the latest Athlon architectural revisions have expanded the DDR signaling technique to the memory bus. DDR timing rates can be confusing. Remember that the base frequency is simply one-half the effective MHz frequency. For current Athlon systems 200, 266, and 66 MHz effective frequencies yield base frequencies of 100, 133, and 33 MHz, respectively.

Athlon K7

The first K7 Athlon design uses a Slot A motherboard interface that resembles Intel's Slot 1 standard. Slot A Athlons feature a custom casing. This must be removed before installing aftermarket cooling solutions or overclocking boards. Front-side and voltage adjustments are possible from the motherboard, but AMD did implement a physically locked multiplier determined by the configuration of certain resistors found on the backside of the processor circuit board. These resistors can by modified to set multiplier values, but overclockers needed a better way to manipulate the multiplier given the amount of experimentation required to realize overclocking potential.

Enthusiasts soon realized that the electrical connector found along the topside of the processor board was actually connected to the same circuitry as the backside resistor array. A specialized circuit board can be connected to the electrical interface and used to manipulate the multiplier value. These aftermarket boards are commonly called Gold Finger Devices (or GFDs). Several manufacturers have produced GFD designs using dials, switches, and jumpers. Regardless of their configuration, all GFD products operate by the same practical method. Some GFDs even include support for processor voltage manipulation, for those possessing the soldering skills needed to install this extra option.

Some overclocking-friendly Slot A motherboards allow configuration of the cache divider from the BIOS Setup interface, but this is not the norm for consumer-grade models. Many GFDs also include the capability to alter the Level 2 cache divider rate. The Athlon derives its L2 cache operational frequency through a fractional process, as the comparatively slow cache memory is mounted on the processor's printed circuit board. The cache memory is incapable of sustaining operation at the processor's core rate, thus AMD was forced into a frequency-scaling paradigm for the Slot A Athlon K7.

Cache rates can be defined at several intervals from 1/4 to 1/2 the processor's core rate. Decreasing the fractional rate often allows for greater processor overclocking, though the performance impact could actually be negative. The bandwidth-hungry Athlon core requires a consistent supply of information from the L2 cache to sustain optimal operation. Any decrease in the cache rate lowers bandwidth and increases latency, stalling the processor at higher operating speeds. The only way to measure performance impact is through benchmark testing.

Processor-to-chipset bus overclocking of the Athlon K7 is only minimally effective. Most Slot A motherboards contain early revision chipsets, which commonly fail at operation rates beyond 112 MHz (224 DDR). Increasing the motherboard's input/output voltage from 3.3 to 3.5 volts may offer additional returns, but increased cooling of the Northbridge chipset will likely be required. The addition of a 50 to 60 millimeter fan often works well, as many motherboards already have a heatsink cooler. Some Slot A boards reach speeds above 124 MHz when properly cooled.

Athlon K7 Overclocking

Table 7-1: Athlon K7 Specifications

Processor Family	Model Name	AMD Athlon K7
	Performance Rating	500 – 700 MHz
	Generation	Seventh: 80686 IA-32
Operational Rates	L1 Cache Speed	1.0x Core Rate
	L2 Cache Speed	Fraction of Core Rate
		1/2.0x, 1/2.5x, 1/3.0x
	Front-side Bus Speed	100 MHz (200 DDR)
	Multiplier Ratio	5.0x – 7.0+x (14x maximum)
Physical Design	Interface Packing	242-Pin Slot A Cartridge
	Core Die Size	.25 micron, 184 mm
	Transistor Count	22 Million
	Voltage Interface	Split Core and I/O
	Core Voltage	1.6 volts
	L2 Cache Voltage	2.8 volts – 3.3 volts
	Power Consumption	38 – 45 watts
	Maximum Power	42 – 50 watts
Architectural Design	Core Technology	OOO and Speculative Execution RISC
	Register Support	Integer = 32 bit
		Floating-Point = 80 bit
		MM = 64 bit
	Execution Units	3 x IEU
		3 x AGU
		3 x FP
	Data Bus Width	64 (+8) bit
	Max Memory Support	Physical = 16 Gigabyte
		Virtual = 64 Terabyte
	Multi-Processor Support	SMP via EV6 Bus
	Level 1 Code Cache	64 KB 2-way
	Level 1 Data Cache	64 KB 2-way
	Level 2 Cache	512 KB Inclusive
	Pre-fetch Queue	16 Byte
	Static Branch Prediction	Supported

(continued on next page)

Table 7-1: Athlon K7 Specifications (continued)

Processor Family	Model Name	AMD Athlon K7
	Dynamic Branch Prediction	2048 Entry
	RSB Branch Prediction	12 Entry
	Floating-Point Processor	Integrated
	Multimedia Extensions	MMX, 3DNow!, Extended 3DNow!

Athlon K7 500

Table 7-2: Athlon K7 500 Specifications

Processor Family	Model Name	AMD Athlon K7
	Performance Rating	500 MHz
	Front-side Bus Speed	100 MHz (200 DDR)
	Multiplier Ratio	5.0x
Physical Design	Interface Packing	242-Pin Slot A Cartridge
	Core Die Size	.25 micron, 184 mm
	Transistor Count	22 Million
	Voltage Interface	Split Core and I/O
	Core Voltage	1.6 volts
	Power Consumption	38 watts
	Maximum Power	42 watts

Table 7-3: Athlon K7 500 Overclocking

Athlon K7	Model Rating	500 MHz
Overclocking Potential	Multiplier Lock Support	Unlocked Multiplier via External GFD
	Typical Multiplier O/C	5.5 – 7.0x
	Typical Front-side Bus O/C	103 – 108 MHz
	Typical O/C Potential	600 – 650 MHz
	Maximum O/C Potential	700 – 750 MHz
Overclocking Tolerances	Recommended Cooling Type	Forced-Air Heatsink
	Recommended Heatsink Coolers	GlobalWin VOS-32 Alpha P7125
	Recommended Peltier Active Cooler	Swifttech MC1501
	Maximum Core Voltage	1.85 volts with Heatsink Cooler
	Maximum Core Temperature	70° Celsius

Strategy

AMD entered the high-performance computing marketplace, a segment traditionally controlled by Intel, with the Athlon K7 500 processor. Built by a .25-micron fabrication process, the original K7 offers only modest overclocking scalability compared to later designs. Maximum scalability for the entire K7 series falls in the 750 to 850 MHz range, with the occasional unit offering slightly improved potential with extreme cooling.

The K7's power demand always attracts attention. Though it runs at 500 MHz, this unit demands 42 watts at peak operation. Cooling is thus a big concern. The factory heatsink is well designed, but any attempts at overclocking should include the use of a quality aftermarket forced-air heatsink. Average scalability for this speed grade falls in the 600 to 650 MHz range.

Athlon K7 550

Table 7-4: Athlon K7 550 Specifications

Processor Family	Model Name	AMD Athlon K7
	Performance Rating	550 MHz
	Front-side Bus Speed	100 MHz (200 DDR)
	Multiplier Ratio	5.5x
Physical Design	Interface Packing	242-Pin Slot A Cartridge
	Core Die Size	.25 micron, 184 mm
	Transistor Count	22 Million
	Voltage Interface	Split Core and I/O
	Core Voltage	1.6 volts
	Power Consumption	41 watts
	Maximum Power	46 watts

Table 7-5: Athlon K7 550 Overclocking

Athlon K7	Model Rating	550 MHz
Overclocking Potential	Multiplier Lock Support	Unlocked Multiplier via External GFD
	Typical Multiplier O/C	6.0 – 7.5x
	Typical Front-side Bus O/C	103 – 108 MHz
	Typical O/C Potential	600 – 700 MHz
	Maximum O/C Potential	~ 750 MHz
Overclocking Tolerances	Recommended Cooling Type	Forced-Air Heatsink
	Recommended Heatsink Coolers	GlobalWin VOS-32 Alpha P7125
	Recommended Peltier Active Cooler	Swifttech MC15
	Maximum Core Voltage	1.85 volts with Heatsink Cooler
	Maximum Core Temperature	70° Celsius

Strategy

The K7 550 MHz processor further extends the power threshold with a 46-watt peak power demand. As with any K7 chip, cooling is a concern. A quality aftermarket cooler should be installed before you attempt any overclocking beyond 50 MHz, especially when you are bumping core voltages beyond 1.8 volts. Average overclocking for the K7 500 is in the 600 to 700 MHz range.

Athlon K7 600

Table 7-6: Athlon K7 600 Specifications

Processor Family	Model Name	AMD Athlon K7
	Performance Rating	600 MHz
	Front-side Bus Speed	100 MHz (200 DDR)
	Multiplier Ratio	6.0x
Physical Design	Interface Packing	242-Pin Slot A Cartridge
	Core Die Size	.25 micron, 184 mm
	Transistor Count	22 Million
	Voltage Interface	Split Core and I/O
	Core Voltage	1.6 volts
	Power Consumption	45 watts
	Maximum Power	50 watts

Table 7-7: Athlon K7 600 Overclocking

Athlon K7	Model Rating	600 MHz
Overclocking Potential	Multiplier Lock Support	Unlocked Multiplier via External GFD
	Typical Multiplier O/C	6.5 – 7.5x
	Typical Front-side Bus O/C	103 – 108 MHz
	Typical O/C Potential	650 – 700 MHz
	Maximum O/C Potential	~ 750 MHz
Overclocking Tolerances	Recommended Cooling Type	Forced-Air Heatsink
	Recommended Heatsink Coolers	GlobalWin VOS-32 Alpha P7125
	Recommended Peltier Active Cooler	Swifttech MC1501
	Maximum Core Voltage	1.85 volts with Heatsink Cooler
	Maximum Core Temperature	70° Celsius

Strategy

The K7 600 begins to show the limitations inherent in a .25-micron processor. The peak power demands jump to 50 watts, which is incredibly high for a 600-MHz processor, especially when compared to 34.5 watts for the Intel Pentium III 600 MHz, also a .25-micron based product. Scalability starts to decrease compared to earlier Athlon units, as the K7 600 reaches maximum potential around 700 to 750 MHz.

Athlon K7 650

Table 7-7: Athlon K7 650 Specifications

Processor Family	Model Name	AMD Athlon K7
	Performance Rating	650 MHz
	Front-side Bus Speed	100 MHz (200 DDR)
	Multiplier Ratio	6.5x
Physical Design	Interface Packing	242-Pin Slot A Cartridge
	Core Die Size	.25 micron, 184 mm
	Transistor Count	22 Million
	Voltage Interface	Split Core and I/O
	Core Voltage	1.6 volts
	Power Consumption	48 watts
	Maximum Power	54 watts

Table 7-8: Athlon K7 650 Overclocking

Athlon K7	Model Rating	650 MHz
Overclocking Potential	Multiplier Lock Support	Unlocked Multiplier via External GFD
	Typical Multiplier O/C	7.0 – 7.5x
	Typical Front-side Bus O/C	103 – 108 MHz
	Typical O/C Potential	700 – 750 MHz
	Maximum O/C Potential	750+ MHz
Overclocking Tolerances	Recommended Cooling Type	Forced-Air Heatsink
	Recommended Heatsink Coolers	GlobalWin VOS-32 Alpha P7125
	Recommended Peltier Active Cooler	Swifttech MC1501
	Maximum Core Voltage	1.85 volts with Heatsink Cooler
	Maximum Core Temperature	70° Celsius

Strategy

The Athlon K7 650 MHz processor starts the downslide in effective per-MHz overclocking. Expect maximum returns in the 700 to 750 MHz range, even when applying maximum core voltage and the best heatsink cooler. The .25-micron core architecture was nearing its maximum potential for the Athlon when the K7 650 was produced. AMD introduced only one more speed grade before shifting to the .18-micron core fabrication process.

Athlon K7 700

Table 7-9: Athlon K7 700 Specifications

Processor Family	Model Name	AMD Athlon K7
	Performance Rating	700 MHz
	Front-side Bus Speed	100 MHz (200 DDR)
	Multiplier Ratio	7.0x
Physical Design	Interface Packing	242-Pin Slot A Cartridge
	Core Die Size	.25 micron, 184 mm
	Transistor Count	22 Million
	Voltage Interface	Split Core and I/O
	Core Voltage	1.6 volts
	Power Consumption	38 watts
	Maximum Power	42 watts

Table 7-10: Athlon K7 700 Overclocking

Athlon K7	Model Rating	700 MHz
Overclocking Potential	Multiplier Lock Support	Unlocked Multiplier via External GFD
	Typical Multiplier O/C	7.5x – 8.0x
	Typical Front-side Bus O/C	103 – 108 MHz
	Typical O/C Potential	750 – 800 MHz
	Maximum O/C Potential	~ 800 MHz
Overclocking Tolerances	Recommended Cooling Type	Forced-Air Heatsink
	Recommended Heatsink Coolers	GlobalWin VOS-32 Alpha P7125
	Recommended Peltier Active Cooler	Swifttech MC1501
	Maximum Core Voltage	1.85 volts with Heatsink Cooler
	Maximum Core Temperature	70° Celsius

Strategy

Oddly enough, the Athlon K7 700 MHz requires slightly less wattage than its 650-MHz counterpart. The revision of the core allowed for slightly improved scalability, with overclocking returns approaching 800 MHz for many units. While not overly impressive in per-MHz scalability, the K7 700 does represent the highest possible overclock (850+ MHz potential) of any .25-micron processor ever manufactured.

Athlon K75 Background

AMD required a new idea as Intel rapidly moved its Pentium III architecture to a .18-micron fabrication process. The solution arrived in the form of the Athlon K75 processor. While nearly identical to the original Athlon, the K75 extended operating frequencies by implementing .18-micron core trace routes. While higher clock ratings are possible, K75 models remain functionally identical to the first-generation Athlon processors.

Table 7-11: Athlon K75 Specifications

Processor Family	Model Name	AMD Athlon K75
	Performance Rating	550 – 1000 MHz
	Generation	Seventh: 80686 IA-32
Operational Rates	L1 Cache Speed	1.0x Core Rate
	L2 Cache Speed	Fraction of Core Rate
		1/2.0x, 1/2.5x, 1/3.0x
	Front-side Bus Speed	100 MHz (200 DDR)
	Multiplier Ratio	5.5x – 10.0+x (14x maximum)
Physical Design	Interface Packing	242-Pin Slot A Cartridge
	Core Die Size	.18 micron, 102 mm
	Transistor Count	22 Million
	Voltage Interface	Split Core and I/O
	Core Voltage	1.6 volts
	L2 Cache Voltage	2.8 – 3.3 volts
	Power Consumption	28 – 60 watts
	Maximum Power	31 – 65 watts
Architectural Design	Core Technology	OOO and Speculative Execution RISC
	Register Support	Integer = 32 bit
		Floating-Point = 80 bit
		MM = 64 bit
	Execution Units	3 x IEU
		3 x AGU
		3 x FP
	Max Execution Rate	5 Micro-Ops per Cycle
	Data Bus Width	64 bit
	Max Memory Support	Physical = 16 Gigabyte
		Virtual = 64 Terabyte
	Multi-Processor Support	SMP via EV6 Bus
	Level 1 Code Cache	64 KB 2-way
	Level 1 Data Cache	64 KB 2-way
	Level 2 Cache	512 KB Inclusive
	Pre-fetch Queue	16 Byte
	Static Branch Prediction	Supported
	Dynamic Branch Prediction	2048 Entry
	RSB Branch Prediction	12 Entry
	Floating-Point Processor	Integrated
	Multimedia Extensions	MMX, 3DNow!, Extended 3DNow!

Athlon K75 550

Table 7-12: Athlon K75 550 Specifications

Processor Family	Model Name	AMD Athlon K75
	Performance Rating	550 MHz
	Front-side Bus Speed	100 MHz (200 DDR)
	Multiplier Ratio	5.5x
Physical Design	Interface Packing	242-Pin Slot A Cartridge
	Core Die Size	.18 micron, 102 mm
	Transistor Count	22 Million
	Voltage Interface	Split Core and I/O
	Core Voltage	1.6 volts
	Power Consumption	28 watts
	Maximum Power	31 watts

Table 7-13: Athlon K75 550 Overclocking

Athlon K75	Model Rating	550 MHz
Overclocking Potential	Multiplier Lock Support	Unlocked Multiplier via External GFD
	Typical Multiplier O/C	6.5x – 7.5+x
	Typical Front-side Bus O/C	103 – 108+ MHz
	Typical O/C Potential	650 – 750 MHz
	Maximum O/C Potential	750 – 800 MHz
Overclocking Tolerances	Recommended Cooling Type	Forced-Air Heatsink
	Recommended Heatsink Coolers	GlobalWin VOS-32 Alpha P7125
	Recommended Peltier Active Cooler	Swifttech MC1501
	Maximum Core Voltage	1.85 volts with Heatsink Cooler
	Maximum Core Temperature	70° Celsius

Strategy

The Athlon K75 550 fairs better than its original K7 counterpart. The newly redesigned .18-micron core requires less than 60% of the wattage demanded by the .25-micron design. Overclocking potential is similarly affected, with potential returns up to 800 MHz for the best chips. Note that the K75 retains a relatively low 70° Celsius maximum core temperature; thus cooling remains an important concern. The factory heatsink should prove adequate for an additional 50 to 100 MHz, but will fail to provide the cooling needed for stability at higher overclocking ranges.

Athlon K75 600

Table 7-14: Athlon K75 600 Specifications

Processor Family	Model Name	AMD Athlon K75
	Performance Rating	600 MHz
	Front-side Bus Speed	100 MHz (200 DDR)
	Multiplier Ratio	6.0x
Physical Design	Interface Packing	242-Pin Slot A Cartridge
	Core Die Size	.18 micron, 102 mm
	Transistor Count	22 Million
	Voltage Interface	Split Core and I/O
	Core Voltage	1.6 volts
	Power Consumption	30 watts
	Maximum Power	34 watts

Table 7-15: Athlon K75 600 Overclocking

Athlon K75	Model Rating	600 MHz
Overclocking Potential	Multiplier Lock Support	Unlocked Multiplier via External GFD
	Typical Multiplier O/C	6.5x – 8.0x
	Typical Front-side Bus O/C	103 – 108+ MHz
	Typical O/C Potential	700 – 800 MHz
	Maximum O/C Potential	800+ MHz
Overclocking Tolerances	Recommended Cooling Type	Forced-Air Heatsink
	Recommended Heatsink Coolers	GlobalWin VOS-32 Alpha P7125
	Recommended Peltier Active Cooler	Swifttech MC1501
	Maximum Core Voltage	1.85 volts with Heatsink Cooler
	Maximum Core Temperature	70° Celsius

Strategy

The K75 600 MHz processor proves the effective scalability of the .18-micron process. The power demands are only a few percent above those for the K7 550. This is an excellent chip to overclock, and you can expect overclocking returns approaching 800 MHz.

Athlon K75 650

Table 7-16: Athlon K75 650 Specifications

Processor Family	Model Name	AMD Athlon K75
	Performance Rating	650 MHz
	Front-side Bus Speed	100 MHz (200 DDR)
	Multiplier Ratio	6.5x
Physical Design	Interface Packing	242-Pin Slot A Cartridge
	Core Die Size	.18 micron, 102 mm
	Transistor Count	22 Million
	Voltage Interface	Split Core and I/O
	Core Voltage	1.6 volts
	Power Consumption	32 watts
	Maximum Power	46 watts

Table 7-17: Athlon K75 650 Overclocking

Athlon K75	Model Rating	650 MHz
Overclocking Potential	Multiplier Lock Support	Unlocked Multiplier via External GFD
	Typical Multiplier O/C	7.5x – 8.5x
	Typical Front-side Bus O/C	103 – 108+ MHz
	Typical O/C Potential	700 – 800 MHz
	Maximum O/C Potential	850+ MHz
Overclocking Tolerances	Recommended Cooling Type	Forced-Air Heatsink
	Recommended Heatsink Coolers	GlobalWin VOS-32 Alpha P7125
	Recommended Peltier Active Cooler	Swifttech MC1501
	Maximum Core Voltage	1.85 volts with Heatsink Cooler
	Maximum Core Temperature	70° Celsius

Strategy

The Athlon K75 650-MHz processor offers an attractive solution for overclocking beyond 800 MHz. Most units from this K75 speed grade offer effective scalability to 200 MHz beyond factory settings, when using an external GFD overclocking device to manipulate the internal processor multiplier values. The Level 2 cache divider may also require adjustment for reaching 800 MHz and beyond, so a quality GFD can make the difference with this processor.

Athlon K75 700

Table 7-18: Athlon K75 700 Specifications

Processor Family	Model Name	AMD Athlon K75
	Performance Rating	700 MHz
	Front-side Bus Speed	100 MHz (200 DDR)
	Multiplier Ratio	7.0x
Physical Design	Interface Packing	242-Pin Slot A Cartridge
	Core Die Size	.18 micron, 102 mm
	Transistor Count	22 Million
	Voltage Interface	Split Core and I/O
	Core Voltage	1.6 volts
	Power Consumption	34 watts
	Maximum Power	39 watts

Table 7-19: Athlon K75 700 Overclocking

Athlon K75	Model Rating	700 MHz
Overclocking Potential	Multiplier Lock Support	Unlocked Multiplier via External GFD
	Typical Multiplier O/C	7.5x – 8.5x
	Typical Front-side Bus O/C	103 – 108+ MHz
	Typical O/C Potential	750 – 850 MHz
	Maximum O/C Potential	~ 900 MHz
Overclocking Tolerances	Recommended Cooling Type	Forced-Air Heatsink
	Recommended Heatsink Coolers	GlobalWin VOS-32 Alpha P7125
	Recommended Peltier Active Cooler	Swifttech MC1501
	Maximum Core Voltage	1.85 volts with Heatsink Cooler
	Maximum Core Temperature	70° Celsius

Strategy

The K75 700-MHz processor represents the first good chance of scaling to 900 MHz with the Athlon architecture. This processor offers an opportunity for overclocking, but only with the introduction of a good forced-air heatsink cooler. Nominal returns with factory cooling are often in the 750 to 800 MHz range, with the best units scaling beyond 900 MHz, given a quality aftermarket cooler.

Athlon K75 750

Table 7-20: Athlon K75 750 Specifications

Processor Family	Model Name	AMD Athlon K7
	Performance Rating	750 MHz
	Front-side Bus Speed	100 MHz (200 DDR)
	Multiplier Ratio	7.5x
Physical Design	Interface Packing	242-Pin Slot A Cartridge
	Core Die Size	.18 micron, 102 mm
	Transistor Count	22 Million
	Voltage Interface	Split Core and I/O
	Core Voltage	1.6 volts
	Power Consumption	35 watts
	Maximum Power	40 watts

Table 7-21: Athlon K75 750 Overclocking

Athlon K75	Model Rating	750 MHz
Overclocking Potential	Multiplier Lock Support	Unlocked Multiplier via External GFD
	Typical Multiplier O/C	8.0x – 9.0x
	Typical Front-side Bus O/C	103 – 108+ MHz
	Typical O/C Potential	800 – 900 MHz
	Maximum O/C Potential	950 MHz
Overclocking Tolerances	Recommended Cooling Type	Forced-Air Heatsink
	Recommended Heatsink Coolers	GlobalWin VOS-32 Alpha P7125
	Recommended Peltier Active Cooler	Swifttech MC1501
	Maximum Core Voltage	1.85 volts with Heatsink Cooler
	Maximum Core Temperature	70° Celsius

Strategy

The Athlon K75 750 offers a decent possibility of reaching upwards of 1000 MHz with the use of Peltier or liquid-based cooling technologies. Traditional cooling can net returns exceeding 900 MHz with little effort beyond the installation of a replacement forced-air heatsink. Operating temperatures need to be monitored closely at speeds approaching 1 GHz. Even the efficient .18-micron Athlon core can produce high thermal loads at this level.

Athlon K75 800

Table 7-22: Athlon K75 800 Specifications

Processor Family	Model Name	AMD Athlon K75
	Performance Rating	800 MHz
	Front-side Bus Speed	100 MHz (200 DDR)
	Multiplier Ratio	8.0x
Physical Design	Interface Packing	242-Pin Slot A Cartridge
	Core Die Size	.18 micron, 102 mm
	Transistor Count	22 Million
	Voltage Interface	Split Core and I/O
	Core Voltage	1.6 volts
	Power Consumption	43 watts
	Maximum Power	48 watts

Table 7-23: Athlon K75 800 Overclocking

Athlon K75	Model Rating	800 MHz
Overclocking Potential	Multiplier Lock Support	Unlocked Multiplier via External GFD
	Typical Multiplier O/C	8.5x – 9.5x
	Typical Front-side Bus O/C	103 – 108+ MHz
	Typical O/C Potential	850 – 950 MHz
	Maximum O/C Potential	1000+ MHz
Overclocking Tolerances	Recommended Cooling Type	Forced-Air Heatsink
	Recommended Heatsink Coolers	GlobalWin VOS-32 Alpha P7125
	Recommended Peltier Active Cooler	Swifttech MC1501
	Maximum Core Voltage	1.85 volts with Heatsink Cooler
	Maximum Core Temperature	70° Celsius

Strategy

Notice the major change in wattage requirements for the K75 800 at default settings compared to its 750 MHz sibling. With a peak power demand of 48 watts, this processor can produce extreme heat at its factory set speed. Accordingly, a quality heatsink should be installed before attempting an overclock. Expect returns in the 900 to 1000 MHz range with traditional forced-air heatsink coolers.

Athlon K75 850

Table 7-24: Athlon K75 850 Specifications

Processor Family	Model Name	AMD Athlon K75
	Performance Rating	850 MHz
	Front-side Bus Speed	100 MHz (200 DDR)
	Multiplier Ratio	8.5x
Physical Design	Interface Packing	242-Pin Slot A Cartridge
	Core Die Size	.18 micron, 102 mm
	Transistor Count	22 Million
	Voltage Interface	Split Core and I/O
	Core Voltage	1.6 volts
	Power Consumption	45 watts
	Maximum Power	50 watts

Table 7-25: Athlon K75 850 Overclocking

Athlon K75	Model Rating	850 MHz
Overclocking Potential	Multiplier Lock Support	Unlocked Multiplier via External GFD
	Typical Multiplier O/C	9.0x – 10.0x
	Typical Front-side Bus O/C	103 – 108+ MHz
	Typical O/C Potential	900 – 1000 MHz
	Maximum O/C Potential	1000+ MHz
Overclocking Tolerances	Recommended Cooling Type	Forced-Air Heatsink
	Recommended Heatsink Coolers	GlobalWin VOS-32 Alpha P7125
	Recommended Peltier Active Cooler	Swifttech MC1501
	Maximum Core Voltage	1.85 volts with Heatsink Cooler
	Maximum Core Temperature	70° Celsius

Strategy

The Athlon K75 850-MHz processor represents the turning point in this series toward per-MHz overclocking scalability. Returns diminish at speeds beyond this range, with most peaking in the 1000 to 1100 MHz range. Wattage requirements also increase for each additional speed grade; thus cooling is a dominant concern for these higher-end chips. Expect returns upwards of 1000 MHz.

Athlon K75 900

Table 7-26: Athlon K75 900 Specifications

Processor Family	Model Name	AMD Athlon K75
	Performance Rating	900 MHz
	Front-side Bus Speed	100 MHz (200 DDR)
	Multiplier Ratio	9.0x
Physical Design	Interface Packing	242-Pin Slot A Cartridge
	Core Die Size	.18 micron, 102 mm
	Transistor Count	22 Million
	Voltage Interface	Split Core and I/O
	Core Voltage	1.6 volts
	Power Consumption	53 watts
	Maximum Power	60 watts

Table 7-27: Athlon K75 Overclocking

Athlon K75	Model Rating	900 MHz
Overclocking Potential	Multiplier Lock Support	Unlocked Multiplier via External GFD
	Typical Multiplier O/C	9.5x – 10.0+x
	Typical front-side Bus O/C	103 – 108+ MHz
	Typical O/C Potential	950 – 1000 MHz
	Maximum O/C Potential	1000+ MHz
Overclocking Tolerances	Recommended Cooling Type	Forced-Air Heatsink
	Recommended Heatsink Coolers	GlobalWin VOS-32 Alpha P7125
	Recommended Peltier Active Cooler	Swifttech MC1501
	Maximum Core Voltage	1.85 volts with Heatsink Cooler
	Maximum Core Temperature	70° Celsius

Strategy

Per-MHz overclocking returns quickly recede as the K75 core approaches the gigahertz level. The Athlon K75 900 proves this rule, as most units from this speed grade will peak around 1000 MHz. Overclocking returns can scale upwards to the 1050 to 1000 MHz range for those willing to undertake more radical cooling procedures.

Athlon K75 950

Table 7-28: Athlon K75 950 Specifications

Processor Family	Model Name	AMD Athlon K75
	Performance Rating	950 MHz
	Front-side Bus Speed	100 MHz (200 DDR)
	Multiplier Ratio	9.5x
Physical Design	Interface Packing	242-Pin Slot A Cartridge
	Core Die Size	.18 micron, 102 mm
	Transistor Count	22 Million
	Voltage Interface	Split Core and I/O
	Core Voltage	1.6 volts
	Power Consumption	55 watts
	Maximum Power	62 watts

Table 7-29: Athlon K75 950 Overclocking

Athlon K75	Model Rating	950 MHz
Overclocking Potential	Multiplier Lock Support	Unlocked Multiplier via External GFD
	Typical Multiplier O/C	10.0x – 10.5x
	Typical Front-side Bus O/C	103 – 108+ MHz
	Typical O/C Potential	1000 – 1050 MHz
	Maximum O/C Potential	1050+ MHz
Overclocking Tolerances	Recommended Cooling Type	Forced-Air Heatsink
	Recommended Heatsink Coolers	GlobalWin VOS-32 Alpha P7125
	Recommended Peltier Active Cooler	Swifttech MC1501
	Maximum Core Voltage	1.85 volts with Heatsink Cooler
	Maximum Core Temperature	70° Celsius

Strategy

The Athlon K75 950-MHz processor typifies the tradeoffs inherent at the upper limits of the K75 core. Overclocking potential usually falls in the 1000 to 1050 MHz range with traditional cooling. Radical cooling and heavy tweaking can sometimes yield more than 1100 MHz, but the costs involved in reaching such a goal are often prohibitive.

Athlon K75 1000

Table 7-30: Athlon K75 1000 Specifications

Processor Family	Model Name	AMD Athlon K75
	Performance Rating	500 MHz
	Front-side Bus Speed	100 MHz (200 DDR)
	Multiplier Ratio	10.0x
Physical Design	Interface Packing	242-Pin Slot A Cartridge
	Core Die Size	.18 micron, 102 mm
	Transistor Count	22 Million
	Voltage Interface	Split Core and I/O
	Core Voltage	1.6 volts
	Power Consumption	60 watts
	Maximum Power	65 watts

Table 7-31: Athlon K75 1000 Overclocking

Athlon K7	Model Rating	1000 MHz
Overclocking Potential	Multiplier Lock Support	Unlocked Multiplier via External GFD
	Typical Multiplier O/C	10.5x – 11.0+x
	Typical Front-side Bus O/C	103 – 108+ MHz
	Typical O/C Potential	1050 – 1100 MHz
	Maximum O/C Potential	1100+ MHz
Overclocking Tolerances	Recommended Cooling Type	Forced-Air Heatsink
	Recommended Heatsink Coolers	GlobalWin VOS-32 Alpha P7125
	Recommended Peltier Active Cooler	Swifttech MC1501
	Maximum Core Voltage	1.85 volts with Heatsink Cooler
	Maximum Core Temperature	70° Celsius

Strategy

The Athlon K75 series comes to an end at 1000 MHz. Impressive in raw performance, this processor has only mild overclocking potential. Most units will reach 1100 MHz with quality cooling, but only a small percentage of chips will ever approach 1200 MHz. Note that this chip requires 65 watts at its default speed, so only the best heatsink cooler should be considered for overclocking.

Athlon Thunderbird

Realizing scalability beyond 1000 MHz would be problematic, AMD opted to integrate the Level 2 cache memory in the processor core for the Athlon Thunderbird. Actual memory size was halved to 256 kilobytes, but the internal cache operates at the core frequency rate. The increase in bandwidth and decrease in latency improved performance dramatically compared to the old Athlon K7.

The Thunderbird also represented AMD's first socket-type processor-to-motherboard interface since the K6. The move toward a socket interconnect ended the Athlon's original Slot A interface, though a few Slot A Thunderbirds did enter the market before the standard was completely abandoned. The Socket A format was welcomed by overclocking enthusiasts, because it ended the need to disassemble slot processors to add boards or coolers.

The Athlon Thunderbird and its successors have become the processors of choice for most overclocking enthusiasts. The Socket A interface allows easy installation of large forced-air heatsink coolers. The Thunderbird also heralded a batch of overclocking-friendly motherboard designs once unavailable to AMD supporters. Most importantly, GFDs were replaced by jumpers, dipswitches, and BIOS settings.

Unlocking the Athlon Thunderbird

The Thunderbird architecture is an overclocking paradise for those with a motherboard that supports multiplier configuration. The Athlon remains an unlocked processor, though AMD has tried to lock its Socket A chips. Most of today's Thunderbird processors ship with no multiplier locking mechanism, while many of the earlier models require a modest amount of work to bypass the AMD locking technique.

Unlocking Thunderbird chips of the Socket A variety requires reconnecting a series of trace routes along the topside of the processor substrate. These tiny bridge connections were severed by a laser, which locked the multiplier. Luckily, AMD has stopped making such cuts because the company feared increasing processor failure rates due to the heat and stress associated with the laser-cutting process.

L1 Bridge Circuit

Figure 7-1: Athlon Thunderbird L1 bridge circuit

Reconnecting the L1 trace routes is a relatively minor operation. The routes must be connected using a conductive transfer medium. Some vendors, such as HighspeedPC.com, offer a specialized adhesive tape with tiny metal strips already embedded at the required connection points. This may offer the simplest solution.

Another quick fix is simply to redraw the bridge connections with a regular number-2 pencil. Each point of the circuit must be connected to the point directly across from it, creating a series of parallel lines. Lead pencils should be avoided. A standard wooden pencil with a finely sharpened tip works best. Sharpen the lead with sandpaper first to insure accuracy. Some hardcore enthusiasts may opt to use a silver-fluid compound instead, but be warned this often creates a permanent connection. The pencil trick is preferred because the marks can easily be erased if something goes wrong during the unlocking procedure.

Each of the L1 circuit pathways must be connected using a straight-line approach. Take great care to ensure that each pencil mark connects the intended circuit points with no overlapping of any lines. An overlapped line can cause a short circuit and consequent unusual results or even processor failure. Examine each pencil line, once it is drawn, under a magnifying glass.

Successful pencil modification allows unrestricted multiplier manipulation. Partial or no success is common on the first try. A less-than-perfect redrawing usually results in allowable multiplier manipulation in the .5 to 1x range. Erasing and redrawing the lines can fix such problems.

Once unlocked, the Thunderbird offers standard multiplier options from 5 to 12.5x, in .5x increments. Some motherboards allow 13x and possibly 13.5 to 14x multipliers, though these cause problems for most Thunderbird models. AMD does produce a 14x Thunderbird, but the multiplier is configured internally through the regular autodetection routine.

The Athlon Thunderbird fares much better for processor-to-chipset bus overclocking compared to its older Slot 1 K7 sibling. Most early Socket A chipsets can successfully reach the 115 to 120 MHz range (230 to 240 DDR). The latest generation offers scalability to 166 MHz and beyond. Most manufacturers now equip their Athlon motherboards with active chipset cooling, as thermal regulation is necessary to maintain stability when overclocking.

Another excellent way to maximize performance of 100-MHz Thunderbird models is to lower the internal multiplier, and then raise the processor bus to 133 MHz. The Athlon is a bandwidth-intensive design that can benefit from processor bus overclocking. All the latest chipsets from ALI, SIS, and VIA allow 133-MHz processor bus support.

Athlon Thunderbird Overclocking

Table 7-32: Athlon Thunderbird Specifications

Processor Family	Model Name	AMD Athlon Thunderbird
	Performance Rating	650 – 1400 MHz
	Generation	Seventh: 80686 IA-32
Operational Rates	L1 Cache Speed	1.0x Core Rate
	L2 Cache Speed	1.0x Core Rate
	Front-side Bus Speed	100 MHz (200 DDR)
	Multiplier Ratio	6.0x – 14.0x
Physical Design	Interface Packing	462-Pin Socket A
		242-Pin Slot A Cartridge
	Core Die Size	.18 micron, 102 mm
	Transistor Count	37 Million
	Voltage Interface	Split Core and I/O
	Core Voltage	Socket A = 1.75 volts
		Slot A = 1.6 volts
	Power Consumption	32.4 – 65 watts
	Maximum Power	36.1 – 72 watts
Architectural Design	Core Technology	OOO and Speculative Execution RISC
	Register Support	Integer = 32 bit
		Floating-Point = 80 bit
		MM = 64 bit
	Execution Units	3 x IEU
		3 x AGU
		3 x FP
	Data Bus Width	64 (+8) bit
	Max Memory Support	Physical = 16 Gigabyte
		Virtual = 64 Terabyte
	Multi-Processor Support	SMP via EV6 Bus
	Level 1 Code Cache	64 KB 2-way
	Level 1 Data Cache	64 KB 2-way
	Level 2 Cache	256 KB Inclusive
	Pre-fetch Queue	16 Byte
	Static Branch Prediction	Supported
	Dynamic Branch Prediction	2048 Entry
	RSB Branch Prediction	12 Entry
	Floating-Point Processor	Integrated
	Multimedia Extensions	MMX, 3DNow!, Extended 3DNow!

Athlon Thunderbird 650

Table 7-33: Athlon Thunderbird 650 Specifications

Processor Family	Model Name	AMD Athlon Thunderbird
	Performance Rating	650 MHz
	Front-side Bus Speed	100 MHz (200 DDR)
	Multiplier Ratio	6.5x
Physical Design	Interface Packing	462-Pin Socket A
		242-Pin Slot A Cartridge
	Core Die Size	.18 micron, 120 mm
	Transistor Count	37 Million
	Voltage Interface	Split Core and I/O
	Core Voltage	Socket A = 1.75 volts
		Slot A = 1.6 volts
	Power Consumption	32.4 watts
	Maximum Power	36.1 watts

Table 7-34: Athlon Thunderbird 650 Overclocking

Athlon Thunderbird	Model Rating	650 MHz
Overclocking Potential	Multiplier Lock Support	Unlocked Multiplier
	Typical Multiplier O/C	7.5x – 8.0x
	Typical Front-side Bus O/C	103 – 115+ MHz
	Typical O/C Potential	750 – 800 MHz
	Maximum O/C Potential	850+ MHz
Overclocking Tolerances	Recommended Cooling Type	Forced-Air Heatsink
	Recommended Heatsink Coolers	Thermalright SK-6
		Alpha PAL-8045
		TaiSol CGK742092
		GlobalWin VOS-32
		Alpha P7125
	Recommended Peltier Active Cooler	Swifttech MCX370
		Swifttech MC1501
	Maximum Core Voltage	1.85 volts with Heatsink Cooler
	Maximum Core Temperature	Socket A = 90° Celsius
		Slot A = 70° Celsius

Strategy

The Thunderbird specifications reveal clear advantages to the Socket A interface. The Socket A format can withstand an additional 20° Celsius compared to the same Thunderbird Slot A processor. The Slot A Thunderbird does hold a slight advantage in voltage efficiency, but 1.6 volts were required by AMD to support existing slot-type motherboards.

The Athlon Thunderbird 650-MHz processor is a relative oddity in the industry, as only a small number escaped AMD fabrication facilities. AMD produced two variants of the Socket A version of this chip: one at 1.7 volts and another at 1.75 volts. Demand for this speed grade was small, as AMD already offered more powerful K75 Slot A designs. Those who possess this early revision Thunderbird processor can expect overclocking returns up to 800 MHz under good cooling conditions.

Athlon Thunderbird 700

Table 7-35: Athlon Thunderbird 700 Specifications

Processor Family	Model Name	AMD Athlon Thunderbird
	Performance Rating	700 MHz
	Front-side Bus Speed	100 MHz (200 DDR)
	Multiplier Ratio	7.0x
Physical Design	Interface Packing	462-Pin Socket A
		242-Pin Slot A Cartridge
	Core Die Size	.18 micron, 120 mm
	Transistor Count	37 Million
	Voltage Interface	Split Core and I/O
	Core Voltage	Socket A = 1.75 volts
		Slot A = 1.6 volts
	Power Consumption	34.4 watts
	Maximum Power	38.3 watts

Table 7-36: Athlon Thunderbird 700 Overclocking

Athlon Thunderbird	Model Rating	700 MHz
Overclocking Potential	Multiplier Lock Support	Unlocked Multiplier
	Typical Multiplier O/C	7.5x – 8.0x
	Typical Front-side Bus O/C	103 – 115+ MHz
	Typical O/C Potential	750 – 800 MHz
	Maximum O/C Potential	850+ MHz
Overclocking Tolerances	Recommended Cooling Type	Forced-Air Heatsink
	Recommended Heatsink Coolers	Thermalright SK-6
		Alpha PAL-8045
		TaiSol CGK742092
		GlobalWin VOS-32
		Alpha P7125
	Recommended Peltier Active Cooler	Swifttech MCX370
		Swifttech MC1501
	Maximum Core Voltage	1.85 volts with Heatsink Cooler
	Maximum Core Temperature	Socket A = 90° Celsius
		Slot A = 70° Celsius

Strategy

The Athlon Thunderbird 700 shares much in common with its 650-MHz sibling. This processor was available in limited quantities, and this speed grade was never officially launched by AMD. Overclocking returns are in line with expectations for the Thunderbird 650.

Athlon Thunderbird 750

Table 7-37: Athlon Thunderbird 750 Specifications

Processor Family	Model Name	AMD Athlon Thunderbird
	Performance Rating	750 MHz
	Front-side Bus Speed	100 MHz (200 DDR)
	Multiplier Ratio	7.5x
Physical Design	Interface Packing	462-Pin Socket A
		242-Pin Slot A Cartridge
	Core Die Size	.18 micron, 120 mm
	Transistor Count	37 Million
	Voltage Interface	Split Core and I/O
	Core Voltage	Socket A = 1.75 volts
		Slot A = 1.6 volts
	Power Consumption	36.3 watts
	Maximum Power	40.4 watts

Table 7-38: Athlon Thunderbird 750 Overclocking

Athlon Thunderbird	Model Rating	750 MHz
Overclocking Potential	Multiplier Lock Support	Unlocked Multiplier
	Typical Multiplier O/C	8.5x – 9.0+x
	Typical Front-side Bus O/C	103 – 115+ MHz
	Typical O/C Potential	800 – 900 MHz
	Maximum O/C Potential	900+ MHz
Overclocking Tolerances	Recommended Cooling Type	Forced-Air Heatsink
	Recommended Heatsink Coolers	Thermalright SK-6
		Alpha PAL-8045
		TaiSol CGK742092
		GlobalWin VOS-32
		Alpha P7125
	Recommended Peltier Active Cooler	Swifttech MCX370
		Swifttech MC1501
	Maximum Core Voltage	1.85 volts with Heatsink Cooler
	Maximum Core Temperature	Socket A = 90° Celsius
		Slot A = 70° Celsius
		Gd

Strategy

750 MHz marks the first official entry in the Athlon Thunderbird series of processors. The Thunderbird 750 also represents a great overclocking choice, as this processor can scale beyond 900 MHz with little effort. A small percentage of the Socket A version of this processor can even offer scalability toward 1 gigahertz with good cooling.

Athlon Thunderbird 800

Table 7-39: Athlon Thunderbird 800 Specifications

Processor Family	Model Name	AMD Athlon Thunderbird
	Performance Rating	800 MHz
	Front-side Bus Speed	100 MHz (200 DDR)
	Multiplier Ratio	8.0x
Physical Design	Interface Packing	462-Pin Socket A
		242-Pin Slot A Cartridge
	Core Die Size	.18 micron, 120 mm
	Transistor Count	37 Million
	Voltage Interface	Split Core and I/O
	Core Voltage	Socket A = 1.75 volts
		Slot A = 1.6 volts
	Power Consumption	38.3 watts
	Maximum Power	42.6 watts

Table 7-40: Athlon Thunderbird 800 Overclocking

Athlon Thunderbird	Model Rating	800 MHz
Overclocking Potential	Multiplier Lock Support	Unlocked Multiplier
	Typical Multiplier O/C	8.5x – 9.5x
	Typical Front-side Bus O/C	103 – 115+ MHz
	Typical O/C Potential	850 – 950 MHz
	Maximum O/C Potential	1000+ MHz
Overclocking Tolerances	Recommended Cooling Type	Forced-Air Heatsink
	Recommended Heatsink Coolers	Thermalright SK-6
		Alpha PAL-8045
		TaiSol CGK742092
		GlobalWin VOS-32
		Alpha P7125
	Recommended Peltier Active Cooler	Swifttech MCX370
		Swifttech MC1501
	Maximum Core Voltage	1.85 volts with Heatsink Cooler
	Maximum Core Temperature	Socket A = 90° Celsius
		Slot A = 70° Celsius

Strategy

The Athlon Thunderbird 800-MHz processor offers a real chance of attaining a successful overclock to 1000 MHz. This is especially true for the Socket A version, as it features much-improved thermal efficiency compared to its Slot-A counterpart. In any case, most Thunderbird 800 chips can scale past 900 MHz with little difficulty.

Athlon Thunderbird 850

Table 7-41: Athlon Thunderbird 850 Specifications

Processor Family	Model Name	AMD Athlon Thunderbird
	Performance Rating	850 MHz
	Front-side Bus Speed	100 MHz (200 DDR)
	Multiplier Ratio	8.5x
Physical Design	Interface Packing	462-Pin Socket A
		242-Pin Slot A Cartridge
	Core Die Size	.18 micron, 120 mm
	Transistor Count	37 Million
	Voltage Interface	Split Core and I/O
	Core Voltage	Socket A = 1.75 volts
		Slot A = 1.6 volts
	Power Consumption	40.2 watts
	Maximum Power	44.8 watts

Table 7-42: Athlon Thunderbird 850 Overclocking

Athlon Thunderbird	Model Rating	850 MHz
Overclocking Potential	Multiplier Lock Support	Unlocked Multiplier
	Typical Multiplier O/C	9.0x – 10.0x
	Typical Front-side Bus O/C	103 – 115+ MHz
	Typical O/C Potential	900 – 1000 MHz
	Maximum O/C Potential	1000+ MHz
Overclocking Tolerances	Recommended Cooling Type	Forced-Air Heatsink
	Recommended Heatsink Coolers	Thermalright SK-6
		Alpha PAL-8045
		TaiSol CGK742092
		GlobalWin VOS-32
		Alpha P7125
	Recommended Peltier Active Cooler	Swifttech MCX370
		Swifttech MC1501
	Maximum Core Voltage	1.85 volts with Heatsink Cooler
	Maximum Core Temperature	Socket A = 90° Celsius
		Slot A = 70° Celsius

Strategy

The Athlon Thunderbird 850-MHz processor provides a good chance of reaching one gigahertz with little more than the use of a good heatsink cooler. As expected, the Socket-A version offers the best overclocking potential. For comparison, the Slot-A version should be capable of reaching 950 MHz, often cooled with the factory-installed heatsink.

Athlon Thunderbird 900

Table 7-43: Athlon Thunderbird 900 Specifications

Processor Family	Model Name	AMD Athlon Thunderbird
	Performance Rating	900 MHz
	Front-side Bus Speed	100 MHz (200 DDR)
	Multiplier Ratio	9.0x
Physical Design	Interface Packing	462-Pin Socket A
		242-Pin Slot A Cartridge
	Core Die Size	.18 micron, 120 mm
	Transistor Count	37 Million
	Voltage Interface	Split Core and I/O
	Core Voltage	Socket A = 1.75 volts
		Slot A = 1.6 volts
	Power Consumption	44.6 watts
	Maximum Power	49.7 watts

Table 7-44: Athlon Thunderbird 900 Overclocking

Athlon Thunderbird	Model Rating	900 MHz
Overclocking Potential	Multiplier Lock Support	Unlocked Multiplier
	Typical Multiplier O/C	9.5x – 10.5x
	Typical Front-side Bus O/C	103 – 115+ MHz
	Typical O/C Potential	950 – 1050 MHz
	Maximum O/C Potential	1050+ MHz
Overclocking Tolerances	Recommended Cooling Type	Forced-Air Heatsink
	Recommended Heatsink Coolers	Thermalright SK-6
		Alpha PAL-8045
		TaiSol CGK742092
		GlobalWin VOS-32
		Alpha P7125
	Recommended Peltier Active Cooler	Swifttech MCX370
		Swifttech MC1501
	Maximum Core Voltage	1.85 volts with Heatsink Cooler
	Maximum Core Temperature	Socket A = 90° Celsius
		Slot A = 70° Celsius

Strategy

The Athlon Thunderbird 900-MHz processor almost guarantees 1000 MHz for most configurations. Many chips in this speed grade can scale effectively to the gigahertz level, but most reach their limit around 1100 MHz without extreme cooling.

Athlon Thunderbird 950

Table 7-45: Athlon Thunderbird 950 Specifications

Processor Family	Model Name	AMD Athlon Thunderbird
	Performance Rating	950 MHz
	Front-side Bus Speed	100 MHz (200 DDR)
	Multiplier Ratio	9.5x
Physical Design	Interface Packing	462-Pin Socket A
		242-Pin Slot A Cartridge
	Core Die Size	.18 micron, 120 mm
	Transistor Count	37 Million
	Voltage Interface	Split Core and I/O
	Core Voltage	Socket A = 1.75 volts
		Slot A = 1.6 volts
	Power Consumption	46.7 watts
	Maximum Power	52 watts

Table 7-46: Athlon Thunderbird 950 Overclocking

Athlon Thunderbird	Model Rating	950 MHz
Overclocking Potential	Multiplier Lock Support	Unlocked Multiplier
	Typical Multiplier O/C	10.0x – 11.0x
	Typical Front-side Bus O/C	103 – 115+ MHz
	Typical O/C Potential	1000 – 1100 MHz
	Maximum O/C Potential	1100+ MHz
Overclocking Tolerances	Recommended Cooling Type	Forced-Air Heatsink
	Recommended Heatsink Coolers	Thermalright SK-6
		Alpha PAL-8045
		TaiSol CGK742092
		GlobalWin VOS-32
		Alpha P7125
	Recommended Peltier Active Cooler	Swifttech MCX370
		Swifttech MC1501
	Maximum Core Voltage	1.85 volts with Heatsink Cooler
	Maximum Core Temperature	Socket A = 90° Celsius
		Slot A = 70° Celsius

Strategy

The Athlon Thunderbird 950-MHz processor offers mild overclocking potential. Nearly all chips from this speed grade can reach 1000 MHz with no additional voltage and cooling required. On a less positive note, the Thunderbird 950 offers minimal overclocking headroom in per-MHz analysis. This model was the last model in its particular revision.

Athlon Thunderbird 1000

Table 7-47: Athlon Thunderbird 1000 Specifications

Processor Family	Model Name	AMD Athlon Thunderbird
	Performance Rating	1000 MHz
	Front-side Bus Speed	100 MHz (200 DDR)
	Multiplier Ratio	6.5x
Physical Design	Interface Packing	462-Pin Socket A
		242-Pin Slot A Cartridge
	Core Die Size	.18 micron, 120 mm
	Transistor Count	37 Million
	Voltage Interface	Split Core and I/O
	Core Voltage	Socket A = 1.75 volts
		Slot A = 1.6 volts
	Power Consumption	48.7 watts
	Maximum Power	54.3 watts

Table 7-48: Athlon Thunderbird 1000 Overclocking

Athlon Thunderbird	Model Rating	1000 MHz
Overclocking Potential	Multiplier Lock Support	Unlocked Multiplier
	Typical Multiplier O/C	11.0x – 12.5x
	Typical Front-side Bus O/C	103 – 115+ MHz
	Typical O/C Potential	1100 – 1250 MHz
	Maximum O/C Potential	1250+ MHz
Overclocking Tolerances	Recommended Cooling Type	Forced-Air Heatsink
	Recommended Heatsink Coolers	Thermalright SK-6
		Alpha PAL-8045
		TaiSol CGK742092
		GlobalWin VOS-32
		Alpha P7125
	Recommended Peltier Active Cooler	Swifttech MCX370
		Swifttech MC1501
	Maximum Core Voltage	1.85 volts with Heatsink Cooler
	Maximum Core Temperature	Socket A = 90° Celsius
		Slot A = 70° Celsius

Strategy

The Athlon Thunderbird 1000-MHz processor ushered in a new core revision with greater overclocking potential than previous models. A large percentage of the Socket-A version of this chip can effectively scale past 1200 MHz with the addition of a quality heatsink cooler. A smaller number has reached toward 1400 MHz with extreme cooling. The Thunderbird 1000 is also the last Slot A Athlon to be released.

Athlon Thunderbird 1100

Table 7-49: Athlon Thunderbird 1100 Specifications

Processor Family	Model Name	AMD Athlon Thunderbird
	Performance Rating	1100 MHz
	Front-side Bus Speed	100 MHz (200 DDR)
	Multiplier Ratio	11.0x
Physical Design	Interface Packing	462-Pin Socket A
		242-Pin Slot A Cartridge
	Core Die Size	.18 micron, 120 mm
	Transistor Count	37 Million
	Voltage Interface	Split Core and I/O
	Core Voltage	1.75 volts
	Power Consumption	49.5 watts
	Maximum Power	55.1 watts

Table 7-50: Athlon Thunderbird 1100 Overclocking

Athlon Thunderbird	Model Rating	1100 MHz
Overclocking Potential	Multiplier Lock Support	Unlocked Multiplier
	Typical Multiplier O/C	12.0 – 14.0x
	Typical Front-side Bus O/C	103 – 115+ MHz
	Typical O/C Potential	1200 – 1300 MHz
	Maximum O/C Potential	1300+ MHz
Overclocking Tolerances	Recommended Cooling Type	Forced-Air Heatsink
	Recommended Heatsink Coolers	Thermalright SK-6
		Alpha PAL-8045
		TaiSol CGK742092
	Recommended Peltier Active Cooler	Swifttech MCX370
	Maximum Core Voltage	1.85 volts with Heatsink Cooler
	Maximum Core Temperature	95° Celsius

The Athlon Thunderbird 1100-MHz processor offers significant scalability, especially given the fact that it introduces a new thermal rating of 95° Celsius. Most models from this speed grade offer overclocking potential beyond 1250 MHz. Some rare models are known to reach 1400 MHz, but only after the implementation of quality cooling.

Athlon Thunderbird 1200

Table 7-51: Athlon Thunderbird 1200 Specifications

Processor Family	Model Name	AMD Athlon Thunderbird
	Performance Rating	1200 MHz
	Front-side Bus Speed	100 MHz (200 DDR)
	Multiplier Ratio	12.0x
Physical Design	Interface Packing	462-Pin Socket A
	Core Die Size	.18 micron, 120 mm
	Transistor Count	37 Million
	Voltage Interface	Split Core and I/O
	Core Voltage	1.75 volts
	Power Consumption	59 watts
	Maximum Power	66 watts

Table 7-52: Athlon Thunderbird 1200 Overclocking

Athlon Thunderbird	Model Rating	1200 MHz
Overclocking Potential	Multiplier Lock Support	Unlocked Multiplier
	Typical Multiplier O/C	13.0 – 14.0x
	Typical Front-side Bus O/C	103 – 115+ MHz
	Typical O/C Potential	1300 – 1400 MHz
	Maximum O/C Potential	1400+ MHz
Overclocking Tolerances	Recommended Cooling Type	Forced-Air Heatsink
	Recommended Heatsink Coolers	Thermalright SK-6
		Alpha PAL-8045
		TaiSol CGK742092
	Recommended Peltier Active Cooler	Swifttech MCX370
	Maximum Core Voltage	1.85 volts with Heatsink Cooler
	Maximum Core Temperature	95° Celsius

Strategy

The Athlon Thunderbird 1200 remains a popular choice for overclocking enthusiasts, mainly due to its widespread availability. This chip offers excellent opportunities. A small number of units scale toward 1500 MHz when paired with a chipset offering 133-MHz processor bus compatibility. Most chips from this speed grade peak around 1400 MHz, whatever the chipset or overclocking method.

Athlon Thunderbird 1300

Table 7-53: Athlon Thunderbird 1300 Specifications

Processor Family	Model Name	AMD Athlon Thunderbird
	Performance Rating	1300 MHz
	Front-side Bus Speed	100 MHz (200 DDR)
	Multiplier Ratio	13.0x
Physical Design	Interface Packing	462-Pin Socket A
	Core Die Size	.18 micron, 120 mm
	Transistor Count	37 Million
	Voltage Interface	Split Core and I/O
	Core Voltage	1.75 volts
	Power Consumption	61 watts
	Maximum Power	68 watts

Table 6-54: Athlon Thunderbird 1300 Overclocking

Athlon Thunderbird	Model Rating	1300 MHz
Overclocking Potential	Multiplier Lock Support	Unlocked Multiplier
	Typical Multiplier O/C	13.5x – 14.0x
	Typical Front-side Bus O/C	103 – 115+ MHz
	Typical O/C Potential	1350 – 1400 MHz
	Maximum O/C Potential	1400+ MHz
Overclocking Tolerances	Recommended Cooling Type	Forced-Air Heatsink
	Recommended Heatsink Coolers	Thermalright SK-6
		Alpha PAL-8045
		TaiSol CGK742092
	Recommended Peltier Active Cooler	Swifttech MCX370
	Maximum Core Voltage	1.85 volts with Heatsink Cooler
	Maximum Core Temperature	95° Celsius

Strategy

While not quite as popular as its 1200 MHz sibling, the Athlon Thunderbird 1300 MHz processor does offer a near guarantee of 1400 MHz. Most models will reach this level with nothing more than the factory AMD heatsink cooler and a modest bump in core voltage. As with the 1200, motherboards offering 133-MHz processor bus support will perform best when overclocked.

Athlon Thunderbird 1400

Table 7-55: Athlon Thunderbird 1400 Specifications

Processor Family	Model Name	AMD Athlon Thunderbird
	Performance Rating	1400 MHz
	Front-side Bus Speed	100 MHz (200 DDR)
	Multiplier Ratio	14.0x
Physical Design	Interface Packing	462-Pin Socket A
	Core Die Size	.18 micron, 120 mm
	Transistor Count	37 Million
	Voltage Interface	Split Core and I/O
	Core Voltage	1.75 volts
	Power Consumption	65 watts
	Maximum Power	72 watts

Table 7-56: Athlon Thunderbird 1400 Overclocking

Athlon Thunderbird	Model Rating	1400 MHz
Overclocking Potential	Multiplier Lock Support	Unlocked Multiplier
	Typical Multiplier O/C	14.0x
	Typical Front-side Bus O/C	103 – 115+ MHz
	Typical O/C Potential	1450 – 1550 MHz
	Maximum O/C Potential	1550+ MHz
Overclocking Tolerances	Recommended Cooling Type	Forced-Air Heatsink
	Recommended Heatsink Coolers	Thermalright SK-6
		Alpha PAL-8045
		TaiSol CGK742092
	Recommended Peltier Active Cooler	Swifttech MCX370
	Maximum Core Voltage	1.85 volts with Heatsink Cooler
	Maximum Core Temperature	95° Celsius

Strategy

The Athlon Thunderbird 1400-MHz processor is a rarity in OEM markets. Enthusiasts with 100-MHz processor bus systems have upgraded to this model, the last 100-MHz Thunderbird produced. Most chips of this speed grade are distributed in the retail market segment. Average overclocking returns are in the 1500 to 1550 MHz range, with the occasional model surpassing 1600 MHz when combined with a later-generation motherboard chipset.

Athlon Thunderbird B Overclocking

Table 7-57: Athlon Thunderbird B Specifications

Processor Family	Model Name	AMD Athlon Thunderbird B
	Performance Rating	1000 – 1400 MHz
	Generation	Seventh: 80686 IA-32
Operational Rates	L1 Cache Speed	1.0x Core Rate
	L2 Cache Speed	1.0x Core Rate
	Front-side Bus Speed	133 MHz (266 DDR)
	Multiplier Ratio	7.5x – 10.5x (14x Max)
Physical Design	Interface Packing	462-Pin Socket A
	Core Die Size	.18 micron, 120 mm
	Transistor Count	37 Million
	Voltage Interface	Split Core and I/O
	Core Voltage	1.75 volts
	Power Consumption	49 – 65 watts
	Maximum Power	54 – 72 watts
Architectural Design	Core Technology	OOO and Speculative Execution RISC
	Register Support	Integer = 32 bit
		Floating-Point = 80 bit
		MM = 64 bit
	Execution Units	3 x IEU
		3 x AGU
		3 x FP
	Data Bus Width	64 (+8) bit
	Max Memory Support	Physical = 16 Gigabyte
		Virtual = 64 Terabyte
	Multi-Processor Support	SMP via EV6 Bus
	Level 1 Code Cache	64 KB 2-way
	Level 1 Data Cache	64 KB 2-way
	Level 2 Cache	256 KB Exclusive
	Pre-fetch Queue	16 Byte
	Static Branch Prediction	Supported
	Dynamic Branch Prediction	2048 Entry
	RSB Branch Prediction	12 Entry
	Floating-Point Processor	Integrated
	Multimedia Extensions	MMX, 3DNow!, Extended 3DNow!

Athlon Thunderbird 1000B

Table 7-58: Athlon Thunderbird 1000B Specifications

Processor Family	Model Name	AMD Athlon Thunderbird B
	Performance Rating	1000 MHz
	Front-side Bus Speed	133 MHz (266 DDR)
	Multiplier Ratio	7.5x
Physical Design	Interface Packing	462-Pin Socket A
	Core Die Size	.18 micron, 120 mm
	Transistor Count	37 Million
	Voltage Interface	Split Core and I/O
	Core Voltage	1.75 volts
	Power Consumption	49 watts
	Maximum Power	54 watts

Table 7-59: Athlon Thunderbird 1000B Overclocking

Athlon Thunderbird B	Model Rating	1000 MHz
Overclocking Potential	Multiplier Lock Support	Unlocked Multiplier
	Typical Multiplier O/C	8.5x – 10x
	Typical Front-side Bus O/C	140 – 150+ MHz
	Typical O/C Potential	1200 – 1300 MHz
	Maximum O/C Potential	1300+ MHz
Overclocking Tolerances	Recommended Cooling Type	Forced-Air Heatsink
	Recommended Heatsink Coolers	Thermalright SK-6
		Alpha PAL-8045
		TaiSol CGK742092
	Recommended Peltier Active Cooler	Swifttech MCX370
	Maximum Core Voltage	1.85 volts with Heatsink Cooler
	Maximum Core Temperature	90° Celsius

Strategy

The Athlon Thunderbird 1000B-MHz processor promises moderate overclocking success. Most models from this speed grade can scale well beyond 1200 MHz with the factory heatsink. Better cooling can yield results exceeding 1300 MHz. Be careful when monitoring temperatures: the Thunderbird 1000B retains the 90° Celsius rating of its earlier cousins.

Athlon Thunderbird 1130B

Table 7-60: Athlon Thunderbird 1130B Specifications

Processor Family	Model Name	AMD Athlon Thunderbird B
	Performance Rating	1130 MHz
	Front-side Bus Speed	133 MHz (266 DDR)
	Multiplier Ratio	8.5x
Physical Design	Interface Packing	462-Pin Socket A
	Core Die Size	.18 micron, 120 mm
	Transistor Count	37 Million
	Voltage Interface	Split Core and I/O
	Core Voltage	1.75 volts
	Power Consumption	56 watts
	Maximum Power	63 watts

Table 7-61: Athlon Thunderbird 1130B Overclocking

Athlon Thunderbird B	Model Rating	1130 MHz
Overclocking Potential	Multiplier Lock Support	Unlocked Multiplier
	Typical Multiplier O/C	9.0x – 10.0+x
	Typical Front-side Bus O/C	140 – 150+ MHz
	Typical O/C Potential	1200 – 1333 MHz
	Maximum O/C Potential	1400+ MHz
Overclocking Tolerances	Recommended Cooling Type	Forced-Air Heatsink
	Recommended Heatsink Coolers	Thermalright SK-6
		Alpha PAL-8045
		TaiSol CGK742092
	Recommended Peltier Active Cooler	Swifttech MCX370
	Maximum Core Voltage	1.85 volts with Heatsink Cooler
	Maximum Core Temperature	95° Celsius

Strategy

The Athlon Thunderbird 1130B-MHz processor expanded the design by means of a core revision, including a higher thermal rating to 95° Celsius. Average overclocking returns for this model tend to reach above 1300 MHz with factory cooling. Quality cooling can extend the potential to 1400 MHz and beyond, though only a small portion of this grade will realize such a level of return.

Athlon Thunderbird 1200B

Table 7-62: Athlon Thunderbird 1200B Specifications

Processor Family	Model Name	AMD Athlon Thunderbird B
	Performance Rating	1200 MHz
	Front-side Bus Speed	133 MHz (266 DDR)
	Multiplier Ratio	9.0x
Physical Design	Interface Packing	462-Pin Socket A
	Core Die Size	.18 micron, 120 mm
	Transistor Count	37 Million
	Voltage Interface	Split Core and I/O
	Core Voltage	1.75 volts
	Power Consumption	59 watts
	Maximum Power	66 watts

Table 7-63: Athlon Thunderbird 1200B Overclocking

Athlon Thunderbird B	Model Rating	1200 MHz
Overclocking Potential	Multiplier Lock Support	Unlocked Multiplier
	Typical Multiplier O/C	10.0x – 11.0x
	Typical Front-side Bus O/C	140 – 150+ MHz
	Typical O/C Potential	1333 – 1400 MHz
	Maximum O/C Potential	1500+ MHz
Overclocking Tolerances	Recommended Cooling Type	Forced-Air Heatsink
	Recommended Heatsink Coolers	Thermalright SK-6
		Alpha PAL-8045
		TaiSol CGK742092
	Recommended Peltier Active Cooler	Swifttech MCX370
	Maximum Core Voltage	1.85 volts with Heatsink Cooler
	Maximum Core Temperature	95° Celsius

Strategy

The Athlon Thunderbird 1200B offers essentially the same potential as its 100-MHz processor bus counterpart. The average overclocking return extends to 1400 MHz with traditional cooling. Massive heatsink cooling may yield results in the 1500 to 1600 MHz range, but this is not common.

Athlon Thunderbird 1333B

Table 7-64: Athlon Thunderbird 1333B Specifications

Processor Family	Model Name	AMD Athlon Thunderbird B
	Performance Rating	1333 MHz
	Front-side Bus Speed	133 MHz (266 DDR)
	Multiplier Ratio	10.0x
Physical Design	Interface Packing	462-Pin Socket A
	Core Die Size	.18 micron, 120 mm
	Transistor Count	37 Million
	Voltage Interface	Split Core and I/O
	Core Voltage	1.75 volts
	Power Consumption	63 watts
	Maximum Power	70 watts

Table 7-65: Athlon Thunderbird 1333B Overclocking

Athlon Thunderbird B	Model Rating	1333 MHz
Overclocking Potential	Multiplier Lock Support	Unlocked Multiplier
	Typical Multiplier O/C	10.5x – 11.0x
	Typical Front-side Bus O/C	140 – 150+ MHz
	Typical O/C Potential	1400 – 1500 MHz
	Maximum O/C Potential	1500+ MHz
Overclocking Tolerances	Recommended Cooling Type	Forced-Air Heatsink
	Recommended Heatsink Coolers	Thermalright SK-6
		Alpha PAL-8045
		TaiSol CGK742092
	Recommended Peltier Active Cooler	Swifttech MCX370
	Maximum Core Voltage	1.85 volts with Heatsink Cooler
	Maximum Core Temperature	95° Celsius

Strategy

The Athlon Thunderbird 1333B offers essentially the same overclocking potential as its 1200-MHz sibling. As with every processor, the Thunderbird displays a maximum point of return, above which it will begin to offer less and less. Expect results in the 1400 to 1500 MHz range. Additional scalability is possible with extreme cooling techniques, but most units reach their limits around 1600 MHz.

Athlon Thunderbird 1400B

Table 7-66: Athlon Thunderbird 1400B Specifications

Processor Family	Model Name	AMD Athlon Thunderbird B
	Performance Rating	1400 MHz
	Front-side Bus Speed	133 MHz (266 DDR)
	Multiplier Ratio	10.5x
Physical Design	Interface Packing	462-Pin Socket A
	Core Die Size	.18 micron, 120 mm
	Transistor Count	37 Million
	Voltage Interface	Split Core and I/O
	Core Voltage	1.75 volts
	Power Consumption	65 watts
	Maximum Power	72 watts

Table 7-67: Athlon Thunderbird 1400B Overclocking

Athlon Thunderbird B	Model Rating	1400 MHz
	Typical Multiplier O/C	11.5x – 12.0x
	Typical Front-side Bus O/C	140 – 150+ MHz
	Typical O/C Potential	1530 – 1600 MHz
	Maximum O/C Potential	~1600+ MHz
Overclocking Tolerances	Recommended Cooling Type	Forced-Air Heatsink
	Recommended Heatsink Coolers	Thermalright SK-6
		Alpha PAL-8045
		TaiSol CGK742092
	Recommended Peltier Active Cooler	Swifttech MCX370
	Maximum Core Voltage	1.85 volts with Heatsink Cooler
	Maximum Core Temperature	95° Celsius

Strategy

The Athlon 1400B closes the Thunderbird family. At a default frequency of 1400 MHz, this processor is near the maximum potential for the Thunderbird core. Overclocking scales to 1600 MHz; extreme cooling has netted returns above 1700 MHz for a small number of chips when they are used in a configuration that is optimized for overclocking.

Athlon Duron Spitfire Background

The Duron stands as the official AMD entry into budget-class computing. Though it competes directly with the Intel Celeron II in price, the Duron often beats even the Pentium III in popular benchmark tests. The Duron's processing core architecture is the same as the Thunderbird's, but AMD limits the Duron's on-die Level 2 cache to 64 KB (compared to the Thunderbird's 256 KB).

The performance impact of the smaller cache size is minimal for most popular desktop applications. The difference only arises in professional applications or for server environments, systems in which large amounts of data move between the processor and memory. In these situations the Thunderbird's additional cache memory boosts performance significantly.

Duron Spitfire Overclocking

The Duron Spitfire offers essentially the same overclocking potential as the Athlon Thunderbird at equivalent clock ratings. The only appreciable difference is improved power efficiency for the Duron, about 80 to 90% better than the Thunderbird. The difference is derived from a smaller transistor count due to the smaller Level 2 cache of the Duron architecture. Accordingly, the Spitfire requires a marginally lower 1.60 core voltage.

All other concerns are the same for both processors. The maximum thermal rating of 90° Celsius applies to all Duron Spitfire processors. The maximum "safe" core voltage of the Duron Spitfire is 1.85 volts, the same as that for the Thunderbird. Each chip is nearly identical to its Thunderbird counterpart in both average and peak overclocking potential.

Table 7-68: Athlon Duron Spitfire Specifications

Processor Family	Model Name	AMD Duron Spitfire
	Performance Rating	550 – 950 MHz
	Generation	Seventh: 80686 IA-32
Operational Rates	L1 Cache Speed	1.0x Core Rate
	L2 Cache Speed	1.0x Core Rate
	Front-side Bus Speed	100 MHz (200 DDR)
	Multiplier Ratio	5.5x – 9.5x (14.0x Max)
Physical Design	Interface Packing	462-Pin Socket A
	Core Die Size	.18 micron, 100 mm
	Transistor Count	25 Million
	Voltage Interface	Split Core and I/O
	Core Voltage	1.6 volts
	Power Consumption	18.9 – 37.2 watts
	Maximum Power	21.1 – 41.5 watts
Architectural Design	Core Technology	OOO and Speculative Execution RISC
	Register Support	Integer = 32 bit
		Floating-Point = 80 bit
		MM = 64 bit
	Execution Units	3 x IEU
		3 x AGU
		3 x FP
	Data Bus Width	64 (+8) bit
	Max Memory Support	Physical = 16 Gigabyte
		Virtual = 64 Terabyte

(continued on next page)

Table 7-68: Athlon Duron Spitfire Specifications (continued)

Processor Family	Model Name	AMD Duron Spitfire
	Multi-Processor Support	SMP via EV6 Bus
	Level 1 Code Cache	64 KB 2-way
	Level 1 Data Cache	64 KB 2-way
	Level 2 Cache	64 KB Exclusive
	Pre-fetch Queue	16 Byte
	Static Branch Prediction	Supported
	Dynamic Branch Prediction	2048 Entry
	RSB Branch Prediction	12 Entry
	Floating-Point Processor	Integrated
	Multimedia Extensions	MMX, 3DNow!, Extended 3DNow!

Athlon Palomino/MP/XP

The Athlon Palomino represented the first major redesign of the Athlon core since the introduction of the Socket A processor-to-motherboard interface. The most significant new feature is a hardware data pre-fetch mechanism in the execution pipeline. This pre-fetch circuitry allows the Palomino to speculate and buffer certain data packets, increasing per MHz efficiency and performance compared to the Thunderbird.

AMD also introduced a new streaming multimedia instruction set with the Palomino architecture. 3DNow! Professional offers all the functions in previous 3DNow! instruction sets, but expands the base set to include binary compatibility with the Intel SSE specification. Because it can process both standards, the Athlon Palomino proves a formidable market competitor.

As expected with any core revision, AMD further refined the Athlon core to improve power efficiency. Core voltage remains consistent with the Thunderbird, but power consumption rates are improved by an average of 5 to 15%. Thermal generation loads have decreased accordingly. Maximum thermal ratings vary within the 90 to 95° Celsius range.

The first Palomino core processor arrived in the form of the Athlon MP. The MP stands for multiprocessing. This processor will operate in symmetric multiprocessing configurations. Oddly enough, nearly all Socket A AMD processors support SMP. The difference is that AMD tests and certifies its MP processors for stability. The Athlon MP usually commands a higher price due to this additional testing.

The Palomino architecture debuted in the consumer market under the designation Athlon XP. The term XP is derived from the marketing of this processor as the Athlon eXPerience. However, many enthusiasts believe AMD planned to correlate the naming of its chip with the release of Windows XP. Whatever the reason, the Athlon XP reigns as AMD's flagship consumer chip.

The most controversial aspect of the Athlon Palomino is the way it has been marketed. Labeled by comparative speed grades instead of raw MHz ratings, the Palomino's model numbers are reminiscent of those in the older K5 series.

Some speculate that these performance-rating values are somehow correlated to the performance of the Intel Pentium 4 models. In reality, the PR numbers compare the performance of the Athlon XP and the Athlon Thunderbird on a per-MHz basis. Only the 1000MP and 1200MP processors in the Palomino series feature true MHz counts in their naming conventions.

Unlocking the Athlon Palomino

AMD introduced a new wrinkle in multiplier locking with the Athlon Palomino. The primary way to unlock this chip remains the same as for the Athlon Thunderbird: simply reconnect the L1 trace-route circuitry. This process is difficult to apply to the Palomino, however, because the design features a ceramic base, containing small pits, which short to a grounded gold foil between the connection points of the L1 circuit range.

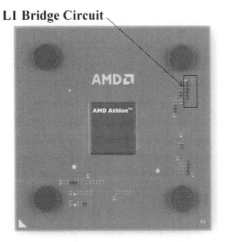

Figure 7-2: Athlon Palomino L1 bridge circuit

Common sense dictates that these grounded pits be filled to allow connection of the L1 circuitry. Simply drawing a connection line with a pencil will not work. Even without the holes, a pencil would be ineffective: the Palomino requires a low-impedance connection between the L1 bridges to communicate the unlocking directive. Conductive paint, intended for use in the repair of printed circuit boards, will connect the L1 bridges. This paint can be purchased from most electronics retailers. It can even be found in window defroster repair kits. A small amount goes a long way, so use conductive paint sparingly.

The Palomino needs additional hardware hacking to fill the holes between the L1 interconnects. Various methods have been used. Some enthusiasts have developed painstaking procedures for applying glues and epoxies, for example. Silicon thermal paste, available and inexpensive, works just as well for most configurations. Just apply the paste to the pits, then use a tiny, flat plastic scraper or pencil eraser to remove any excess paste that protrudes above the ceramic surface. You can also buy an XP unlocking kit that includes a cleaning agent, a non-conductive gap filler, conductive grease, an applicator, a magnifying glass, tape, and instructions, from HighspeedPC.com.

With the voids properly filled, the Palomino can be unlocked. Using a narrow needle or pin, draw connections between each L1 circuit bridge with conductive paint. As in the Thunderbird pencil trick, avoid overlapping any lines. Be patient and accomplish this procedure correctly the first time. You can try again, but removing the conductive paint is tedious. Some overclockers have taken it off with isopropyl alcohol or a pencil eraser. Neither method is easy.

Athlon Palomino/MP/XP Overclocking

Table 7-69: Athlon Palomino/MP/XP Specifications

Processor Family	Model Name	AMD Athlon Palomino/MP/XP
	Performance Rating	1000 – 1730 MHz
	Generation	Seventh: 80686 IA-32
Operational Rates	L1 Cache Speed	1.0x Core Rate
	L2 Cache Speed	1.0x Core Rate
	Front-side Bus Speed	133 MHz (266 DDR)
	Multiplier Ratio	7.5x – 13.0x (14.0+x Max)
Physical Design	Interface Packing	462-Pin Socket A
	Core Die Size	.18 micron, 128 mm
	Transistor Count	37.5 Million
	Voltage Interface	Split Core and I/O
	Core Voltage	1.75 volts
	Power Consumption	41.3 – 64.3 watts
	Maximum Power	46.1 – 72 watts
Architectural Design	Core Technology	OOO and Speculative Execution RISC
	Register Support	Integer = 32 bit
		Floating-Point = 80 bit
		MM = 64 bit
	Execution Units	3 x IEU
		3 x AGU
		3 x FP
	Data Bus Width	64 (+8) bit
	Max Memory Support	Physical = 16 Gigabyte
		Virtual = 64 Terabyte
	Multi-Processor Support	SMP via EV6 Bus
	Level 1 Code Cache	64 KB 2-way
	Level 1 Data Cache	64 KB 2-way
	Level 2 Cache	256 KB Exclusive
	Hardware Date Pre-fetch	Supported
	Pre-fetch Queue	16 Byte

(continued on next page)

Table 7-69: Athlon Palomino/MP/XP Specifications (continued)

Processor Family	Model Name	AMD Athlon Palomino/MP/XP
	Static Branch Prediction	Supported
	Dynamic Branch Prediction	2048 Entry
	RSB Branch Prediction	12 Entry
	Floating-Point Processor	Integrated
	Multimedia Extensions	MMX, 3DNow!, Extended 3DNow!, 3DNow! Professional (SSE)

Athlon Palomino 1000

Table 7-70: Athlon Palomino 1000 Specifications

Processor Family	Model Name	AMD Athlon Palomino
	Performance Rating	1000 MHz
	Front-side Bus Speed	133 MHz (266 DDR)
	Multiplier Ratio	7.5x
Physical Design	Interface Packing	462-Pin Socket A
	Core Die Size	.18 micron, 128 mm
	Transistor Count	37.5 Million
	Voltage Interface	Split Core and I/O
	Core Voltage	1.75 volts
	Power Consumption	MP = 41.3 watts
	Maximum Power	MP = 46.1 watts

Table 7-71: Athlon Palomino 1000 Overclocking

Athlon Palomino	Model Rating	1000 MHz
	Typical Multiplier O/C	9.0x – 10.5+x
	Typical Front-side Bus O/C	140 – 150 MHz
	Typical O/C Potential	1200 – 1400 MHz
	Maximum O/C Potential	1400+ MHz
Overclocking Tolerances	Recommended Cooling Type	Forced-Air Heatsink
	Recommended Heatsink Coolers	Thermalright SK-6
		Alpha PAL-8045
		TaiSol CGK742092
	Recommended Peltier Active Cooler	Swifttech MCX370
	Maximum Core Voltage	1.85 volts with Heatsink Cooler
	Maximum Core Temperature	95° Celsius

Strategy

The Athlon Palomino is represented at 1000 MHz by the Athlon MP processor. This is an early-generation design, which debuted prior to the introduction of AMD's performance rating designations. Effective overclocking scalability of this unit often falls in the 1200 to 1400 MHz realm, though a few rare samples have been know to exceed 1400 MHz under extreme cooling conditions.

Athlon Palomino 1200

Table 7-72: Athlon Palomino 1200 Specifications

Processor Family	Model Name	AMD Athlon Palomino
	Performance Rating	1200 MHz
	Front-side Bus Speed	133 MHz (266 DDR)
	Multiplier Ratio	9.0x
Physical Design	Interface Packing	462-Pin Socket A
	Core Die Size	.18 micron, 128 mm
	Transistor Count	37.5 Million
	Voltage Interface	Split Core and I/O
	Core Voltage	1.75 volts
	Power Consumption	MP = 49.1 watts
	Maximum Power	MP = 54.7 watts

Table 7-73: Athlon Palomino 1200 Overclocking

Athlon Palomino	Model Rating	1200 MHz
	Typical Multiplier O/C	10.0x – 11.0+x
	Typical Front-side Bus O/C	140 – 150 MHz
	Typical O/C Potential	1333 – 1530 MHz
	Maximum O/C Potential	1550+ MHz
Overclocking Tolerances	Recommended Cooling Type	Forced-Air Heatsink
	Recommended Heatsink Coolers	Thermalright SK-6
		Alpha PAL-8045
		TaiSol CGK742092
	Recommended Peltier Active Cooler	Swifttech MCX370
	Maximum Core Voltage	1.85 volts with Heatsink Cooler
	Maximum Core Temperature	95° Celsius

Strategy

The Athlon MP 1200 has much in common with its 1000-MHz counterpart. It too arrived before the performance-rating marketing initiative, and also reigned in as the premier choice in Athlon multiprocessing environments for several months. By offering decent power efficiency, this processor can often scale beyond 1500 MHz in dedicated overclocking configurations.

Athlon Palomino 1333 (XP/MP 1500+)

Table 7-74: Athlon Palomino 1333 Specifications

Processor Family	Model Name	AMD Athlon Palomino
	Performance Rating	Real = 1333 MHz
		XP/MP = 1500+
	Front-side Bus Speed	133 MHz (266 DDR)
	Multiplier Ratio	10.0x
Physical Design	Interface Packing	462-Pin Socket A
	Core Die Size	.18 micron, 128 mm
	Transistor Count	37.5 Million
	Voltage Interface	Split Core and I/O
	Core Voltage	1.75 volts
	Power Consumption	53.8 watts
	Maximum Power	60 watts

Table 7-75: Athlon Palomino 1333 Overclocking

Athlon Palomino	Model Rating	Real = 1333 MHz XP/MP = 1500+
	Typical Multiplier O/C	10.5x – 11.5+x
	Typical Front-side Bus O/C	140 – 150 MHz
	Typical O/C Potential	1450 – 1500 MHz
	Maximum O/C Potential	1500 – 1600+ MHz
Overclocking Tolerances	Recommended Cooling Type	Forced-Air Heatsink
	Recommended Heatsink Coolers	Thermalright SK-6
		Alpha PAL-8045
		TaiSol CGK742092
	Recommended Peltier Active Cooler	Swifttech MCX370
	Maximum Core Voltage	1.85 volts with Heatsink Cooler
	Maximum Core Temperature	XP = 90° Celsius
		MP = 95° Celsius

Strategy

The dreaded comparative performance ratings debuted with the release of the Palomino at 1333 MHz. Both the Athlon XP and MP designs at this speed grade carry the marketing designation 1500+. This model name describes the overclocking potential of this processor quite accurately. Many units from this speed grade can scale beyond 1500 MHz when paired with an effective heatsink cooler.

Athlon Palomino 1400 (XP/MP 1600+)

Table 7-76: Athlon Palomino 1400 Specifications

Processor Family	Model Name	AMD Athlon Palomino
	Performance Rating	Real = 1400 MHz
		XP/MP = 1600+
	Front-side Bus Speed	133 MHz (266 DDR)
	Multiplier Ratio	10.5x
Physical Design	Interface Packing	462-Pin Socket A
	Core Die Size	.18 micron, 128 mm
	Transistor Count	37.5 Million
	Voltage Interface	Split Core and I/O
	Core Voltage	1.75 volts
	Power Consumption	56.3 watts
	Maximum Power	62.8 watts

Table 7-77: Athlon Palomino Overclocking

Athlon Palomino	Model Rating	Real = 1400 MHz XP/MP = 1600+
	Typical Multiplier O/C	11.0x – 12.0+x
	Typical Front-side Bus O/C	140 – 150 MHz
	Typical O/C Potential	1500 – 1600 MHz
	Maximum O/C Potential	1600+ MHz
Overclocking Tolerances	Recommended Cooling Type	Forced-Air Heatsink
	Recommended Heatsink Coolers	Thermalright SK-6
		Alpha PAL-8045
		TaiSol CGK742092
	Recommended Peltier Active Cooler	Swifttech MCX370
	Maximum Core Voltage	1.85 volts with Heatsink Cooler
	Maximum Core Temperature	XP = 90° Celsius
		MP = 95° Celsius

Strategy

The Palomino 1400-MHz core is marketed under the 1600+ designation for both the Athlon MP and XP series of processors. Overclocking falls in line with expectations; this core is capable of operation exceeding 1600 MHz. While the factory-supplied heatsink can often push this processor an additional 50 to 100 MHz, a quality aftermarket cooler should always be installed when pushing beyond 1600 MHz, especially if any increase in core voltage is required.

Athlon Palomino 1466 (XP 1700+)

Table 7-78: Athlon Palomino 1466 Specifications

Processor Family	Model Name	AMD Athlon Palomino
	Performance Rating	Real = 1466 MHz XP = 1700+
	Front-side Bus Speed	133 MHz (266 DDR)
	Multiplier Ratio	11.0x
Physical Design	Interface Packing	462-Pin Socket A
	Core Die Size	.18 micron, 128 mm
	Transistor Count	37.5 Million
	Voltage Interface	Split Core and I/O
	Core Voltage	1.75 volts
	Power Consumption	57.4 watts
	Maximum Power	64 watts

Table 7-79: Athlon Palomino 1466 Overclocking

Athlon Palomino	Model Rating	Real = 1466 MHz XP = 1700+
	Typical Multiplier O/C	11.5x – 12.5+x
	Typical Front-side Bus O/C	140 – 150 MHz
	Typical O/C Potential	1550 – 1650 MHz
	Maximum O/C Potential	1650+ MHz
Overclocking Tolerances	Recommended Cooling Type	Forced-Air Heatsink
	Recommended Heatsink Coolers	Thermalright SK-6 Alpha PAL-8045 TaiSol CGK742092
	Recommended Peltier Active Cooler	Swifttech MCX370
	Maximum Core Voltage	1.85 volts with Heatsink Cooler
	Maximum Core Temperature	90° Celsius

Strategy

The Athlon XP 1700+ is based on a 1466-MHz Palomino core. Oddly enough, AMD has never officially released an MP 1700+ processor, skipping this speed grade in its production schedule. Despite the marketing glitch, this processor offers decent overclocking potential. Most 1466-MHz units are scalable beyond 1600 MHz with quality cooling and a slight bump in core voltage.

Athlon Palomino 1533 (XP 1800+)

Table 7-80: Athlon Palomino 1533 Specifications

Processor Family	Model Name	AMD Athlon Palomino
	Performance Rating	Real = 1533 MHz XP = 1800+
	Front-side Bus Speed	133 MHz (266 DDR)
	Multiplier Ratio	11.5x
Physical Design	Interface Packing	462-Pin Socket A
	Core Die Size	.18 micron, 128 mm
	Transistor Count	37.5 Million
	Voltage Interface	Split Core and I/O
	Core Voltage	1.75 volts
	Power Consumption	59.2 watts
	Maximum Power	66 watts

Table 7-81: Athlon Palomino 1533 Overclocking

Athlon Palomino	Model Rating	Real = 1533 MHz XP/MP = 1800+
	Typical Multiplier O/C	12.0x – 13.0x
	Typical Front-side Bus O/C	140 – 150 MHz
	Typical O/C Potential	1600 – 1700 MHz
	Maximum O/C Potential	1700+ MHz
Overclocking Tolerances	Recommended Cooling Type	Forced-Air Heatsink
	Recommended Heatsink Coolers	Thermalright SK-6 Alpha PAL-8045 TaiSol CGK742092
	Recommended Peltier Active Cooler	Swifttech MCX370
	Maximum Core Voltage	1.85 volts with Heatsink Cooler
	Maximum Core Temperature	XP = 90° Celsius MP = 95° Celsius

Strategy

Just as quickly as the Athlon MP dropped out for the Palomino 1446-MHz core, it reappeared as the Athlon 1800+, with the 1553-MHz iteration of the MP and XP families. The overclocking limits of the .18-micron Athlon architecture are evident with the Athlon 1800+. Most units from this speed grade see overclocking returns in the 1600 to 1700 MHz range with traditional cooling techniques.

Athlon Palomino 1600 (XP/MP 1900+)

Table 7-82: Athlon Palomino 1600 Specifications

Processor Family	Model Name	AMD Athlon Palomino
	Performance Rating	Real = 1600 MHz XP/MP = 1900+
	Front-side Bus Speed	133 MHz (266 DDR)
	Multiplier Ratio	12.0x
Physical Design	Interface Packing	462-Pin Socket A
	Core Die Size	.18 micron, 128 mm
	Transistor Count	37.5 Million
	Voltage Interface	Split Core and I/O
	Core Voltage	1.75 volts
	Power Consumption	60.7 watts
	Maximum Power	68 watts

Table 7-83: Athlon Palomino 1600 Overclocking

Athlon Palomino	Model Rating	Real = 1600 MHz XP/MP = 1900+
	Typical Multiplier O/C	12.xx – 13.0+x
	Typical Front-side Bus O/C	140 – 150 MHz
	Typical O/C Potential	1650 – 1750 MHz
	Maximum O/C Potential	1750+ MHz
Overclocking Tolerances	Recommended Cooling Type	Forced-Air Heatsink
	Recommended Heatsink Coolers	Thermalright SK-6 Alpha PAL-8045 TaiSol CGK742092
	Recommended Peltier Active Cooler	Swifttech MCX370
	Maximum Core Voltage	1.85 volts with Heatsink Cooler
	Maximum Core Temperature	XP = 90° Celsius MP = 95° Celsius

Strategy

Both the Athlon MP and XP 1900+ are built on a 1600-MHz Palomino processing core. The Athlon 1900+ offers modest scalability. Most units post overclocking returns approaching, and sometimes exceeding, 1700 MHz. Cooling is a definite concern when pushing into that frequency range. Use only a quality cooler when increasing the core voltage.

Athlon Palomino 1667 (XP/MP 2000+)

Table 7-84: Athlon Palomino 1667 Specifications

Processor Family	Model Name	AMD Athlon Palomino
	Performance Rating	Real = 1667 MHz
		XP/MP = 2000+
	Front-side Bus Speed	133 MHz (266 DDR)
	Multiplier Ratio	12.5x
Physical Design	Interface Packing	462-Pin Socket A
	Core Die Size	.18 micron, 128 mm
	Transistor Count	37.5 Million
	Voltage Interface	Split Core and I/O
	Core Voltage	1.75 volts
	Power Consumption	62.5 watts
	Maximum Power	70 watts

Table 7-85: Athlon Palomino 1667 Overclocking

Athlon Palomino	Model Rating	Real = 1667 MHz XP/MP = 2000+
	Typical Multiplier O/C	13.0x – 13.5+x
	Typical Front-side Bus O/C	140 – 150 MHz
	Typical O/C Potential	1700 – 1800 MHz
	Maximum O/C Potential	1800+ MHz
Overclocking Tolerances	Recommended Cooling Type	Forced-Air Heatsink
	Recommended Heatsink Coolers	Thermalright SK-6
		Alpha PAL-8045
		TaiSol CGK742092
	Recommended Peltier Active Cooler	Swifttech MCX370
	Maximum Core Voltage	1.85 volts with Heatsink Cooler
	Maximum Core Temperature	XP = 90° Celsius
		MP = 95° Celsius

Strategy

The Athlon 2000+ is a popular choice in computing communities. This processor ushered AMDs into the 2 gigahertz arena—at least in marketing theory. This chip is built atop a 1667-MHz Palomino processing core. Expect overclocking returns around 1800 MHz for the better chips in this grade. Take note of the 1667-MHz rating. It appears that AMD avoided the whole "666" issue the same way Intel did.

Athlon Palomino 1733 (XP/MP 2100+)

Table 7-86: Athlon Palomino 1733 Specifications

Processor Family	Model Name	AMD Athlon Palomino
	Performance Rating	Real = 1733 MHz XP/MP = 2100+
	Front-side Bus Speed	133 MHz (266 DDR)
	Multiplier Ratio	13.0x
Physical Design	Interface Packing	462-Pin Socket A
	Core Die Size	.18 micron, 128 mm
	Transistor Count	37.5 Million
	Voltage Interface	Split Core and I/O
	Core Voltage	1.75 volts
	Power Consumption	64.3 watts
	Maximum Power	72 watts

Table 7-87: Athlon Palomino 1733 Overclocking

Athlon Palomino	Model Rating	Real = 1733 MHz XP/MP = 2100+
	Typical Multiplier O/C	13.5x – 14.0x
	Typical Front-side Bus O/C	140 – 150 MHz
	Typical O/C Potential	1750 – 1850 MHz
	Maximum O/C Potential	1900+ MHz
Overclocking Tolerances	Recommended Cooling Type	Forced-Air Heatsink
	Recommended Heatsink Coolers	Thermalright SK-6 Alpha PAL-8045 TaiSol CGK742092
	Recommended Peltier Active Cooler	Swifttech MCX370
	Maximum Core Voltage	1.85 volts with Heatsink Cooler
	Maximum Core Temperature	XP = 90° Celsius MP = 95° Celsius

Strategy

The Athlon XP 2100+ offers marginal overclocking returns in the 1800 to 1900 MHz range for the majority of configurations. A dedicated overclocking system designed around cooling can achieve 2000 MHz, but this is not common.

Duron Morgan Background

The AMD Morgan core architecture is a Palomino-derived extension to the Duron series of budget-oriented microprocessors. Upgrades include 3DNow! Professional, hardware data pre-fetching, and various core improvements for better regulation of both thermal and power consumption rates. The scaled-back cache architecture comes over from the Spitfire, as the Morgan still features 64 KB to the Palomino's 256 KB. The addition of a hardware data pre-fetch mechanism works well to offset the Morgan's cache deficiency. This latest-model Duron can boast performance exceeding that of the supposedly more powerful Athlon Thunderbird. The Morgan is expected to be the last Duron core marketed by AMD. The impressive Athlon Thoroughbred will soon relegate the XP to entry-level systems.

Table 7-88: Duron Morgan Specifications

Processor Family	Model Name	AMD Duron Morgan
	Performance Rating	1000 – 1300 MHz
	Generation	Seventh: 80686 IA-32
Operational Rates	L1 Cache Speed	1.0x Core Rate
	L2 Cache Speed	1.0x Core Rate
	Front-side Bus Speed	100 MHz (200 DDR)
	Multiplier Ratio	9.0x – 13.0x (14.0x Max)
Physical Design	Interface Packing	462-Pin Socket A
	Core Die Size	.18 micron, 106 mm
	Transistor Count	25.2 Million
	Voltage Interface	Split Core and I/O
	Core Voltage	1.75 volts
	Power Consumption	39.2 – 42.7 watts
	Maximum Power	55.2 – 60 watts
Architectural Design	Core Technology	OOO and Speculative Execution RISC
	Register Support	Integer = 32 bit
		Floating-Point = 80 bit
		MM = 64 bit
	Execution Units	3 x IEU
		3 x AGU
		3 x FP
	Data Bus Width	64 (+8) bit
	Max Memory Support	Physical = 16 Gigabyte
Virtual = 64 Terabyte		
	Multi-Processor Support	SMP via EV6 Bus
	Level 1 Code Cache	64 KB 2-way
	Level 1 Data Cache	64 KB 2-way
	Level 2 Cache	64 KB Exclusive
	Hardware Date Pre-fetch	Supported

(continued on next page)

Table 7-88: Duron Morgan Specifications (continued)

Processor Family	Model Name	AMD Duron Morgan
	Pre-fetch Queue	16 Byte
	Static Branch Prediction	Supported
	Dynamic Branch Prediction	2048 Entry
	RSB Branch Prediction	12 Entry
	Floating-Point Processor	Integrated
	Multimedia Extensions	MMX, 3DNow!, Extended 3DNow!, 3DNow! Professional (SSE)

Table 7-89: Duron Morgan Overclocking

Duron Morgan	Model Rating	1000 – 1300 MHz
	Typical O/C Potential	1300 – 1400+ MHz
Overclocking Tolerances	Recommended Cooling Type	Forced-Air Heatsink
	Recommended Heatsink Coolers	Thermalright SK-6
		Alpha PAL-8045
		TaiSol CGK742092
	Recommended Peltier Active Cooler	Swifttech MCX370
	Maximum Core Voltage	1.85 volts with Heatsink Cooler
	Maximum Core Temperature	90° Celsius

Strategy

The Duron Morgan processor offers an overclocking opportunity for most configurations. Many Duron Morgan processors are able to exceed 1300 MHz with quality forced-air heatsink cooling. Some of the higher speed processors in the series have been known to overclock past 1400 MHz with relative ease. This Palomino-derived processor displays great thermal and electrical efficiency.

Athlon Thoroughbred

The Athlon Thoroughbred is AMD's successor to the Palomino. Featuring a smaller 0.13 micron core, the Thoroughbred is a cooler running processor than the Palomino and it has other physical improvements. It debuted with an XP 2200+ version, though AMD later backtracked, releasing several slower processors in the Thoroughbred core as well.

Like the Palomino, the Thoroughbreds below the XP 2400+ are clock multiplier locked. The L1 bridges must be reconnected to allow multiplier changes. You can freely change the multiplier of XP 2400+ and newer Thoroughbreds using KT400 based motherboards without any processor alteration.

The Thoroughbred is currently available in two model revisions: Revision A and Revision B. The Revision A models (at speeds of XP 1700+ to XP 2200+, or 1.47 GHz to 1.80 GHz) are not all that impressive in their overclocking ability, though the lower speed models such as the XP 1700+ do offer better potential than the higher speed models. The entire speed range of the Revision B models is improved and their overclocking potential is significant. Having learned from the Revision A model, AMD implemented a few physical improvements for the Revision B model, such as additional transistors and an additional metal layer within the processor to optimize its electrical properties and increase its maximum clock speed potential.

If you own (or plan to purchase) an Athlon XP 2400+ or faster, you can be assured that it is a Revision B type since those processors were never manufactured as the Revision A type. Otherwise, if you own or plan to buy anywhere from an Athlon XP 1800+ to an XP 2200+, the only way to tell the difference between a Revision A and Revision B Thoroughbred is by knowing the CPUID of the processor, though some retailers may specifically sell Revision B processors, so be sure to look for a "B" designation.

Revision A processors are known by their CPUID of 680, and Revision B by their CPUID of 681. Revision B Thoroughbreds are definitely better overclockers, with a potential upwards of 2.4 GHz, and lower speed Revision B models are recommended (such as the 1800+ XP, Rev. B), since they have a bigger potential than the higher speed models that are already operating near their maximums.

Note that as of November 2002, the Thoroughbred became available in a 166MHz DDR (333MHz) FSB variety. The new 166MHz variant offers more bandwidth and extra future expandability as processor speeds increase, though you could accomplish the same thing by increasing the FSB of a proc.

Athlon Thoroughbred 1467 Rev. A (XP 1700+)

Table 7-90: Athlon Thoroughbred 1467 Rev. A Specifications

Processor Family	Model Name	AMD Athlon Thoroughbred, Rev. A
	Performance Rating	Real = 1467 MHz XP/MP = 1700+
	Front-side Bus Speed	133 MHz (266 DDR)
	Multiplier Ratio	11.0x
Physical Design	Interface Packing	462 Pin Socket A
	Core Die Size	.13-micron, 80mm^2
	Transistor Count	37.2 Million
	Voltage Interface	Split Core and I/O
	Core Voltage	1.50v
	Power Consumption	44.9 watts
	Maximum Power	49.4 watts

Table 7-91: Athlon Thoroughbred 1467 Rev. A Overclocking

Athlon Thoroughbred	Model Rating	Real = 1467 MHz XP = 1700+
	Typical Multiplier O/C	12.0x – 13.0x
	Typical FSB O/C	145 – 150 MHz
	Typical O/C Potential	1600 – 1667 MHz
	Maximum O/C Potential	1733+ MHz
Overclocking Tolerances	Recommended Cooling Type	Forced-Air Heatsink
	Recommended Heatsink Coolers	Thermalright SK-6
		Alpha PAL-8045
		TaiSol CGK742092
	Recommended Peltier Active Cooler	Swifttech MCX370
	Maximum Core Voltage	1.80v with Heatsink Cooler
	Maximum Core Temperature	90° Celsius

Strategy

The slowest Thoroughbred available, the Athlon XP 1700+ offers good over-clocking capabilities and is popular due to its low cost and good quality, despite it being available in the "A" revision only. Some users have reported overclocks as high as 2000 MHz with extreme cooling and extreme voltages of 2.0v+, but that voltage level is not recommended and you will more realistically see around 1700 MHz with 1.7v.

Athlon Thoroughbred 1533 Rev. A (XP 1800+)

Table 7-92: Athlon Thoroughbred 1533 Rev. A Specifications

Processor Family	Model Name	AMD Athlon Thoroughbred, Rev. A
	Performance Rating	Real = 1533 MHz XP = 1800+
	Front-side Bus Speed	133 MHz (266 DDR)
	Multiplier Ratio	11.5x
Physical Design	Interface Packing	462 Pin Socket A
	Core Die Size	.13-micron, 80mm²
	Transistor Count	37.2 Million
	Voltage Interface	Split Core and I/O
	Core Voltage	1.50v
	Power Consumption	46.3 watts
	Maximum Power	51.0 watts

Table 7-93: Athlon Thoroughbred 1533 Rev. A Overclocking

Athlon Thoroughbred	Model Rating XP = 1800+	Real = 1533 MHz
	Typical Multiplier O/C	12.0x – 13.5x
	Typical FSB O/C	145 – 150 MHz
	Typical O/C Potential	1600 – 1800 MHz
	Maximum O/C Potential	1862 MHz
Overclocking Tolerances	Recommended Cooling Type	Forced-Air Heatsink
	Recommended Heatsink	Thermalright SK-6
	Cooleres	Alpha PAL-8045
		TaiSol CGK742092
	Recommended Peltier Active Cooler	Swifttech MCX370
	Maximum Core Voltage	1.80v with Heatsink Cooler
	Maximum Core Temperature	90° Celsius

Strategy

The Athlon XP 1800+ offers slightly better results than the Thoroughbred 1467, as you are likely to see around 1800 MHz with this processor, using approximately 1.75v, or 1700 MHz with a less aggressive voltage and cooling.

Athlon Thoroughbred 1600 Rev. A (XP 1900+)

Table 7-94: Athlon Thoroughbred 1600 Rev. A Specifications

Processor Family	Model Name	AMD Athlon Thoroughbred, Rev. A
	Performance Rating	Real = 1600 MHz
		XP = 1900+
	Front-side Bus Speed	133 MHz (266 DDR)
	Multiplier Ratio	12.0x
Physical Design	Interface Packing	462 Pin Socket A
	Core Die Size	.13-micron, 80mm^2
	Transistor Count	37.2 Million
	Voltage Interface	Split Core and I/O
	Core Voltage	1.50v
	Power Consumption	47.7 watts
	Maximum Power	52.5 watts

Table 7-95: Athlon Thoroughbred 1600 Rev. A Overclocking

Athlon Thoroughbred	Model Rating	Real = 1600 MHz XP = 1900+
	Typical Multiplier O/C	12.5x – 13.5x
	Typical FSB O/C	140 – 150 MHz
	Typical O/C Potential	1662 – 1795 MHz
	Maximum O/C Potential	1862 MHz
Overclocking Tolerances	Recommended Cooling Type	Forced-Air Heatsink
	Recommended Heatsink	Thermalright SK-6
	Coolers	Alpha PAL-8045
		TaiSol CGK742092
	Recommended Peltier Active Cooler	Swifttech MCX370
	Maximum Core Voltage	1.80v with Heatsink Cooler
	Maximum Core Temperature	90° Celsius

Strategy

The Athlon XP 1900+ offers decent overclocking potential, but real world results may be on the low end, closer to 1700 MHz, than the high end, such as 1800+ MHz, without major voltage increases and extreme cooling.

Athlon Thoroughbred 1667 Rev. A (XP 2000+)

Table 7-96: Athlon Thoroughbred 1667 Rev. A Specifications

Processor Family	Model Name	AMD Athlon Thoroughbred, Rev. A
	Performance Rating	Real = 1667 MHz
		XP = 2000+
	Front-side Bus Speed	133 MHz (266 DDR)
	Multiplier Ratio	12.5x
Physical Design	Interface Packing	462 Pin Socket A
	Core Die Size	.13-micron, 80mm^2
	Transistor Count	37.2 Million
	Voltage Interface	Split Core and I/O
	Core Voltage	1.60v-1.65v
	Power Consumption	54.7 watts
	Maximum Power	60.3 watts

Table 7-97: Athlon Thoroughbred 1667 Rev. A Overclocking

Athlon Thoroughbred	Model Rating	Real = 1667 MHz XP = 2000+
	Typical Multiplier O/C	13.0x – 14.0x
	Typical FSB O/C	136 – 144 MHz
	Typical O/C Potential	1700 – 1800 MHz
	Maximum O/C Potential	1862+ MHz
Overclocking Tolerances	Recommended Cooling Type	Forced-Air Heatsink
	Recommended Heatsink Coolers	Thermalright SK-6
		Alpha PAL-8045
		TaiSol CGK742092
	Recommended Peltier Active Cooler	Swifttech MCX370
	Maximum Core Voltage	1.80v with Heatsink Cooler
	Maximum Core Temperature	90° Celsius

Strategy

The XP 2000+ is marginally overclockable by about 100 MHz, which is decent in case you already own one, but don't go out and buy one of these processors, as there are other models with better price to performance ratios than this one. Some users have reported overclocks up to 1900+ MHz but this is not typical, and better results have been obtained using processors with the "AGOIA" stepping than without.

Athlon Thoroughbred 1733 Rev. A (XP 2100+)

Table 7-98: Athlon Thoroughbred 1733 Rev. A Specifications

Processor Family	Model Name	AMD Athlon Thoroughbred, Rev. A
	Performance Rating	Real = 1733 MHz XP = 2100+
	Front-side Bus Speed	133 MHz (266 DDR)
	Multiplier Ratio	13.0x
Physical Design	Interface Packing	462 Pin Socket A
	Core Die Size	.13-micron, 80mm^2
	Transistor Count	37.2 Million
	Voltage Interface	Split Core and I/O
	Core Voltage	1.60v
	Power Consumption	56.4 watts
	Maximum Power	62.1 watts

Table 7-99: Athlon Thoroughbred 1733 Rev. A Overclocking

Athlon Thoroughbred	Model Rating	Real = 1733 MHz XP = 2100+
	Typical Multiplier O/C	12.0x – 13.0x
	Typical FSB O/C	145 – 150 MHz
	Typical O/C Potential	1750 – 1800 MHz
	Maximum O/C Potential	1850+ MHz
Overclocking Tolerances	Recommended Cooling Type	Forced-Air Heatsink
	Recommended Heatsink Coolers	Thermalright SK-6
		Alpha PAL-8045
		TaiSol CGK742092
	Recommended Peltier Active Cooler	Swifttech MCX370
	Maximum Core Voltage	1.80v with Heatsink Cooler
	Maximum Core Temperature	90° Celsius

Strategy

Overclocking returns begin to diminish at this speed level and this processor is therefore not recommended for overclockers. Cheaper, slower rated Throughbreds have a higher performance to price ratio than the XP 2100+.

Athlon Thoroughbred 1800 Rev. A (XP 2200+)

Table 7-100: Athlon Thoroughbred 1800 Rev. A Specifications

Processor Family	Model Name	AMD Athlon Thoroughbred, Rev. A
	Performance Rating	Real = 1800 MHz XP = 2200+
	Front-side Bus Speed	133 MHz (266 DDR)
	Multiplier Ratio	13.5x
Physical Design	Interface Packing	462 Pin Socket A
	Core Die Size	.13-micron, 80mm^2
	Transistor Count	37.2 Million
	Voltage Interface	Split Core and I/O
	Core Voltage	1.65v
	Power Consumption	61.7 watts
	Maximum Power	67.9 watts

Table 7-101: Athlon Thoroughbred 1800 Rev. A Overclocking

Athlon Thoroughbred	Model Rating	Real = 1800 MHz XP = 2200+
	Typical Multiplier O/C	12.0x – 13.0x
	Typical FSB O/C	145 – 150 MHz
	Typical O/C Potential	1825 – 1850 MHz
	Maximum O/C Potential	1900 MHz
Overclocking Tolerances	Recommended Cooling Type	Forced-Air Heatsink
	Recommended Heatsink	Thermalright SK-6
	Coolers	Alpha PAL-8045
		TaiSol CGK742092
	Recommended Peltier Active Cooler	Swifttech MCX370
	Maximum Core Voltage	1.80v with Heatsink Cooler
	Maximum Core Temperature	85° Celsius

Strategy

The Revision A core is pushed to its limits with the XP 2200+, and overclocking returns are therefore not impressive. This processor's Maximum Core Temperature also decreased by 5° Celsius over the other speed grades in the Thoroughbred Revision A class, making heat tolerance a bigger factor.

Athlon Thoroughbred 2000 Rev. B (XP 2400+)

Table 7-102: Athlon Thoroughbred 2000 Rev. B Specifications

Processor Family	Model Name	AMD Athlon Thoroughbred, Rev. B
	Performance Rating	Real = 2000 MHz XP = 2400+
	Front-side Bus Speed	133 MHz (266 DDR)
	Multiplier Ratio	15x
Physical Design	Interface Packing	462 Pin Socket A
	Core Die Size	.13-micron, 84mm^2
	Transistor Count	37.6 Million
	Voltage Interface	Split Core and I/O
	Core Voltage	1.65v
	Power Consumption	62 watts
	Maximum Power	68.3 watts

Table 7-103: Athlon Thoroughbred 2000 Rev. B Overclocking

Athlon Thoroughbred	Model Rating	Real = 2000 MHz XP = 2400+
	Typical Multiplier O/C	16.5x – 17.5x
	Typical FSB O/C	145 – 155 MHz
	Typical O/C Potential	2200 – 2327 MHz
	Maximum O/C Potential	2450 MHz
Overclocking Tolerances	Recommended Cooling Type	Forced-Air Heatsink
	Recommended Heatsink	Thermalright SK-6
	Coolers	Alpha PAL-8045
		TaiSol CGK742092
	Recommended Peltier Active Cooler	Swifttech MCX370
	Maximum Core Voltage	1.80v with Heatsink Cooler
	Maximum Core Temperature	85° Celsius

Strategy

The Athlon XP 2400+ offers a good price/performance ratio and is a favorite amongst Thoroughbred overclocking enthusiasts. Extreme cooling will get you to 2400 MHz (though HardOCP.com, for instance, did achieve 2500 MHz with the Thermalright SLK-800 and a very aggressive 1.95v, and they also achieved 2400 MHz with average cooling), but 2200MHz or so is more likely with standard to moderate cooling. The XP 2400+ is the first Thoroughbred to be L1 factory unlocked, and you can therefore adjust the multiplier freely if you have a KT400 based motherboard.

Athlon Thoroughbred 2133 Rev. B (XP 2600+)

Table 7-104: Athlon Thoroughbred 2133 Rev. B Specifications

Processor Family	Model Name	AMD Athlon Thoroughbred, Rev. B
	Performance Rating	Real = 2133 MHz
		XP = 2600+
	Front-side Bus Speed	133 MHz (266 DDR)
	Multiplier Ratio	16x
Physical Design	Interface Packing	462 Pin Socket A
	Core Die Size	.13-micron, 84mm²
	Transistor Count	37.6 Million
	Voltage Interface	Split Core and I/O
	Core Voltage	1.65v
	Power Consumption	62 watts
	Maximum Power	68.3 watts

Table 7-105: Athlon Thoroughbred 2133 Rev. B Overclocking

Athlon Thoroughbred	Model Rating	Real = 2133 MHz XP = 2600+
	Typical Multiplier O/C	16.5x – 17.5x
	Typical FSB O/C	145 – 155 MHz
	Typical O/C Potential	2200 – 2350 MHz
	Maximum O/C Potential	2450 MHz
Overclocking Tolerances	Recommended Cooling Type	Forced-Air Heatsink
	Recommended Heatsink	Thermalright SK-6
	Coolers	Alpha PAL-8045
		TaiSol CGK742092
	Recommended Peltier Active Cooler	Swifttech MCX370
	Maximum Core Voltage	1.80v with Heatsink Cooler
	Maximum Core Temperature	85° Celsius

Strategy

Like the XP 2400+, the XP 2600+ is L1 factory unlocked, and the multiplier can be freely changed with KT400 based motherboards. This processor is reasonably comparable to the XP 2400+, though you may be able to overclock the XP 2600+ by the same speed increase as the XP 2400+ while using a lower voltage with the XP 2600+.

8

VIA/CYRIX OVERCLOCKING

One Chip, Many Names

VIA Technologies, a Taiwan-based computing giant, acquired the aging Cyrix processing platform in June 1999. In the same timeframe, the company bought rights to the Centaur WinChip architecture, allowing it to enter the processor design business. While VIA is now actively developing processing platforms, it still relies on outside resources to produce its models.

Many computer users have never heard of a VIA processor. This lack of visibility can best be attributed to poor marketing, though the quality of the processors has also been in question. The original VIA Cyrix III processor never shipped to market; its architecture simply could not compete with similarly priced offerings from Intel and AMD.

In acquiring Centaur, VIA moved to redesign its failed chip. The Centaur design team had posted moderate success with WinChip; VIA was hoping to leverage that success into a viable processor design. The VIA Cyrix III, called Samuel, was derived from Centaur; it shared little technology with any earlier Cyrix design. The Samuel was underpowered, but it did establish VIA's presence in the microprocessor market.

Figure 8-1: The VIA C3 processor

The current VIA processing platform is called C3, a name derived from Cyrix III but shortened to neutralize the stigma associated with earlier Cyrix models. The VIA C3 is essentially a fifth-generation 80586 core architecture, with extensions for compatibility with MMX and 3DNow! instruction sets. 3DNow! support is a real blessing, as the base floating-point unit of the C3 leaves much to be desired. The C3 fairs slightly better in desktop applications; it usually performs within a few percentage points of the popular Intel Celeron II for most integer-based calculations. Comparing the C3 against the AMD Duron is pointless; the entry-level Duron often outperforms even the powerful Pentium III.

Table 8-1: VIA C3 Specifications

Processor Family	Model Name	VIA C3
	Performance Rating	733 – 933+ MHz
	Generation	Fifth: 80586 IA-32
Operational Rates	Level 1 Cache Speed	1.0x Core Rate
	Level 2 Cache Speed	1.0x Core Rate
	Front-side Bus Speed	100 – 133 MHz
	Multiplier Ratio	4.5x – 8.0+x
Physical Design	Interface Packing	370 Pin Socket
	Core Die Size	.15 micron, 52 mm^2
		.13 micron, 52 mm^2
	Transistor Count	15.8 Million
	Voltage Interface	Split Core and I/O
	Core Voltage	.15 micron: 1.6 volts
		.13 micron: 1.35 volts

(continued on next page)

Table 8-1: VIA C3 Specifications (continued)

Processor Family	Model Name	VIA C3
	I/O Voltage	3.3 volts
	Power Consumption	6.8 – 10.6 watts
	Maximum Power	9.6 – 17.7 watts
Architectural Design	Core Technology	In-order and Pipelined Execution RISC
	Register Support	Integer = 32 bit
		Floating-Point = 80 bit
		MM = 64 bit
	Execution Units	1x Integer
		1x FPU (1/2 Speed)
	Data Bus Width	64 bit
	Max Memory Support	Physical = 4 Gigabyte
		Virtual = 64 Terabyte
	Multi-Processor Support	Not Supported
	Level 1 Code Cache	64 KB 4-way
	Level 1 Data Cache	64 KB 4-way
	Level 2 Cache	64 KB Exclusive
	Pre-fetch Queue	3x 16 Byte
	Static Branch Prediction	Supported
	Dynamic Branch Prediction	128 Entry
	RSB Branch Prediction	16 Entry
	Floating-Point Processor	Integrated
	Multimedia Extensions	MMX, 3DNow!

VIA C3 Overclocking

The VIA C3 processor's specifications suggest great overclocking opportunities. The C3 boasts a small core die size and extremely low thermal loads, even at its highest frequency ratings. It is compatible with the widest variety of popular socket-370 motherboards, plus it offers a decent execution pipeline. Sadly, though, the C3 remains a modest overclocking option for most configurations.

The C3's overclocking potential is highest with lower processor-speed grades. Users may find that the chip responds unfavorably to front-side bus overclocking. Most C3 chips are multiplier unlocked, however, and can scale to an additional 100 MHz. Overclocks can peak at 950 to 1000 MHz for the best .13-micron processors. Multiplier adjustments can be performed directly within Windows using H.Oda's popular WCPUID freeware testing application, which can be obtained at http://www.h-oda.com.

Proper voltage can be a serious concern for the C3. Unlike competing designs from Intel, the C3 is not well suited for large increases in core voltage rates. The fastest .13-micron models are designed for 1.35 core volts; pushing these units beyond 1.4 volts is discouraged because it seriously increases potential for core failure. Earlier .15-micron units typically operate at .16 volts, though it is not wise to attempt more than 1.7 to 1.75 volts when overclocking them.

Expensive cooling solutions are not really necessary when overclocking the VIA C3. This chip accommodates thermal generation loads unparalleled by anything other than the mobile processor families from Intel. However, junking the passive heatsink cooler that many companies ship with the C3 is a good idea. This cheap heatsink can barely pass for a decent socket-7 cooler, it is not a cooler for the overclocking enthusiast. Any quality socket-370 forced-air heatsink should work well for overclocking the C3.

9

BENCHMARK TESTING

Testing Methodology

Benchmark testing is essential in evaluating performance gains or losses from overclocking. Two types of benchmarking techniques are available: synthetic and real world. Synthetic benchmarks use a series of performance-testing algorithms and enable you to compare your system's results with results generated from other systems, across all platforms. Synthetic benchmark results for a single system are not useful; they must be compared to results obtained on other systems. Real-world benchmarks test actual performance for common operating scenarios, in real time. Results are often measured in *frames per second* or *operations per second*.

Benchmark results can provide a foundation for determining the best combination of multiplier and bus overclocking techniques. Increasing system bus rates, while decreasing or maintaining processor multiplier settings, may produce better performance than raising multiplier values alone. A thorough benchmarking process can help you analyze the various impacts on performance and stability introduced by overclocking.

It is important to establish baseline performance numbers on your system before you do any overclocking, so that you can make before-and-after comparisons. Overclocking does not always improve computing results; sometimes it brings negligible gains or even declines in performance. Before-and-after comparisons will help you determine whether or not your overclocking efforts have succeeded and if further adjustments are necessary.

System stability is often affected by overclocking, so it is valuable to determine what impact your efforts have had on stability without having to experience failures (that is, system hang-ups and crashes) in your real-world applications. Benchmarking apps involve strenuous system tests that exceed the level of CPU power and resources required by typical applications in everyday use. During such tests, a system can be pushed to its limits. If the system fails, it is probably either overclocked beyond its capabilities or in need of additional tweaks. Increasing CPU voltage, improving the cooling, or reducing bus speed while increasing the CPU multiplier may yield better results.

A few simple steps will ensure that your system is properly configured for benchmarking.

1. Your desktop display resolution should always be set to the same value for each pass or test run of a given application. A resolution of 1024 x 768 pixels with 16-bit color is recommended for consistency and comparable results.

2. All hard disks in your system should be thoroughly defragmented before testing to ensure maximum bandwidth, low access latencies, and a consistent data flow among each of the system components and the drive array.

3. Finally, all components (video, chipset, etc.) should be installed using the latest software drivers from each hardware manufacturer.

SiSoft Sandra

SiSoft Sandra is one of the most widely used synthetic benchmarking applications. Sandra offers performance testing for many subsystems and components. It also provides detailed analyses of system performance, capabilities, and stability. Overclockers will appreciate Sandra's dedicated tests designed for specific areas, such as processor, memory, and drive systems. These tests will help determine the best combination of settings for memory bus rates, front-side bus rates, and processor multiplier values.

Sandra's processor testing is broken down into two benchmarking modules. The primary processor-testing module provides instructions-per-second ratings for both integer and floating-point math operations. The multimedia module tests any enhanced streaming instruction capabilities the processor may offer, including Intel's SSE2 or AMD's 3DNow!. While synthetic processor testing may not represent real-world performance, it is a good place to start in identifying changes that result from overclocking.

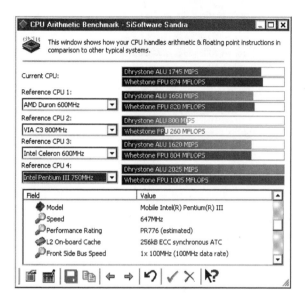

Figure 9-1: Sandra processor benchmark

The Sandra memory module lets you benchmark the available bandwidth between the memory and processor buses via the chipset bus. The results are displayed in megabytes per second for both integer and floating-point operations. Increases in front-side bus and memory bus rates offer greater bandwidth improvements than multiplier-only overclocking.

The Sandra file system benchmark provides both stability and performance testing. Front-side bus overclocking can produce higher drive bandwidth, with less read/write latency, through consequent overclocking of the PCI bus transfer rate. Stability can be evaluated by way of multiple-loop drive testing (i.e., running the test multiple times) to verify that data integrity is maintained during operation at extended PCI bus frequencies.

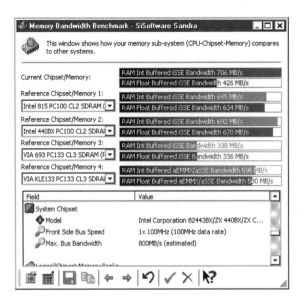

Figure 9-2: Sandra memory bandwidth benchmark

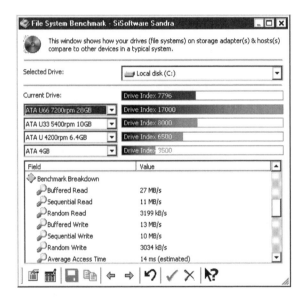

Figure 9-3: Sandra file system benchmark

MadOnion 3DMark

MadOnion is the publisher of several popular synthetic benchmark applications. Its 3DMark series analyzes system performance at both the processor and subsystem levels. Though it was originally designed to evaluate 3D video performance, the stress 3DMark places on the processor, chipset, and memory buses allows 3DMark to effectively benchmark of overall system performance.

3DMark2000 can test the effectiveness of the processor alone. It separates the video card's advanced 3D functions from the rendering pipeline in order to isolate the processor's performance independent of the video card. Be sure to disable any hardware transform-and-lighting (T&L) operations when configuring the test environment, so that the processor-related tests rely totally on software rendering routines. The 3DMark2000 also offers a looping demo mode that can be used to test system stability over time. In the *SE* version, internal rendering pipelines have been updated to support Microsoft's DirectX 8.1 D3D hardware acceleration routines.

Figure 9-4: 3DMark2001 testing

Ziff Davis WinBench 99

Ziff Davis, the popular content publishing and hardware testing corporation, provides WinBench 99, version 2.0, as a free download. All WinBench testing routines are performed through 32-bit operations, with benchmarks designed to stress and evaluate graphics, video, and disk performance. The numbers generated by Graphics WinMark tests are based on comparative normalized scores, while the Disk WinMark scores represent actual drive transfer rates in thousands of bytes per second. Test results can be saved for later system-to-system comparisons or to analyze performance changes induced by various overclocking settings compared to your system's baseline performance.

	Compaq Deskpro	Cyrix	Cyrix Media GX	Dell OptiPlex GX1	
WinBench 99/Business Disk WinMark 99 (Thousand l	2280	1330	1230	2290	2
WinBench 99/Business Graphics WinMark 99	54.9	58.2	22.2	118	5
WinBench 99/CPUmark 99	20.1	14.1	6.93	30.4	1
WinBench 99/DirectDraw/Animate BLT size, 256 pixel	17.8	30.7	20.9	47.8	
WinBench 99/DirectDraw/Animate BLT size, 1024 pixe	32.5	92.9	51.9	183	
WinBench 99/DirectDraw/Animate BLT size, 4096 pixe	41.8	152	71.2	223	
WinBench 99/DirectDraw/Animate Blt:Pixels Drawn (M	41.7	152	67.7	223	
WinBench 99/DirectDraw/Animate BltFast:Pixels Draw	41.8	152	71.6	223	
WinBench 99/DirectDraw/Animate Clipped:Pixels Draw	20.8	54.9	NoResult	79	
WinBench 99/DirectDraw/Animate Color Depth, 8 bit:F	41.8	152	71.8	223	
WinBench 99/DirectDraw/Animate Color Depth, 16 bit:	22	71.8	40.4	112	
WinBench 99/DirectDraw/Animate Color Depth, 24 bit:	14.8	9.44	NoResult	40.1	

Figure 9-5: WinBench 99 comparison tables

Real-world Testing: 3D Games

Complex 3D games can test real-world performance by measuring rendering rates in frames per second. ID Software's Quake 3 remains the dominant choice for such testing, even though its rendering engine is aging. Other popular games, like Unreal Tournament, Aquanox, and any other game with a frames-per-second benchmark capability, should prove equally acceptable. DirectX and OpenGL games lack internal testing functions, but they can still be benchmarked using the FRAPS performance measurement utility (http://www.fraps.com).

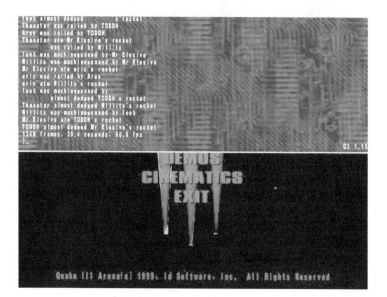

Figure 9-6: Quake 3 time demo results

Quake 3 frames-per-second testing is performed via the console command line interface.

1. Press the tilde (˜) key while the game is running. This will invoke the interface.

2. At the command line, type **timedemo 1** and press the ENTER key.

3. Close the console interface by pressing the tilde key (˜) a second time.

4. Perform frames-per-second testing by selecting either available demo via the main menu. The average rates will be returned to the console interface when the demo is completed.

5. Record the values for later analysis.

6. Return the game to the original timedemo 0 state via the console interface to re-establish normal play.

Real-world Testing: Applications

Many multimedia applications can be used for real-world performance testing. Encoding sample video clips with Microsoft Windows Media Encoder, VirtualDub, or Adobe Premiere can be a very effective comparative test, as long as each encoding pass is accomplished under the same system configuration. Each of these applications can return values that indicate the amount of time elapsed during encoding. Similar operations can also measure the time required to apply transforms or filters to graphics in applications such as GIMP or Adobe Photoshop.

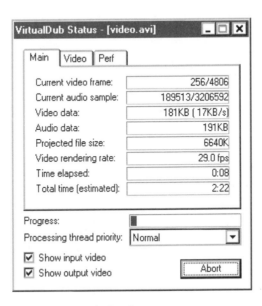

Figure 9-7: VirtualDub video compression

10

TROUBLESHOOTING

Troubleshooting Overview

The need for system troubleshooting arises when an overclocking attempt is not successful. In the world of overclocking, the word *successful* is subjectively defined. Success, or lack thereof, is usually measured by whether or not the system boots and whether or not it remains stable over time. Symptoms of system instability include software applications that freeze, crash (with or without an error message), or otherwise produce unexpected and unwelcome results. Some users are content with a system that crashes once a day. Others require complete system stability for weeks at a time before they are satisfied. Whatever "success" means to you, it is possible to turn overclocking failures into successes by understanding what went wrong and taking the right steps to correct problems.

Overclocking can create system stability problems that would not occur at default settings. Deviations from normal (or default) temperatures, voltages, and operating frequencies of various system components can lead to instability, or even failure, after prolonged operation. To correct such problems, or to fix a system that will not boot after an overclocking attempt, it may be necessary to restore the system to its default configuration, or at least to a more stable configuration. Ways to do this include clearing the computer's CMOS data via a motherboard jumper, changing motherboard dipswitches or jumpers back to defaults, or reflashing the BIOS to force default settings. The risk of device failure is minimal if you exercise care and patience during overclocking. System instability is the larger concern. Nevertheless, failure or damage to hardware is a possibility. Troubleshooting can shed light on the causes of instability and help you get the kinks out of any overclocking attempt.

Proper Cooling and Thermal Monitoring

The main cause of system instability or damage that arises from overclocking is poor cooling, because increased operating speeds produce higher thermal loads. The excess heat must be adequately dissipated, usually by means of a heatsink combined with a forced-air fan cooler. To know whether or not your system is being cooled sufficiently, you must monitor its operating temperatures.

Most quality motherboards permit onboard temperature monitoring through a variety of sensors mounted in strategic locations. The most valuable sensor point is underneath the base of the processor inside the socket interface (if there is one) or adjacent to the processor on slot-interface boards. Some architectures offer an additional layer of security by embedding a thermal sensing circuit in the processor's die substrate layers. A chipset or third-party circuit then actively monitors the hardware, passing temperatures and other relevant data to the CMOS for analysis and display on the BIOS Setup's user interface. Software applications can also extract temperature data from the sensor circuitry and move it directly to the operating system for real-time monitoring.

Most motherboards that offer thermal monitoring also support user-defined temperature limits to safeguard against damage to the processor and other components. Suggested maximums vary with processor designs. Exceeding temperature limits may trigger a warning or cause the system to shut down. Although stability problems can occur, even at low temperatures, you should avoid exceeding 60° Celsius when overclocking any current generation processor.

Maximum recommended operating temperatures for a variety of processors can be found in Chapters 5 and 6. Just as you should establish a performance baseline when benchmarking your system, you should also establish a processor or system case temperature baseline before overclocking. Of course, you can be quite confident that processor and system case temperatures will increase when your processor is overclocked. Instability will not necessarily follow increased temperature, but it is important to know where your system started out. Such knowledge will make troubleshooting easier down the road.

Overclocking tends to be a trial-and-error process. The more data you can gather about your system, the better. If an overclocking attempt is successful, in the sense that the system remains stable, you can record the processor's temperature during that attempt. If you later overclock your processor to a higher speed, and that produces instability, you'll know what temperature to seek via improved cooling to improve stability.

Processor Voltage

An increase in processor speed sometimes requires an increase in processor voltage to improve stability or to make a system boot at all. Unfortunately, increasing voltage is perhaps the most dangerous aspect of overclocking. Next to excessive temperatures, it is the quickest way to kill your processor. Increasing the voltage improves a processor's ability to operate at higher speeds, but take care: increase voltage levels by tiny increments and monitor every aspect of system operation—temperature, performance, and stability—after each increase. High voltage means a greater likelihood of electromigration, which can destroy a processor's circuit pathways. Although rare, electromigration is impossible to measure or predict. Unless your processor is expendable, the best rule of thumb is to deviate from the processor's default voltage as little as possible. Slight changes in voltage are usually well tolerated, whereas large changes are more troublesome. As with all overclocking attempts, quality cooling should be in place before you raise processor voltage.

Bus Overclocking: Drives

Increased stress on system components, due to overclocking via the front-side bus, often generates instability. Components built with low-quality manufacturing or design standards are most likely to suffer, though even the best components have limits. Hard drives, video cards, and memory are the most susceptible to instability introduced by overclocking.

Overclocking the front-side bus affects the operating speeds of all system buses, as discussed in Chapter 4. Each bus rate is affected differently, according to the front-side bus speed. The exact deviation in operating speed depends on the chipset being used with each motherboard's specific design. In general, all system bus speeds increase as front-side bus rates increase, although most x86 architectures employ multiplier division to derive bus speeds. Devices attached to each of the various buses must be able to sustain operation at extended speeds introduced through the overclocking process.

Drive arrays are the most susceptible to problems in an overclocked system. Loss of data integrity is a real concern. PCI bus speeds that exceed the normal specification of 33 MHz can cause problems, especially above 40 MHz. Drives based on the IDE standard are most likely to suffer data corruption, while SCSI-based devices are less worrisome.

Decreasing the drive controller's transfer rates through the BIOS Setup interface will often prevent data corruption problems. You'll have to experiment to find optimum stability, but most drive problems cease when the controller's transfer rate is lowered by one or two levels. For example, ATA/66 DMA 4 could be taken down to ATA/33 DMA 2. While you can lower drive transfer rates without devastating performance, you should never disable direct memory access (DMA) transfers in current generation systems. DMA bypasses the processor during data transfers; this valuable feature should be enabled at all times.

Examine any changes in performance that result when drive transfer rates are lowered. System performance could be degraded due to decreases in drive data throughput. Bandwidth gained through overclocking the bus rate may be negated by reduced signaling rates. You must maintain a balance between maximum operating frequency and available bandwidth. A quality benchmarking utility, such as SiSoft Sandra, will help you assess drive bandwidth as you make overclocking decisions.

Bus Overclocking: Graphics Accelerators

Graphics accelerators can be very susceptible to bus overclocking, especially the older generations of AGP video cards. Based on a 66-MHz PCI bus design, AGP cards store graphical texture data in the system's main memory. This improves 3D rendering by speeding up access to more graphical information than can be stored in the video card's onboard memory. Subsequent revisions have extended the AGP standard to include an advanced data signaling technique, which transfers information at up to eight times the rate of the original specification.

The latest generation of video cards can usually sustain AGP speeds approaching 90 MHz, though earlier models often fail above 75 MHz. Lowering the effective data transfer rate can neutralize the stress of extended speeds. AGP 4x cards must often be lowered to 2x for successful operation. In addition, disabling side-band transfers and fast-write capabilities can limit the effects of bus overclocking on stability in the AGP subsystem. AGP bus configuration can usually be altered from within a system's BIOS interface, though some video cards feature onboard jumpers.

Most games and other 3D applications will see only mild performance losses from lowered transfer rates or disabled advanced AGP. The latest graphics accelerators feature 64 to 128 megabytes of onboard memory, so the need to perform texturing operations in the system's main memory is reduced. Even the most advanced 3D games rarely demand more than 32 MB of graphics memory at display resolutions below 1024 x 768. Computer-aided design applications suffer the worst performance degradation, but professionals who use such software rarely resort to overclocking. They prize data integrity and system stability, and tend to obtain speed by upgrading rather than tweaking their systems.

Bus Overclocking: Memory

The memory subsystem is often the first to lose stability during front-side bus overclocking. The quality of the memory itself is important in determining overclocking potential. Generic memory types should be avoided, as the memory chip manufacturer often has no control over the production processes used in building generic components. Small manufacturers purchase memory chips from brand-name corporations and mount them on low-quality printed circuit boards. These boards often fail quality testing at overclocked speeds because they are designed to meet minimum quality standards.

Quality memory modules undergo production and testing within the same manufacturing environment. Large manufacturers, such as Micron's Crucial Technology retail sales division, offer superior quality testing. Each Crucial memory module must meet the same stringent standards as Micron's OEM modules. This high degree of vigilance usually produces an excellent chip.

Some vendors take advantage of the confusion surrounding memory quality. For example, Micron provides memory chips for sale to other manufacturers for assembly on a generic printed circuit board. Some vendors receive the generic memory, then attempt to sell it as a brand-name product because each individual chip is tagged with Micron's manufacturing and model codes. Users expect a quality product, but instead they receive a generic part that may not meet Micron quality assurance standards. Purchasing memory directly from large-scale manufacturers is the best way to avoid low-quality components though some smaller manufacturers do have good testing procedures and warranties.

Type and performance ratings are the two most important things to consider when evaluating whether or not a memory module is suitable for an overclocked configuration. Better-quality PC-133 SDRAM and PC-2100 DDR memory modules can operate up to 33 MHz beyond their factory ratings with good stability. The high-frequency RAMBUS designs can often go 100 MHz beyond their rated speed. Older fast-page and extended data-out technologies are not as scalable, with overclocking potential less than 33 MHz. As with processors, the maximum overclocked speed depends on a number of design, production, and testing factors.

You may need to tweak memory timing values when overclocking the memory bus. Most motherboards allow memory timing rates to be defined in the BIOS Setup interface. While you must use trial and error to determine the best timing pattern, setting CAS (column address strobe) latency can be a valuable overclocking tool. CAS latency determines the rate for memory read, write, and move operations.

Most quality memory will feature a CAS latency of 2 for SDRAM, or up to 2.5 for DDR memory modules. Adjusting this value to 3 will often enable memory modules that would otherwise fail at overclocked bus rates to operate without any problems. As latency increases, bandwidth decreases. However, performance loss is negligible because subsequent overclocking of the memory bus can deliver more available bandwidth to offset latency. Benchmark testing is required to determine the proper relationships among timing, latency, and operating frequencies.

Many motherboards, especially those featuring non-Intel chipsets, give users the ability to specify custom bus rates correlated to the front-side bus. This can prove invaluable when overclocking the front-side bus. Most chipsets feature a fixed multiplier range for PCI, AGP, and other interconnect bus operations, but many chipsets skew the memory bus rate through an additive or subtractive process. The skew value is often derived from the rate of the PCI bus, which is 33 MHz at default clock operation.

Manipulating the memory bus is an important aspect of overclocking. Let's look at the Intel Pentium III *e* series, for example. This processor operates with a 100-MHz front-side bus. Many non-Intel motherboards allow the memory bus to be offset from the front-side bus by 33 MHz. Thus, a high-performance

PC-133 SDRAM in asynchronous mode can replace the original synchronous default. The P3e processor can be overclocked to a front-side bus rate of 133 MHz. If the user already has PC-133 memory, the memory bus can be configured for synchronous operation. However, with low-quality PC-100 memory, the user could opt to use an asynchronous 100 MHz memory bus (133 MHz minus 33 MHz), thus improving stability while allowing the processor to be overclocked to the 133-MHz front-side rate.

The P3e system is only one example. Most chipsets support the skewing of memory bus rates, not only for overclocking but also to improve performance in other ways. In the P3e with PC-100 SDRAM example, assume a user wants to upgrade to PC-166 technology. After changing out the old memory, he or she can use the additive asynchronous mode to maximize memory bandwidth. This process allows the front-side bus to retain its 133-MHz overclocked rate, while the memory bus is skewed to achieve 166 MHz.

Sadly, most Intel chipsets do not allow skewing the memory bus though asynchronous operation, though nearly all non-Intel chipsets do. Remember that lowering operating speeds for system buses, especially the memory bus, may also reduce performance, even when the processor or front-side bus is overclocked.

Resetting the BIOS

Unresponsive or unstable systems can often be rescued by resetting the firmware BIOS to its default configuration. The BIOS is based around a CMOS memory that stores system configuration data on an *EEPROM* (electrically erasable programmable read-only memory) flash memory module. The method for resetting the BIOS to default values differs with the motherboard model, but the basic premise remains the same. The electrical supply to the EEPROM, from the motherboard's onboard battery, must either be removed or shorted to clear the stored memory.

Most motherboards feature a CMOS clear jumper, while others require the user to hold a key during boot to reset BIOS values. If specific instructions are not available, simply removing the CMOS battery for 15 minutes can reset most motherboards. If that isn't successful, shorting the positive-to-negative posts of the battery interface socket with a wire jumper or paper clip may speed up erasure.

If the battery is soldered to the motherboard, it may be possible to drain it by attaching a resistor, with impedance under 100 ohms, between the positive and negative battery poles. Be careful, though: if the motherboard doesn't support battery recharging, this will render the system useless. A new battery will have to be soldered in place of the drained one.

Flash updating of the system BIOS can often restore the default configuration. The command to force such an update option varies by vendor, but most boards featuring popular Award or AMI BIOS routines can be forced to reinstate original CMOS values with a flash and reboot. Upgrading the BIOS can also prove beneficial, as the latest code usually includes compatibility and performance updates.

All user-defined settings are lost once the configuration is reset to factory defaults. Retain a hard-copy version of all BIOS, jumper, and dipswitch settings, as configured when the system is operating in a stable manner. The task of writing down each setting can be tedious, but this extra work ensures your ability to restore the system if it should fail. If you lack a backup list, most motherboard user manuals recommend BIOS settings for common configurations, and most BIOS Setup interfaces contain a Restore to BIOS Defaults option. Reset all motherboard jumpers and dipswitches to their default or recommended values before booting a reset system.

Hardware Failure and Warranties

Device failure is a significant concern. As noted several times throughout this text, only quality components should be used in an overclocked system. If your system is factory built, you may not have the best components, but you can still take care to cool and configure your system properly. Remember that overclocking can void product warranties. Multiplier overclocking voids processor warranties, while front-side bus overclocking voids agreements for nearly all system components. Trying to get product replacements or refunds for damages incurred during overclocking is unethical if not illegal. Deceitful tactics increase hardware costs for everyone and have compelled some companies to implement anti-overclocking technologies.

11

FINAL THOUGHTS

Overclocking Examined

While this book covers most of what you are likely to face when overclocking, the techniques involved can change as new computing architectures appear and technology evolves. Thankfully, the x86 architecture itself imposes some restrictions, which will allow the information here to be used across a wide range of both current and future systems. While each new design introduces additional performance features, overclocking concepts remain relatively similar for all x86 platforms.

Overclocking grows out of qualities inherent in the manufacturing of integrated circuit products. Manufacturers choose to market microprocessors at various speed grades, effectively holding back any given processor from its maximum potential. In turn, overclocking enthusiasts opt to push their systems as far as they can. They do this either because they want to extend the useful life of an existing system or because they want to purchase a slower rated and thus cheaper system and get more performance from it. The process of overclocking can also be addictive: some people thrive on the challenge of attaining maximum performance for the least amount of money.

The premise of overclocking is that it is possible to improve computing performance, either by raising the operating frequency of the primary processor-to-system bus on the motherboard or by remapping the internal clock multiplier of the processor. The methods involved may be different for each specific processor across the wide range of products offered by Intel, AMD, and VIA. The original idea remains the same for all platforms, but its application can vary wildly for each of the popular architectures.

Many secondary factors play key roles in reaching and maintaining peak operating speeds for an overclocked system. Proper thermal regulation, through the implementation of active and passive cooling technologies, builds the foundation for success. Problems can arise, however, even with the best configurations, so troubleshooting will almost certainly be necessary. Once overclocking has been attempted, benchmarking enables enthusiasts to analyze stability problems and measure positive performance returns.

Your Motherboard Won't Let You Overclock?

If your motherboard doesn't support enough (or any) FSB settings or multiplier changes, fear not. Most motherboard manufacturers provide BIOS upgrades that may add new features and BIOS Setup options. Also be sure to try third-party software options such as SoftFSB (discussed in the Appendix) to alter front-side bus speeds from within Windows. Finally, replacing your motherboard in order to gain more overclocking options is a viable choice, and can be done for as little as $50. If you do buy a new motherboard, be sure that it supports all of your existing hardware.

Now You Know How, But Should You Do It?

Overclocking appeals to a wide variety of PC users, but it is not for everyone. If you are easily frustrated by problems with your PC, troubleshooting is an annoyance for you, or you frequently rely on others to help resolve issues with your PC, overclocking can only complicate your life. But if you enjoy (or at least tolerate) troubleshooting and tweaking, and the idea of getting a faster system for practically no extra money sounds pretty slick, consider overclocking as a viable means to an end. It might even become a hobby.

You should begin your experimentation on an extra PC, rather than on your main system. Even if you don't maintain the only copy of a Fortune 100 company's financial records on your main box, you probably don't want to lose data or deal with the frustration of not having a functional and reliable main PC when you need it. Remember, back up everything!

What to Do with the Extra Performance

You will undoubtedly be happy with quicker application response times or higher frame rates in games, but why let the extra performance go to waste when you're not using your PC? Distributed computing projects are popular as a way to solve complex or CPU-intensive problems using the power of PCs around the world.

Projects to find cures for cancer, crack encryption, unlock the secrets of our genetic code, and identify drugs to fight anthrax and smallpox, are just a few of the distributed computing projects out there. What makes these projects irresistible is the fact that they track your PC's number-crunching power and total contribution to the overall effort, so you can see how your PC, or group of PCs, stacks up against others.

Performance junkies can even join teams of users running the same distributed computing effort, combining their forces and engaging in friendly competition against other teams. The teams work toward achieving the project's goal and earn bragging rights as a bonus. Learn about six popular distributed computing projects, which can put your new higher-performing PC to work when you're not using it, at http://www.techimo.com/teams.html.

Be warned, however: because distributed computing projects keep your CPU running at 100% effort around the clock, stability problems are more likely to surface. That can be a good thing if you want to find problems and eliminate them, but it can also be annoying if you're happy with your PC's new level of performance and you don't intend to do any further tweaking.

Smart Shopping

Whether you have decided to buy slower hardware and overclock it, or bite the bullet and pay for speed up front, it's always worthwhile to find good deals and reliable retailers. Although local shops might have decent sales from time to time, on the whole, online shopping will provide the best prices on hardware components.

A site called ResellerRatings (http://www.resellerratings.com), which is owned and maintained by the author of this book, lets you search thousands of online retailers to find the best hardware prices, and then browse customer reviews of retailers to protect you from poor service. Some other price search engines have company ratings as well, but those sites are in the business of providing price searches, not company ratings, and they do not go the extra mile to ensure the integrity and authenticity of the customer reviews of companies to nearly the same degree as ResellerRatings. If you use other price search sites such as iBuyer.net (http://www.ibuyer.net), PriceWatch (http://www.pricewatch.com), PriceGrabber (http://www.pricegrabber.com), or CostUpdate (http://www.costupdate.com) to compare results, be sure to use ResellerRatings.com to evaluate unfamiliar retailers. Once you have made a purchase, help other shoppers by leaving your feedback on the site as well.

BizRate (http://www.bizrate.com) is another site that features ratings and reviews of online retailers. However, BizRate only features 450 or so computer hardware retailers. It is also unclear to this author as to what steps BizRate takes to prevent fraudulent evaluations. Still, the site offers one more resource for your arsenal, especially when coupled with ResellerRatings and various other price search sites.

The AnandTech "Hot Deals" forum, accessible at http://forums.anandtech.com, is another way to find good prices online. As its name implies, this forum is filled with the latest online hardware deals.

Although I do not advocate that you buy from one retailer or another, and that you make full use of price search sites and ResellerRatings before you buy, NewEgg (http://www.newegg.com) has a user reviews feature on its site that you may find useful. It enables customers to submit reviews and ratings for various products, which are helpful when deciding which products to buy. Often, users comment about the overclockability of a motherboard or other product, as well.

Exclusion of Liability

Overclocking should prove a positive experience for PC enthusiasts. However, problems can arise when you deviate from the processor manufacturer's original specifications. Overclocking voids product warranties, so take great care at all stages of the process. Monitor an overclocked system carefully, even if it appears to be stable and functioning properly.

Overclocking is the entire responsibility of the user who actually implements the techniques and information offered in this text and its supplementary resources. Manufacturers offering product warranties for components within an overclocked system are not responsible for any damages suffered, regardless of whether product failure or damage is either directly or indirectly associated with overclocking. Invoking warranties or agreements for components in an overclocked system is an ethical issue. Common sense and law require the user to assume all liability for any part, hardware or software, used in conjunction with overclocking.

All parties involved in the development, production, or sale of this text disclaim any and all liability for problems that may result from the knowledge you gain from *The Book of Overclocking*.

Beware: It's Addictive

Once we have achieved a goal in life, it never seems to be enough, so we adopt a greater goal. The same is true for overclocking. Once you become adept at it, you may find yourself perpetually tweaking your PC, always seeking the smallest performance increase, temperature reduction, or improvement in stability. What started as a desire to save a few bucks and keep from upgrading can turn into a pricey, time-consuming, endless pursuit. Your dollars can disappear into cooling components and case modifications. And you may find yourself spending too many hours on the web discussing the search for maximum performance.

Not to worry, though, you're in good company. Sites like techimo.com (http://www.techimo.com), HardOCP.com (http://www.hardocp.com), Overclockers.com (http://www.overclockers.com) and AnandTech.com (http://forums.anandtech.com) provide support for your new habit, and can help all skill levels with the overclocking process. These community-oriented sites allow a free exchange of ideas about computing on any topic—from daily operations to troubleshooting to overclocking and beyond. Answers to your tough overclocking questions are never more than a mouse click away.

APPENDIX

Frequently Asked Questions

Q: What is overclocking?

A: Overclocking is the process of operating computer hardware at speeds in excess of their manufacturers' ratings.

Q: Can I overclock my OEM system?

A: With the advent of software utilities like SoftFSB, the answer is "possibly." Most OEM systems from the largest manufacturers (Dell, Gateway, Compaq, etc.) cannot sustain a serious overclock. It is possible to obtain a few extra MHz.

Q: What about overclocking my notebook?

A: We do not recommend overclocking for portable computers. Most notebook systems cannot accommodate extra cooling. Even if overclocking were possible, most notebook cases are not designed to dissipate the amount of heat it would generate.

Q: I run important applications on my system on a regular basis and I cannot tolerate system crashes or data loss. Should I overclock my system?

A: No. When system stability and data integrity are of utmost concern, don't overclock. Overclocking is best suited for gamers, who want realistic and smooth play; and speed fanatics, who want bragging rights on having the fastest, cheapest system around.

Q: Will overclocking damage my processor or void my warranty?

A: If you are conscientious enough to observe proper thermal regulation and abide by voltage limits, overclocking is unlikely to damage your processor. It can sometimes shorten the lifespan of a processor, though most chips will become obsolete long before they burn out. But yes, overclocking will void your CPU warranty, and possibly other component warranties as well.

Q: I have seen advertisements for retailers that sell overclocked CPUs. Are they legitimate, and is there an advantage to buying one rather than overclocking my own?

A: Some retailers sell legitimate CPU, motherboard, and memory combos, which come preoverclocked and pretested for less money than you would spend on an analogous system at the manufacturer-rated speed. Buying such a combination could save you some guesswork, as not all processors in any given class can overclock successfully. Some retailers guarantee that these overclocked systems will run; others do not. Ask questions, and know what you are buying. Beware of retailers who sell processor/motherboard combos in an overclocked state without advertising them as being overclocked. These are instances of fraud, which should be reported to the appropriate processor manufacturer.

Q: Why is my overclocked system unstable?

A: This is a complex question. Many factors can create system instabilities. Common causes include:

Core Voltage. Increasing voltage can help stabilize an overclocked processor, but remember that additional cooling will likely be required to offset the extra heat that is generated.

Cooling. Proper thermal regulation is key to maintaining a stable overclocked system. Use a quality processor cooler, combined with an efficient case fan layout. One trick for diagnosing potential thermal problems is to use a cooling spray (found at most electronics vendors for under $10) to directly lower the temperature of specific components, while you operate the system at maximum CPU load. If stability improves when you are cooling a particular component, that component likely needs better cooling.

Memory. Poor quality memory is one of the leading causes of overclocking instability. When overclocking, use only quality memory from trusted manufacturers, not generic modules from unknown vendors. Increasing CAS latency, or decreasing certain memory timings, is sometimes required to stabilize the memory subsystem when overclocking. Benchmark testing can help you evaluate any performance differences that result from changing the various settings.

Buses. Both the PCI and AGP bus standards are built around strict operating specifications. Try to maintain bus rates as close to their default values (PCI = 33 MHz, AGP = 66 MHz) as possible. An AGP bus is more forgiving when overclocked than a PCI, but decreasing AGP transfer rates may be required to achieve stability. Similarly, hard drives attached to the PCI bus may require lowered transfer rates to ensure data integrity when overclocking via the front-side bus.

Power Supply. Overclocking requires more wattage than the default settings require. While most power supplies can easily sustain moderate overclocking, some systems will require a power supply upgrade to maintain stability. Intel- or AMD-approved units with a rating of at least 300 watts are recommended. Brand name power supplies are often preferred over generic power supplies, as brand name units may prove more reliable and have power output voltages that more closely meet the required motherboard voltage specifications.

Firmware/BIOS. Be sure to update the BIOS firmware and hardware drivers for all components. Most manufacturers release updates at regular intervals, so checking the appropriate websites and online file archives for updates is required.

Q: Is my processor running hot?

A: The temperature limits listed in Chapters 5 and 6 indicate failure points, not maximum stable operating temperatures. Processors should never exceed 60° Celsius. The best cooling systems will keep temperatures well below 50° for most configurations.

Q: What can I do for a hot processor?

A: 1. Apply a *thin* layer of thermal paste between the heatsink and processor core.
2. Verify that there is adequate airflow in the system and make sure the fans are moving air in the right direction.
3. Check for proper heatsink-to-processor alignment, as some models can slip during shipping.
4. And finally, install a quality processor cooling solution for better thermal dissipation.

Q: What if my processor does not overclock as expected?

A: Not all chips will overclock the same. This fact is a byproduct of integrated circuit manufacturing techniques. Most individual examples of a specific processor model might overclock to a certain range, but that does not mean your specific processor is guaranteed to reach the same speeds.

Q: How do I "burn in" my processor?

A: The need to burn in a processor is an old overclocking myth. A processor has no mechanical friction, only a type of electrical friction. Electrons will flow through a processor core the same way, regardless of the duration of that flow.

Glossary

AGP   Acronym for accelerated graphics port, a bus interconnect standard designed by Intel for the high-speed transfer of graphics data and the storage of 3D texture data within a system's primary RAM. Most current 2D and 3D graphics accelerators are designed for the AGP bus standard.

AMD   Advanced Micro Devices is the second largest personal computer microprocessor manufacturer, with models covering nearly all market segments in the computing industry. AMD is currently Intel's strongest competitor. Their rivalry helps ensure lower CPU prices across the board.

Athlon   A 32-bit microprocessor architecture manufactured by Advanced Micro Devices. The high-performance Athlon is marketed as direct competition to Intel's Pentium III and Pentium 4 architectures. Both the Pentium and the Athlon lines have undergone multiple revisions since their original release.

Bandwidth   A measurement of the amount of information processed or transferred within a given timeframe, usually measured in megabytes per second. Bandwidth is synonymous with throughput.

Benchmark   A test designed to measure the performance of either hardware or software components.

Binary   A mathematics system composed of ones and zeros that is the basis of modern computing technologies.

Bus   A collection of wires designed to transmit data across various components within a computing platform. The front-side bus connects the processor, memory, and chipset computing components. The back-side bus connects the front-side bus to expansion peripherals, such as drives or graphics accelerators.

Cache   A specialized type of memory designed to store data temporarily so it can be accessed quickly during buffering operations. Cache is generally designed around static random access memory (SRAM) and, unlike similar dynamic random access technologies, it does not require continuous refresh updates.

Capacitance   A measurement of the ratio of electrical charge transferred across two conductors, or the amount of charge an isolated conductor can effectively store.

CFM   Cubic feet per minute, a measure of a fan's ability to move air. The higher the CFM rating, the more volume of air can be moved in any given time and the cooler your system will be. Note that higher CFM generally means greater noise.

Chipset   A combination of integrated circuit devices designed to route, control, and transfer information across various operating buses found in today's systems. Common designs incorporate two distinct but interconnected hubs: the Northbridge and Southbridge controllers.

Circuit   A configuration of electrically or magnetically connected components or devices.

Clock Speed   A measurement of how many times an integrated circuit can change its operating state within a given timeframe, usually measured in megahertz, or millions of cycles per second.

Convection   A process of thermal dissipation using a liquid or gas medium to transfer heat away from a given substance to another region or medium.

Cyrix   Cyrix originally existed as an independent manufacturer of Intel-compatible microprocessors, but this smaller corporation was acquired by VIA Technologies in 1999. The Cyrix product name is often associated with the latest processors offered by VIA, though these newer architectures share little in common with the older Cyrix platforms.

Die Size   A measurement of the width of internal pathways within an integrated circuit device, usually measured in nanometers.

DDR SDRAM   Acronym for double data rate synchronous dynamic random access memory. DDR memory technologies employ a signaling technique capable of transferring data along both the rising and falling edges of each clock cycle, thus offering a theoretical 2x improvement in memory bandwidth over conventional SDRAM.

FSB   An acronym for front-side bus. The FSB connects the processor to the memory and other components in a PC.

GHz   An acronym for gigahertz, or one billion cycles per second. One GHz is equal to 1000 MHz. See MHz.

Integrated Circuit   An electronic device composed of multiple transistor circuits, originally developed by Texas Instruments and Fairchild Semiconductor in the 1950s.

Intel   The world's largest developer and manufacturer of personal computer microprocessors. Intel maintains the dominant market share across all platforms, and is often considered to be the leading authority in microprocessor design.

ISA   An aging bus standard that is rapidly disappearing in today's computing platforms. ISA offers minimal bandwidth and is best suited for low bandwidth devices, such as modems or sound cards.

Latency   The amount of time that elapses for a process to take place, or the time delay involved with one component waiting for another to finish a process.

Memory   A device designed to store data. Primary storage is composed of a series of integrated circuits that hold data short term (while a PC is in operation). Secondary storage is composed of physical disks (hard drive, CD-ROM, etc.) and similar devices designed for the long-term archiving of information.

MHz   An acronym for megahertz. One MHz is equal to one million Hertz, or cycles per second. Processor clock speeds are measured in megahertz, but don't be fooled: there are many other factors that determine a processor's performance than the MHz speed alone.

Microprocessor   A logical controlling integrated circuit chip composed of multiple transistor pathways, generally based on a silicon substrate with aluminum or copper circuit interconnects. Same as processor or central processing unit (CPU).

Multiplier An internal value that correlates the front-side bus speed to the operating speed of the microprocessor. Example: Pentium III 800e = 100 MHz FSB x 8 Multiplier.

Multiplier Lock Implemented by processor manufacturers to prevent users or dishonest retailers from overclocking processors through changes in the CPU multiplier setting.

Nanometer One billionth of a meter.

Overclock To operate a microprocessor at speeds beyond its original equipment manufacturer (OEM) rating.

Pentium A 32-bit microprocessor architecture manufactured by the Intel Corporation. The Pentium series has undergone multiple revisions and redesigns over the years, so the name is more a marketing trademark than an architecture designation.

PCI Acronym for peripheral component interconnect, a bus standard developed by Intel to be scalable to 66 MHz and 64 bits. Most current-generation personal computing architectures employ a 33 MHz, 32–bit PCI bus standard.

RDRAM Acronym for rambus dynamic random access memory. Rambus memory is designed for extreme operating speeds up to and exceeding 800 MHz. It offers a substantial bandwidth advantage over original SDRAM technologies.

SDRAM Acronym for synchronous dynamic random access memory. SDRAM is designed for high-speed operation, and thus provides consistent data flow between the processor and memory buses.

Transistor A semiconductor device designed to archive or amplify signals, thus creating a logic storage and manipulation circuit. The original transistor was developed by Bell Labs in 1947.

Voltage A measurement of a circuit's electromotive force or potential difference.

Wattage A measurement of power required for the operation of a circuit.

Overclocking Software

Hmonitor (http://www.hmonitor.com) is a real-time hardware monitoring application for systems featuring thermal and fan-speed sensors. Hmonitor allows for active monitoring. It can also alert users to potential problems associated with excessive heat generated through overclocking.

SoftFSB (http://www.voodoofiles.com/250) is an advanced application designed to interface with the front-side bus clock controller from within Windows. SoftFSB is a valuable tool for obtaining maximized overclocking of today's most popular platforms.

WCPUID (http://www.h-oda.com) is a freeware application developed to analyze and display detailed information for current-generation processors and chipsets.

WCPUZ (http://www.cpuid.com) is a freeware application that can provide information about most current processors. Categories of information include the following: processor name, vendor, core stepping, packaging, core voltage, internal clocks, external clocks, overclock detection, processing features, cache architecture, and other motherboard information.

Benchmark Software

MadOnion 3DMark (http://www.madonion.com) is the most popular 3D graphics benchmark available today. 3DMark offers effective system testing in both traditional and overclocked environments. The 3DMark 2000 v1.1 is designed for DirectX 7 graphics accelerators, while the 3DMark 2001 is best suited for DirectX 8.1-compatible video cards.

SiSoftware SANDRA (http://www.sisoftware.co.uk) offers effective benchmarking and diagnosis for a multitude of system components. SANDRA is available in multiple versions, though the freeware edition offers all the benchmarking modules required to analyze overclocking performance returns and system stability.

Ziff Davis WinBench (http://www.etestinglabs.com) is a popular benchmark suite designed to test the graphics, video, and disk subsystems under all versions of the Windows operating system. The latest version was released in July 2001, but the highly optimized WinBench99 still provides a superior testing interface compared to competing applications.

Diagnostic Software

Motherboard Monitor (http://mbm.livewiredev.com) is a popular Windows system tray utility that will display information from your motherboard's sensor chip. Details such as fan speeds, processor and motherboard temperatures, and voltage, are displayed to the user. It is a good way to monitor your system and improve your tweaking and troubleshooting capabilities.

TuffTEST #1 (http://www.tufftest.com/Online Resources) offers great diagnostic capabilities. It will help you assess any potential stability problems incurred through overclocking. TuffTEST builds a self-booting disk that requires no external operating system. As a result, this highly effective testing suite can be deployed across all ranges of x86 computing systems.

Helpful Resources

TechIMO (http://www.techimo.com) is the premier online community in which to discuss all aspects of computing technology. TechIMO consists of an informative group of 60,000+ users who are capable of answering even the most challenging of troubleshooting or overclocking questions.

Sandpile (http://www.sandpile.org) is an extensive resource for those interested in the technical aspects of nearly any x86 computing platform. Sandpile is updated regularly to ensure that it contains the best-quality information.

Ace's Hardware (http://www. aceshardware.com) offers a superb mix of both professional and enthusiast computing information. Common topics include the presentation and discussion of new computing technology.

Google (http://www.google.com) is hands down the best search engine on the web. Those who operate other search engines spend their days trying to figure out how to be as good as Google. Google also acquired Deja news, the Usenet newsgroup archiving service, and they archive new newsgroup postings as well. Whenever you have a question, go to Google, click on the Groups tab, and search. You will very likely find threads discussing and solving your question.

HardOCP.com's (http://www.hardocp.com) Kyle Bennett tells it like it is. Read no nonsense reviews of the latest hardware, get timely news and references to performance and overclocking related articles from all around the web, and participate in active discussion forums.

Overclockers.com (http://www.overclockers.com) features timely overclocking related hardware reviews and a great overclocking survey database where users submit their own overclocking results. Use the overclocking database to see how well your CPU type/speed has been overclocked by other users.

AnandTech.com (http://www.anandtech.com) features the very latest hardware reviews. The message board (http://forums.anandtech.com) has many useful forums, with the Hot Deals forum being this author's favorite.

TechTV's "The ScreenSavers" (http://www.thescreensavers.com) is a live daily television show hosted by Leo Laporte and Patrick Norton, that covers hardware, overclocking, and various technology subjects. The show is a lot of fun and is highly recommended for overclocking enthusiasts. It is broadcast live from San Francisco every weekday at 4pm Pacific Time, on DirectTV Channel 354, Dish Network Channel 191, and a wide variety of cable networks.

Cooling and Overclocking Specialty Retailers

Be sure to research these retailers at ResellerRatings.com before you buy:

1COOLPC (http://www.1coolpc.com) offers fans for all CPU types, rounded cables, water cooling kits, lights and window mods, thermal compound, video card coolers.

PCMods (http://www.pcmods.com) offers cases and case accessories, fans and fan accessories, lights and window mod kits, control and monitoring devices, hard drive coolers, noise reduction and sound absorption products.

Highspeed PC (http://www.highspeedpc.com) offers water cooling kits, quiet power supplies, Athlon XP multiplier unlocking kit, high performance fans, pre-tested high-speed DDR memory, case windows, lights and LCD mods.

3DCOOL (http://www.3dcool.com) offers CPU, laptop, and monitor (display) coolers, chipset fans, hard drive fans, RAM fans, silent fans, cases (clear and aluminum), temperature monitors, round cables.

Xoxide Modifications (http://www.xoxide.com) offers water cooled cases, water cooling kits, water cooling accessories, case lighting, CPU coolers, case fans, standard and modified cases.

INDEX

B

C

G

games, 214–15, 220

gate arrays, 16

GFDs (Gold Finger Devices), 142

Gigabyte, 29

gigahertz (GHz), 13, 235

GIMP, 215

Gold Finger Devices (GFDs), 142

Google (search engine), 238

graphics accelerators, 34

Graphics WinMark tests, 213

H

HardOCP, *10*, 229, 238

hardware

    costs of, 2

    failure of, 222

    online retailers, 227–28

    overclockability of, 9–10

heat transfer compounds, 40–41

heatsinks, 37–39

    lapping, 39–40

    and thermal dissipation rate, 15

    troubleshooting, 233

Highspeed PC (specialty

    retailer), 238

Hmonitor (overclocking

    software), 236

Hybrid Celeron processors, *3*

I

IBM-compatible computers, 2

iBuyer.net, 227

ID Software, 214

IDE drives, 219

IDT Centaur, 4

impurities, 16

insulation, 16

integrated circuits, 235

    fabrication, 15–16

    physical properties of, 14–15

    PLL (phase locked loop), 23–24

    thermal dissipation rate, 15

    See also processors

Intel Corp., *3*, 49–51, 235

iron heatsinks, 38

ISA bus, 34, 235

J

jumpers, 10–11, 28–29

K

K5 processors, *3*, 139–40

K6 processors, *3*, 140

K6-2 processors, *3*, 140–41

K6-2/3+ processors, *3*

K6-3 processors, *3*, 141

K7 processors (Athlon), *3*, 143–44

    500 MHz, 144–45

    550 MHz, 145

    600 MHz, 146

    650 MHz, 147

    700 MHz, 148

K75 processors (Athlon), *3*, 149

    550 MHz, 150

    600 MHz, 151

    650 MHz, 152

    700 MHz, 153

    750 MHz, 154

    800 MHz, 155

    850 MHz, 156

    900 MHz, 157

    950 MHz, 158

    1000 MHz, 159

R

RAMBUS memory, *32*, 221

RDRAM (rambus dynamic random access memory), 236

real-world benchmarks, 210, 214–15

replacements, 1

ResellerRatings.com, 227

RTV sealants, 43

S

Samuel (Cyrix processor), 206

sanding, 39–40

Sandpile, 237

SCSI drives, 219

SDRAM (synchronous dynamic random access memory), 32, 221–22, 236

search engines, 238

self-built systems, overclocking of, 8–10

servers, 136

side-band addressing, 34

silicon sealants, 44

silicon substrates, 16

silicon wafers, *17*

silicon-on-insulator (SOI), 17, 19–20

silver pastes, 41

SIMMs (single inline memory modules), 32

SIMOX method, 17

SiSoftware Sandra (benchmark software), 210–12, 237

Slot 1 processors, 117–20

Slot A motherboards, 142

slot coolers, 43

Slotket converters, 118

SoftFSB (overclocking software), 226, 231, 236

software, 236–37

SOI (silicon-on-insulator), 17, 19–20

specialty retailers, 227–28, 232, 238

speed. *See* clock speed

speed binning, 21–22

SSE2 technology, 211

stability, 30

    benchmark testing of, 210

    and overclocking, 217–18, 231

    and voltage levels, 34–35

Styrofoam blocks, 44

submersion cooling, 48

subzero cooling, 44

SwiftTech liquid coolers, *47*

synchronous dynamic random access memory (SDRAM), 32, 221–22, 236

synchronous memory bus, 31–32

synthetic benchmarks, 210–13

T

T&L (transform-and-lighting) operations, 213

TechIMO.com, *10*, 229, 237

technology, 1

TechTV, 238

thermal conductivity, 38, 41

thermal dissipation rate, 15

thermal loads, 27, 37

thermal monitoring, 218

thermal pads, 40

thermal paste, 40–41, 233

thermal regulation, 11

VIRTUAL LEGO®
The Official LDraw.org Guide to LDraw Tools for Windows

by TIM COURTNEY, STEVE BLISS, AND AHUI HERRERA

Introduces you to a suite of software that allows you to create and document computer-generated LEGO models. Written by maintainers of LDraw.org, the official hub of LEGO model-building software, the book includes coverage of popular freeware tools such as LDraw, MLCAD, L3P, L3PAO, LPub, POV-Ray, and MegaPOV. The CD-ROM contains all the software you need to get started, all available LEGO parts models, and templates for building instruction layouts.

MAY 2003, 450 PP. W/CD-ROM, $39.95 ($59.95 CDN)
ISBN 1-886411-94-8

THE BOOK OF WI-FI
Install, Configure, And Use 802.11b Wireless Networking

by JOHN ROSS

This plain English guide to the 802.11b wireless networking standard teaches readers how to use wireless networks at home, work, or in their neighborhood. Includes detailed, practical information on access points, network interface cards, cables and antennas, and wireless software. Readers learn how to protect their wireless access point from unwanted intruders with encryption, password protection, and virtual private networks (VPNs), and how to configure wireless connections for Windows, Macintosh, Linux, Unix, and PDAs.

2003, 504 PP., $39.95 ($59.95 CDN)
ISBN 1-886411-45-X

THE SOUND BLASTER LIVE!™ BOOK
A Complete Guide to the World's Most Popular Sound Card

by LARS AHLZEN AND CLARENCE SONG

Configure your hardware; watch DVDs in surround sound; record and organize digital audio MP3s; and use sequencers, MIDI, and SoundFonts to compose music. The CD-ROM includes music and audio examples, sample sound clips, SoundFonts, and audio software.

2002, 504 PP. W/CD-ROM, $49.95 ($74.95 CDN)
ISBN 1-886411-73-5

STEAL THIS COMPUTER BOOK 3
What They Won't Tell You About The Internet

by WALLACE WANG

This offbeat, non-technical book looks at what hackers do, how they do it, and how readers can protect themselves. The third edition of this bestseller adopts the same informative, irreverent, and entertaining style that made the first two editions a huge success. Thoroughly updated, this edition also covers rootkits, spyware, web bugs, identity theft, hacktivism, wireless hacking (wardriving), biometrics, and firewalls.

"If this book had a soundtrack, it'd be Lou Reed's *Walk on the Wild Side.*"
—*InfoWorld*

2003, 464 PP., $24.95 ($37.95 CDN)
ISBN 1-59327-000-3

THE BOOK OF SCSI, 2ND ED.
I/O for the New Millennium

by GARY FIELD, PETER M. RIDGE, ET AL.

This thoroughly updated second edition offers down-to-earth instructions for installing, implementing, utilizing, and maintaining SCSI on a PC.

"You'd be very hard pressed to find a more complete and readable treatment of the SCSI protocol than this book." —*Slashdot*

2000, 428 PP. W/CD-ROM, $49.95 ($77.50 CDN)
ISBN 1-886411-10-7

Phone:

1 (800) 420-7240 OR
(415) 863-9900
MONDAY THROUGH FRIDAY,
9 A.M. TO 5 P.M. (PST)

Fax:

(415) 863-9950
24 HOURS A DAY,
7 DAYS A WEEK

Email:

SALES@NOSTARCH.COM

Web:

HTTP://WWW.NOSTARCH.COM

Mail:

NO STARCH PRESS
555 DE HARO STREET, SUITE 250
SAN FRANCISCO, CA 94107
USA

Distributed in the U.S. by Publishers Group West

UPDATES

Visit **http://www.nostarch.com/?overclock** for updates, errata, and other information.

ABOUT THE AUTHORS

Scott Wainner founded SysOpt.com, one of the first PC hardware enthusiast sites, and ran it for seven years until in late 2001 he launched TechIMO.com, a knowledge-sharing community of PC hardware enthusiasts, gamers, and web developers.

Wainner's opinions on overclocking have been cited by *PC World,* CNN, the *Toronto Star, Entrepreneur Magazine,* and countless hardware web sites.

Robert Richmond's background experience in IT-related journalism extends to many well-recognized publications, such as SysOpt.com, SharkyExtreme, HardwareCentral, Romulus2, EarthWeb, and as a hardware editor for TechIMO.com. Robert holds Associate of Science degrees in Mathematics, Computer Sciences, and Scientific Application Development. Robert offers a rather untraditional approach to computers, as he is often more interested in "why" a device works rather than "how" it works.